Government and Policy-Making Reform in China

China's rapid economic development has not translated automatically into political development, with many of its institutions still in need of major reform. In the post-Mao era, despite the decentralisation of local government with significant administrative and fiscal authority, China's government and policy-making processes have retained much of the inefficiency and corruption characteristic of the earlier period. This book analyses the implementation of government and policy-making reform in China, focusing in particular on the reform programmes instituted since the early 1990s. It considers all the important areas of reform, including the enhancement of policy-making capacity, reform of taxation and fund transfer policies, tightening of financial control, civil service reform and market deregulation. It assesses the course of policy reform in each of these areas, considers how successful reforms have been, and outlines what remains to be done. In particular, it explores the impact on the reform process of China's entry into the WTO in 2001. It demonstrates that the process of reform in China has been one of continuous conflict between the agenda of political elites in central government, and the priorities of local leaders, with local agents often distorting, delaying or ignoring the policies emanating from the central government.

Bill K.P. Chou is Assistant Professor in the Department of Social Sciences at the University of Macau. His research interests include policy process, public sector and civil service reform, central-local relationships, local government, political economy, governance of China, and public sector reform in Macao.

Comparative development and policy in Asia series
Series Editors:
Ka Ho Mok
Faculty of Social Sciences, The University of Hong Kong, China
Rachel Murphy
Oxford University, UK
Yongjin Zhang
Centre for East Asian Studies, University of Bristol, UK

Government and Policy-Making Reform in China

The implications of governing capacity

Bill K.P. Chou

Routledge
Taylor & Francis Group

LONDON AND NEW YORK

First published 2009
by Routledge
2 Park Square, Milton Park, Abingdon, Oxon OX14 4RN

Simultaneously published in the USA and Canada
by Routledge
270 Madison Ave, New York, NY 10016

Routledge is an imprint of the Taylor & Francis Group, an informa business

Typeset in Times by Wearset Ltd, Boldon, Tyne and Wear
Printed in the UK by the MPG Books Group

British Library Cataloguing in Publication Data
A catalogue record for this book is available from the British Library

Library of Congress Cataloging in Publication Data
Chou, Bill K. P.
Government and policy-making reform in China: the implications of
governing capacity/Bill K.P. Chou.
p. cm. – (Comparative development and policy in Asia series; 6)
Includes bibliographical references and index.
1. China–Politics and government–2002– I. Title.
JQ1510.C48354 2009
320.60951–dc22

2008051956

ISBN10: 0-415-43704-0 (hbk)
ISBN10: 0-203-87634-2 (ebk)

ISBN13: 978-0-415-43704-2 (hbk)
ISBN13: 978-0-203-87634-3 (ebk)

Contents

Figures

Tables

Preface

I started to study the governance of China after I enrolled on the doctoral degree programme at the University of Hong Kong in 1998. A usual approach of researching China is to understand the theories and concepts generated from the Western liberal democracies, and then apply these theories and concepts to the context of China. Without modification, these theories and concepts are often inapplicable to China. In OECD countries, for instance, it is believed that the authority of policy making should be moved closer to the citizens so that the decisions made are more suited to citizens' needs. The belief engenders the devolution from central to local governments. Department managers are given higher autonomy over personnel and financial policies to increase their incentives in economising the use of resources and to hold them responsible for their decisions. However, China follows a different trajectory. Since the mid-1990s, the central government has taken over several important tax bases and substantially increased its tax revenue at the expense of local governments. The authority over tax collection, establishment planning, financial management and regulation of local markets has been removed either from lower-level to upper-level governments, or from spending departments to such supervisory departments as finance bureaux and audit offices. Certain functional departments are made more vertically integrated with the functional departments at upper-level governments (*chuizhi guanli*) in order to reduce the authority of lower-level governments.

One explanation for the difference is that the administration of OECD countries is highly institutionalised; the rigidity and red tape related to a high level of institutionalisation are the roots of administrative problems in OECD governments. Thus government and policy-making reforms are characterised by de-institutionalisation to provide vitality for the administration and incentive for department managers to make decisions and take responsibilities. In China, administrative problems used to originate from a low level of institutionalisation, and therefore more institutions are needed. Those supporting this notion equate institutionalisation with centralisation and concentration of policy-making authority. Looking back to PRC history, we can see that the notion is hardly convincing: During the Maoist era, centralisation and decentralisation took turns at being the guiding principles of economic development, even though the legal system and the policy-making process were un-institutionalised by today's standards. Furthermore, decentralisation and de-concentration in OECD countries do not equate with de-institutionalisation: Decentralisation and de-concentration are often associated with institutionalisation, such as specification of the rights, duties and performance indicators of local governments and department managers in order to hold them accountable for their performance.

The divergence of Chinese practices from the Western paradigm prompted me to investigate this phenomenon and write this book. I found that the issue of centralisation versus decentralisation is path-dependent; the cycle 'centralisation–decentralisation–centralisation' in the reform era is no different from that in Maoist era. The decentralisation since the early 1980s, aimed at motivating local leaders to develop the economy, was a coping strategy to deal with the problems caused by centralisation. Centralisation in China since the mid-1990s, in turn, was a response to the decentralisation problems, such as economy overheat, decline in central government's capacity over taxation and thriving corruption. The cycle follows the trajectory of past policy shifts and cannot be explained merely by the perceived needs of institutionalisation.

Meanwhile, the notion '*shang you zhengce, xia you duice*' (lower-level governments have counter-measures to dilute the policies from upper-level governments) merits investigation. Even under the authoritarian and unitary political systems in which local leaders are supposed to be subservient to central policies, numerous literature and cases have proved otherwise. Centralisation policy may reflect the control mentality of central leaders: Administrative problems are perceived to be a consequence of too much room for local leaders to manoeuvre and undermine central policy. The solutions to the problems include strengthening central control, correcting information asymmetry for supervision purposes and curtailing local leaders' discretionary power. Through reasoning, it is not difficult to conclude that the policies are doomed to fail: Given that China is a huge country and the administrative hierarchy is complex and fragmented, information asymmetry is inevitable. The flow of information is far from free due to the relatively closed political system and tight control on mass media; thus close supervision on local leaders is not easy. Making sure that local leaders always carry out central policies as planned through narrowing the information gap is therefore difficult if not impossible. To prove this reasoning is another purpose of this book.

The literature on China's governing capacity is full of contradictions. Some authors of the literature believe that China's governing capacity is improving. The enormous wealth generated by economic reform enables the Chinese government to tap adequate resources for investing in infrastructure, improving public service, building up armed forces, buying political support and maintaining a powerful dictatorship machinery to crush political dissidents. The Chinese government can use the entry into its vast domestic market as a bargaining chip in trade talks and extracting concessions from Western developed countries. Nevertheless, other authors point to the weakness of food-safety regulation, the high incidence of industrial accidents and collective protests, environmental degradation, the failure of anti-corruption campaigns and the defiance of local leaders against a wide spectrum of central policies, and argue that the governing capacity of the Chinese government is weakening. Such a contradiction is partly due to different understandings on the concept of governing capacity. This book seeks to clarify the concept of governing capacity and link the concept with government and policy-making reforms. By this means, we can understand why discussions on China's governance come to conclusions contradictory with each other. At the same time, we can trace the connections among the seemingly unrelated literature on governance, governing capacity, public-sector reform and policy processes.

Acknowledgements

I am indebted to many people and organisations in the preparation of this book. John Burns inspired me to research the governance of China and set a good example for me in the pursuit of academic excellence. Ka-ho Mok encouraged me to turn my understanding of China into this book project. The University of Macau gave me several research and conference grants to finance my research activities. During the different stages of writing this book, the Asian Development Bank Institute, East Asian Institute of the National University of Singapore and Governance in Asia Research Centre of the City University of Hong Kong offered me sponsorship and excellent research environments. In these institutes, I benefited greatly from the feedback of my colleagues on the drafts of the book chapters, including Douglas Brooks, Wang Gunwu, John Wong, Zou Keyuan, Quan Xiaohong, Lai Hongyi and Wang Zhengxu. Weeli Lian, James Tan, Miyuki Aldrich, Miki Miyako and Virginia Chan provided me with much-needed administrative support. Wang Xin helped a lot in the preparation of the final version of the manuscript, and Stephenie Yoo assisted in proofreading.

Chapter 5, 'Civil service reform', is an updated version of 'Civil service reform in China, 1993–2001: A case implementation failure', *China: An International Journal*, 2, no. 2. Chapter 6, 'Implementation of administrative licensing law', is revised from the book chapter 'Regulatory reform and private sector development in China: A case study of downsizing administrative licenses', in Ka Ho Mok and Ray Forrest (eds.) *Changing Governance and Public Policy in East Asia* (London: Routledge, 2009), which is based on an occasional paper 'Downsizing administrative licensing system and private sector development in China: A preliminary assessment', published by the Asian Development Bank Institute in 2006. I have to thank Singapore University Press, Routledge and the Asian Development Bank Institute for their copyright permission.

On a personal note, special gratitude has to be extended to my parents who always stand by me to get through the most difficult time in my life. My father, orphaned at the age 11, remained uneducated throughout his life. His progression from a coolie to a businessman reminds me of the secret behind every success story which motivate me to strive but not to yield. The company of Frankie is also much appreciated. Without their spiritual and emotional support, I would hardly have finished this book.

1 Introduction

A sound government structure and policy-making process are essential for good governance: They potentially ease the consensus-making process of major policy actors who must define and prioritise public problems and choose appropriate policy tools. Policy implementers are better motivated to translate these consensuses into acts and policy outcomes that both policy elites and the target population desire. Furthermore, such standards ensure that policy elites are able to receive accurate feedback concerning the progress of policy implementation so that timely adjustment of policies is possible when necessary.

The Chinese government has continually reformed its government structure and policy-making process to spur sustainable development and enhance its legitimacy. The reform of government and policy-making in China follows two intertwining trajectories: the first is to refine the technical arrangements of various stages of policy process; the second is more political, entailing power redistribution. It seeks to strengthen central control to solicit the compliance of local agents with central policies. A vast existing literature on the reforms investigates the policy context, policy content and implications of the reform measures, studies policy elites' perceptions of policy-making problems, and examines how policy elites and functional bureaucracies negotiate over the reform measures. However, understanding how the reform measures have improved governing capacity has not been fully explored. Policy-making is a series of activities entailing problem identification and agenda, policy design, policy implementation and policy evaluation. Further research is necessary for answering the questions of whether these reform measures have been carried out as policy elites have planned, and whether the outcome of these reform measures is congruent with their objectives. The core objective of this book is to address these questions.

Concepts of policy making and governing capacity

Policy-making is a process of deciding what to do and what not to do. The process is divided into five stages: agenda setting, policy formulation, policy adoption, policy implementation and policy evaluation. Agenda setting involves defining policy problems and setting policy agenda. To study this stage is to address the questions of why and how some phenomena are construed by policy-makers to be problems and included in political agendas. Policy formulation generates policy options for resolving or ameliorating public problems. What kinds of policy options are generated and the length that this stage lasts are contingent on the number of policy makers in this stage, their constituencies and technical competence. Policy adoption is the selection of policy options among an available range. The adoption of policy options are affected by which policy makers have final say on choosing policy options, as well as what requirements are used for adoption. Policy implementation is the application of adopted policy options. This stage may also be regarded as policy remaking because the policy options adopted may be either too vague or too controversial for implementation. Policy implementers are required to refine or reshape the adopted policy options. Whether the remaking of policy makers is conducive to the accomplishment of policy objectives depends heavily on the alignment of the policy options with the implementers' agenda, and the effectiveness of the policy makers' monitoring over the course of policy implementation. Policy evaluation reveals what policy options have accomplished, and whether they have achieved their goals or have engendered unintended consequences. It is a continuous process throughout all stages of policy making. The specificity of policy objectives, the commitment of policy elites and the amount of resources available may have an impact on the effectiveness of policy evaluation. After policy evaluation is undertaken, the policy options may be modified, killed off or remain unchanged (Dye 2004: 31–59; Anderson 2000: 30–2).

For different purposes, policy actors often try to influence different stages of policy making. Policy implementers may reformulate the adopted policy options when they find the policy options too controversial for a target population. In this case, the policy options have to be modified to make it acceptable for a target population. During policy evaluation, policy elites may abandon original policy options and adopt another after they find that the original policy choices cannot attack the roots of the identified problems. Policy agendas have to be adjusted if the identified problems are no longer a common concern of the public, or if external issues such as a reshuffle of political leadership and/or wars have changed the priorities of the policy communities before the impact of the policies on such agendas have come into being. In other words, the distinctions among different stages are far from clear-cut; the order of different stages of policy making discussed above is not necessarily followed.

We can come up with the following ways of reforming the policy-making process derived from the concept of policy making:

1   Policy makers are provided with assistance to set policy agendas better reflecting citizens' wishes. This involves channelling the opinions of social organisations and individual citizens into the policy-making process. Some of the examples include speeding up democratisation, introducing deliberative democracy and involving citizen participation in the policy process.

2   More feasible and useful policy options are generated for addressing the agenda. This entails extracting enough fiscal resources and economising the use of current fiscal resources to widen the spectrum of possible policy options. Competent think tanks have to be established to provide sound policy advice and options for consideration.

3   Policy makers are provided with assistance to make sensible policy options, using crucial inputs from civil society and think tanks.

4   Policy implementers should be better equipped to put policy options on paper into practice, adapting (or reformulating) policies to local context and citizens' wishes, and mobilising resources to undertake unfunded or partially funded mandates imposed by upper-level governments. To do so, a competent and neutral civil service managed on the principle of professionalism should be established. Public employees should be provided with incentives to work according to the policy makers' agendas. The structure of bureaucracy should be rationalised.

5   Policy makers should be given more information about what the adopted policy options have accomplished, whether they have achieved their goals, and whether they have caused unintended consequences. In addition to more actively soliciting feedback from different policy actors, policy makers have also to establish an effective mechanism for information collection and analysis.

Hilderbrand and Grindle provided a conceptual linkage between governing capacity and policy making that, in turn, made the literature on governance and reform of governing capacity useful for understanding the theme of this book. After reviewing various definitions of governing capacity, Hilderbrand and Grindle pointed out that the definitions range from the broadest view that equates governing capacity with development and the narrowest perspective equating governing capacity with the training of human resources. The definitions at the two extremes of the spectrum are both too vague to be utilised for analytical purposes and too narrow to provide a meaningful focus of study. In view of these definitions' weaknesses, they propose their own definition lying between the two extremes: Governing capacity is defined as the ability to perform appropriate tasks effectively, efficiently and sustainably. Appropriate tasks are those defined by necessity, history or the situation in specific contexts or within a given country (Hilderbrand and Grindle 1997: 34). The definition entails several stages of policy making: Defining appropriate tasks concerns agenda setting, policy formulation and policy adoption. Performing appropriate tasks involves policy implementation. The definition is very close to the catchphrase 'governance' which underlines governments' efforts to achieve the common goals of diverse societal interests. A major weakness of the definition is its lack of adequate specifications for research purposes. The meaning of appropriate tasks remains unclear, and fails to highlight the role of the politico-administrative structure in steering the course of policy making. As pointed out by Keohane and Nye, appropriate formal and informal institutions are able to render the behavioural pattern of various stakeholders favourable for achieving the commonly desired goals (The Commission on Global Governance 1995: 2; Keohane and Nye 2000: 12).

Using China as the context, Wang and Hu defined state capacity as the ability of the state to transform its own will and purposes into reality. Wang and Hu believe that only central/federal governments can represent the will and preferences of the state. Thus they refer to the 'state' as the central/federal governments and exclude local government from analysis. Four categories of state capacity may be identified: financial extraction capacity; steering capacity (or regulatory and control capacity); the capacity of legitimation; and the capacity for coercion. Financial extraction capacity refers to the capacity to mobilise economic resources. Steering capacity refers to the capacity to guide the economic development of society. Legitimation capacity refers to the capacity to employ political symbols to create consensus among the citizens of a nation so as to consolidate the position of the ruling regime. Coercive capacity refers to the capacity to employ violent means, organisations and threats (Wang and Hu 1999: 24–39). The four categories of state capacity echo Almond and Powell's five dimensions of capabilities of a political system: extractive capability; regulative capability; redistributive capability; symbolic capability; and responsive capability (Almond and Powell 1966: 190–212).

While the concept of state capacity by Wang and Hu is more operationalised for research purposes, the concept ignores the significance of local actors in policy making. As discussed widely in the field of China studies, local governments in China have made numerous innovations in developing the economy and generating capital for local investment when no central directives are available, capital is inadequate and market mechanism does not properly function to channel resources for economic construction. It is largely the self-initiative of local governments, rather than the carefully plotted strategy of political elites in central government that contributed to the success of China's economic reform (Oi 1999). Local governments play a very active role in policy formulation and the adaptation of central policies to a local context.

In comparison, Painter and Pierre's analytical framework is more encompassing. Their analytical framework divides the concept of governing capacity into three broad categories: state capacity; policy capacity; and administrative capacity. State capacity concerns the ability of the state to aggregate diverse societal interests and iron out their differences to agree on policy choices. The ability is contingent on the effectiveness of political structures and consultative set-ups in building consensus. Policy capacity is 'the ability to marshal the necessary resources to make intelligent collective choices and set strategic directions for the allocation of scarce resources to public ends'. Building the capacity requires appropriate administrative coordination, accurate information and analysis, as well as sound programme planning and evaluation so that the planned programmes may align with the interests of different stakeholders. Reforms of resource extraction and the reporting system are examples of policy capacity reformation. Administrative capacity refers to 'the ability to efficiently manage the human and physical resources required for delivering the outputs of government'. A merit-based civil service system, appropriate distribution of authority vertically within the administration and horizontally among state, business and society, and sound public financial management are conducive to the improvement in administrative capacity (Painter and Pierre 2005: 2). The three governing capacities correspond with the five stages of policy making, and the strategies of augmenting governing capacities correspond with the reform of the policy-making process (see Table 1.1).

By linking governing capacities with policy making, we may identify numerous literature relevant to the theme of this book. The studies of democratisation, village election and public participation in China revolve around the stages of agenda setting, policy formulation and policy adoption. These studies can be divided into two main study categories: studies of rural context and urban context. Democratisation in rural areas through village elections has been widely publicised by the Chinese government as a showcase of citizen participation and democratisation. Generally speaking, democratisation in rural China may encourage residents to participate in policy making, align the interests of common people with the agendas of village committees, strengthen the monitoring of village cadres and make village governance less abusive. Nevertheless, open and fair village elections are not common. Many township-level governments interfere with the electoral process to support their favourite candidates in the hope of assuring that the elected village chiefs will be more cooperative in implementing the mandates (Bernstein and Lü 2003; Li, L. 2004; O'Brien 2002, 2004; Manion 2000).

The expansion of democracy in cities is not a high priority of any political agenda. Socioeconomic development, however, has encouraged some urban residents to join collective actions and impact public policies in order to protect their own rights. Read (2003) and Derleth and Koldyk (2004) studied the evolution of residents' committees from the tools of the administration for social control to vehicles for residents for tackling community problems. They found that with the extension of property ownership, home owners have incentive to confront and negotiate with local officials and property developers for policy changes when they feel their property rights are infringed and the value of their properties are affected. Meanwhile, pulling the state away from the economic and social sphere has given rise to civil society and social organisations which have impacted state capacity (White *et al.* 1996; Unger and Chan 1995). Ma focused

Table 1.1 Governing capacities and policy making

Governing capacities	*Stages of policy making*
State capacity	Agenda setting, policy formulation and policy adoption
Policy capacity	Policy evaluation
Administrative capacity	Policy implementation

on the emergence of non-governmental organisations in the post-Mao era. Her research highlights how the new institutions and organisations outside the Leninist state system negotiate with government policy actors and shape the process of making such policies on public health, environmental protection, women's rights and poverty reduction (Ma 2006).

With regard to policy capacities, Glaser and Saunders (2002) provided an overview of the key civilian research institutes and their roles as policy advisers and evaluators. They pointed out that the Chinese government's growing involvement in the international community and a more pluralistic policy environment has created the need for more policy advice and provided opportunities for analysts unaffiliated with the traditional research-institute system to influence public policies. Huang (2001, 1995) examined the institutional development of administrative monitoring, information collection and analysis that gave useful information for policy elites to scrutinise policy implementers and evaluate policies. The central government has made substantial progress with institutional development. In 1978, the centre possessed almost no systematic information-collection channels, and its performance-evaluation procedures lacked explicit, enforceable criteria. Compliance depended completely on ideological coercion and terror. During the reform era, Chinese agencies considerably strengthened their staffing and technocratic capabilities. Many agencies established research centres and institutes to sharpen their analytical skills. A series of procedures for considering the appointment of leading officials was specified to overcome nepotism and localism. Provincial general offices were strengthened to supply accurate, up-to-date information about local governments to central general offices. Monitoring of unscrupulous local officials encouraged public petitions. The National Audit Office and State Statistical Bureau were strengthened for auditing the economic affairs of the government and exercising performance checks. Lieberthal's (1992) comment on the policy capacities of the Chinese government was nevertheless more negative. He pointed out that the authority of the government was widely dispersed across badly coordinated functional departments. The fragmentation of authority resulted in numerous veto points in policy implementation, a high incentive for local officials to shirk and hide information, and led to great difficulties in mediating interdepartmental disputes.

Fiscal reform is central to the reform of resource extraction. After examining the evolution of fiscal policy, Wong, Head and Woo concluded that fiscal reforms since the 1980s have failed to meet the increasing demand for government services from lower-level governments. Under the 1994 tax-sharing reform, government revenues were shared between the central government and provincial governments by a formula. While this reform successfully increased the amount of central government revenue and its proportion in the overall government revenue, the expenditure assignments between central and local governments were not clearly defined. Many local governments had to shoulder numerous expenditure assignments and ran into debt. In the face of financial problems, many local governments had to impose heavy taxes and fees on peasants. In addition, they had to cut costs by compromising the quality and quantity of such social services as education and health care (Wong 2000, 1997; Wong *et al.* 1995). Yep investigated tax-for-fee reform – an attempt by the Chinese government to reduce the peasants' tax and fee burden. He concluded that while the reform was successful in reducing the peasants' burden, its sustainability is contingent on central government's continued provision of transfer payment which is far from well-institutionalised, and therefore makes it difficult for local governments to forecast the future revenue.

Most of the studies concerning the reforms of governing capacities are related to public-sector reform, focusing on improving administrative capacities. Manion's (1993) study of cadre retirement policy analysed how the establishment of the cadre retirement system had been put on high agenda. Lee (1991) examined the institutionalisation of meritocracy in the cadre management system. Owing to the greater emphasis on the cadres' work-related knowledge and skill rather than their political credentials, the reform era witnessed the replacement of revolutionary cadres by technocrats. Burns (1994, 1989) studied the *nomenklatura* system and the strengthening of the Chinese Communist Party's (CCP) control over the appointment of the leadership of state organs, state-owned enterprises and public-service units (*shiye danwei*). Chan and Lam (1996, 1995a, 1995b) investigated the elite politics over civil service reform in the late 1980s, and examined how the debate over the problems of personnel management was shaped by political development, most notably the 1989 Tiananmen Square incident. Edin (2003) and Zhong (2003) studied the performance appraisal system which emphasises local leaders' abilities in developing the economy and stabilising society. They point out that the policy priorities of local leaders are under the heavy influence of the performance system. All the reforms discussed by the literature were directed towards the goal of professionalising the civil service without compromising party control.

With regard to resource utilisation and public-spending control, Cheung (2003) and Chou (2006) argued that these administrative processes were undermined by several structural factors: The fragmentation of authority resulted in a lack of coordination and inadequate supervision of budget preparation and execution. The need for extra-budgetary funds to finance capital investment and administrative outlay has kept huge amounts of funds outside the scrutiny of financial bureaux. Due to weak supervision, much of the spending is unlawfully dispensed. The lack of expertise in lower-level governments weakened spending control and offered many opportunities for leading officials to misappropriate public funds.

The linkage of market regulation with administrative capacity lies in the fact that in the context of China, reform of market regulations requires moving the state away from the micro-management of individual enterprises and industries, and building up a regulatory framework for developmental purposes. This entails reducing the scope of administrative interference in the market mechanism and potentially improves the efficiency of administration, as well as the quality of policy output. The reform era witnesses a divestment of state-owned enterprises (bankruptcy and privatisation), the rise of new economic activities (insurance and stock exchange), the emergence of market failure (coalmine accidents, shoddy product quality and environmental pollution), and the perceived threat of foreign competition to domestic enterprises resulting from trade liberalisation (banking and car industries). The evolution of an economic regulatory framework in China is a response to the regulatory need for dealing with these economic issues. Most of the literature about market regulatory reform focuses on particular sectors of an economy. Energy, telecommunications, financial services and the coal industry are widely researched areas (Speed 2004; Mueller and Tan 1996; Laurenceson and Chai 2003; Wang, S. 2006).

As discussed above, the divisions among different stages of policy making are far from clear cut. Accordingly, the stages of policy making will not be discussed separately. The emphasis of this book will be on the dynamics of the process of implementing the reforms of three types of governing capacities. The focus on the process of policy implementation is due to three reasons: First, the reforms are as good as their implementation outcome. A study of the process of implementing the reforms may contribute to identifying the reasons for the success and failure of the reforms.

Second, all the reforms have one common goal: They seek to reform the structure and process of the bureaucracy to achieve the objectives of higher efficiency and effectiveness. The members of the bureaucracy who are charged with implementing the reform policy are much affected by the reforms. Out of inertia and the desire for maintaining vested interests, some of these policy implementers are likely to resist the reforms. The behaviour of shirking responsibilities and bending the policy in their favour portrayed by public choice analysts is expected. What are the vested interests of these implementers? How are their vested interests shaped? How can they manage to shirk responsibilities when political elites successfully narrow the information gap and put them under close scrutiny? These questions can be addressed through investigating the implementation process.

Third, the process of implementing the reforms is under-researched. Most of the existing literature discussed the reforms in the 1980s and 1990s, studied the policy context of the reforms and analysed the dynamics among policy actors in formulating the reform measures. Little is known about what happened in the stage of implementation and how this stage affected policy success and failure. Several features of Chinese administration indicate that the success of the reform is particularly influenced by the stage of policy implementation. Chinese administration is characterised by the huge size of its local governments. Among the 205 countries and regions surveyed by the World Bank, Chinese local bureaucrats account for 93.1 per cent of all bureaucrats, the fourth highest after the 96.74 per cent of Uzbekistan and Russia, and 94.87 per cent of Kazakhstan (The World Bank 2006).[1] The Chinese government hires the largest number of bureaucrats (19.91 million) in the world and the bureaucracy is far bigger than the second-place Indian government (8.21 million). However, its central bureaucracies (a staff of 1.33 million) are slimmer than their counterparts in India (2.74 million), the United States (2.64 million), the United Kingdom (1.80

million), Columbia (2.00 million) and Egypt (1.35 million), even though the geographical size and population of the latter three are much smaller than China's. Central government has to rely on local governments for both manpower and monies to implement most of its policies. China also has 31 provincial-level governments (excluding the two Special Administrative Regions of Hong Kong and Macao), 333 prefectural-level governments, 2,861 county-level governments, and 44,067 township-level governments, all of which have some authority over the implementation of all the reforms of policy making. Given the huge number of local governments within the five-level administration (central, provincial, prefectural, county and township), there are many veto points in the implementation process. Monitoring the implementers is extremely difficult. Local bureaucrats are therefore able to wield high discretionary power and shape national reform policies according to local institutional features and locally defined state objectives.

Institutions and administrative behaviour

The process of implementing reform policies are shaped by institutions. Hall (1992) defined institutions as both the formal rules and informal practices that regularise individual behaviour and structure individual relationships. Institutions may have an impact on the behaviour of public employees through affecting public employees' views of their self-interest, structuring the organisational incentive systems and affecting the possible strategies that public employees may employ to maximise expected individual utility (Rothstein 1996). Institutions not only influence the behaviour of current public employees but also affect the decisions of future policy makers: Hall and Taylor (1996) argued that the institutional choices made early in the development of policy areas and/or political systems have a pervasive effect on the decisions of policy makers and the reactions of other policy stakeholders, such as policy implementers and the target population. Above all, the cost invested in learning how to operate within a known institutional setting is too high to change the institutions. Those concerned with maintaining vested interests in the existing institutional settings also make institutional changes difficult. Once particular institutional designs are adopted, they exhibit a strong tendency to self-reinforcement and are difficult to change.

Institutions can also affect the conflict level of policy context which in turn affects the extent of congruence between policy outcome and policy intentions. Policy context, together with policy content, are the two broad categories of variables determining policy success (Grindle 1980: 12). Matland (1995) perceived policy context as a relative concept along a continuum of high and low level of conflict of policy context. The conflict level of policy context is affected by many institutional factors such as the availability of adequate resources, the number of implementing agencies involved and the incentive of policy implementers to assure the successful implementation of the policies concerned. Matland believed that successful implementation of policy is unlikely if the conflict level of policy context is high, and vice versa. In the context of China, central leaders have long relied on appointing their protégés to both provincial leading positions and important central positions (the CCP Central Committee, the Politburo and the Standing Committee) to reduce the conflict level. Being concurrently central decision makers, provincial leaders will have more incentive to assure the successful implementation of central policies (Naughton and Yang 2004; Huang 2002). Meanwhile, local leaders' incentive to carry out central policies may be further increased through decentralisation. Su (2004) argued that assigning the state coal mines to provincial governments would motivate them to enforce the central policies of protecting such coal mines by closing down small coal mines.

Increasing the clarity of policy content – the second broad category of variables affecting policy success – alleviates the adverse impact of conflictual policy context. Clear policy content helps to reduce the cost of political elites in monitoring policy implementers. The clarity of policy content is contingent on the clarity of policy objectives, the availability of appropriate policy instruments to implement policy, the availability of benchmarks to evaluate the congruence between policy objectives and policy outcome, the effectiveness of the monitoring system and the measurability of policy outcome. Similar to policy context, policy content is a relative concept ranging between high and low ambiguity. Unclear policy content may increase the possibility of policy implementers shirking and hiding their practices from their political elites. This, in turn, is likely to lead to unsuccessful policy implementation.

In China, the central–local relation may be construed as a principal–agent relation. From the principal–agent perspective, local leaders are concurrently agents of central leaders and gatekeepers of information. They have a tendency to hide information or falsify reports to their principals because the information may provide clues about their fault-finding principals and expose their wrongdoings. The problem is especially serious when the implementation of principals' tasks entails many actors, and each actor monopolises certain kinds of information that affects monitoring. The more actors are involved, the more information will be hidden, and thus higher supervision and coordination costs are necessary for soliciting agents' compliance (Lam 2005: 641). To reduce agency costs, the CCP relies on political control to narrow the information gap for monitoring purposes. Central government maintains a *nomenklatura* system which lists the leading positions in local governments under the management of the Organisation Committee of the CCP Central Committee and its local branches. The appointment of the leadership of provincial-level and prefectural-level governments is under the direct control of the Party Centre. Political credentials and loyalty are important considerations in appointment decisions, especially to the positions of party secretaries whose main duties are to carry through central policies and supervise governors and mayors on behalf of the Party Centre. Leading party members' groups (*dangzu*) manned by reliable Party members are set up in the state apparatus for making major decisions. Upper-level Party committees formulate performance contracts for local leaders. Inside the performance contracts are specific performance indicators reflecting the policy priorities of upper-level Party committees. In addition, the CCP uses the schemes of position rotation and avoidance to make local leaders more responsive to central directives. Under the schemes, local leaders change their postings regularly and are assigned locales away from their birthplaces. Since they cannot stay in office for a long time and have to work in a region without kinship connections, building their own patronage is difficult (Bo 2004; Burns 1989). Therefore, in principle, they have little incentive to defend local interests against central directives.

Discussion about institutional designs may be supplemented by the vast literature on implementation studies. Top-down and bottom-up models are the two major models of implementation. The top-down perspective holds that successful policy implementation is based on the congruence of the policy outcome with objectives formulated by decision makers. Divergence between policy objectives and policy outcome are deemed a problem and require rectification. To assess the implementation outcome is to ask whether implementers comply with the predetermined benchmarks, prescribed procedures, timetables and restrictions. Based on the top-down model, institutional settings are steered to increase the clarity of policy content so that policy elites can tap more information, monitor implementers more closely and reduce agency costs (Cline 2000; Hull and Hjern 1987; Weatherly and Lipsky 1977). The following chapters will discuss how the top-down approach characterises the Chinese government and policy-making reform measures.

A major weakness of top-downers is that they overlook the impact of policy context on the outcome of policy implementation. As principal–agent theorists predict, policy implementers do not necessarily carry out their principals' policies as planned. On evaluating the capacity of the Chinese government in policy implementation, Naughton commented that the extensive coercion capacity of the Chinese government enabled it to mobilise vast institutional resources to carry out its policy measures in areas of fundamental state interests. Nevertheless, it was much less effective in implementing differentiated policies due to the conflictual context (Naughton and Yang 2004). Very often, the context of many policies is so conflictual that implementing the policies as planned by policy makers is almost impossible. Policy implementers may reshape, delay or even ignore the policies, especially if the policies conflict with their own agendas and there is an absence of a monitoring mechanism. Besides, clarifying policy content is sometimes difficult or undesirable: clarifying policy content requires *ex ante*, precise specification of behaviour. But such a specification is often costly because of the unobservability of some behaviour. The objectives of some policies may be too vague for policy makers to develop specific performance indicators and make it difficult to collect data for assessing these policies (Palumbo and Nachmias 1987). On some occasions, too much specification of policy objectives and too detailed instruction may be counterproductive because controversy may be caused among policy makers themselves and other stakeholders. Often policy makers do not fully understand local situations. If the means to achieve the policy objectives are clearly specified and no latitude is left for implementers to adapt the policy to a local context, unsuccessful implementation of policy often results. Measurable performance indicators may encourage implementers to opt for execution of the policies with measurable objectives and ignore the policies without, even though these policies may be more important (de Leon 1999; Matland 1995; Sabatier 1991; Elmore 1985).

Top-down advocates assume that the information gap can be eliminated, but this assumption is not yet proven. According to the concept of the 'economic man', public employees are rational actors. They actively seek career advancement within the bureaucracy. Since career advancement depends upon their superiors' recommendations, career-oriented public employees will act to please their superiors. They forward favourable information and suppress unfavourable information. Distortion of information diminishes control and generates unrealistic expectations. Owing to the inevitability of an information gap, even under close scrutiny implementers are often able to preserve certain discretionary powers and reshape the policy programmes based on their own priorities. Accordingly, efforts to correct the malfunctioning of bureaucracies by tightening control will simply magnify errors (Ostrom and Ostrom 2000).

It is out of this context that the bottom-up approach is advocated. Bottom-uppers believe that information gaps are inevitable. Policy implementers are able to resist unpopular policies by holding back information essential for supervision and control. The cooperation from implementers cannot be extracted simply by coercion, command and control. Instead of ignoring implementers' interests and pursuing control over them, bottom-uppers suggest inducing appropriating behaviour on the part of the implementers by aligning implementers' interests with broader collective objectives (O'Toole 1989). Implementation should be understood to be a process that moves towards the attainment of various participants' goals. The desired policy outcomes should be determined through a process of interaction among policy makers, implementers and the target population. Ruttan argued that aligning implementers' interests with broader collective objectives involved building up incentive-compatible institutions – those capable of connecting individuals with organisational objectives. Policy elites should appreciate the priorities of policy implementers and solicit their input from the initial stages of policy making. Then the policies would be able to internalise the aggregate welfare of policy elites and policy implementers (Ruttan 1998: 156). The bottom-up approach is occasionally used in China when central elites fail to reach a consensus on certain policies. The agricultural responsibility system and the experiments of economic reform in the five economic special zones during the early reform era were examples of the bottom-up approach.

This book will illustrate that the Chinese government tends to use the top-down model to reform the government and the policy-making process. The reforms are largely initiated by central government and imposed on local leaders. The reform programmes seek to increase the clarity of reform-policy content, regularise the authority of government officials and increase the information tapped for monitoring and control purposes. Heavy emphasis is placed on strengthening the control mechanism, such as the centralisation of the authority in revenue generation, the use of public funds and the issuance of administrative licence. How to reduce the conflict level of reform-policy context does not receive adequate attention, however. While the reforms are useful for reducing the ambiguities of the reform programme as well as the latitude of policy implementers, they fail to align local interests with the reform objectives and solicit input of local leaders about the policy process. Policy implementers are not provided with adequate incentives to cooperate and carry out the reforms according to policy plans. Some reform policies make policy context conflictual and undermine their implementation.

Structure of the book

The programmes of government and policy-making reform are numerous and extensive; this book will only discuss the most crucial programmes. The book is divided into seven chapters. Chapter 2 examines citizen participation in urban China – an example of reforming state capacity. In comparison to village elections and democracy, which is used by the Chinese government as a showcase of democratisation, this area receives much less scholarly attention and is therefore less extensively researched. For a long time, non-government actors have had very limited institutionalised positions in the earlier stages of the policy-making process. The socioeconomic transformation has resulted in a more liberal policy-making approach and the opinions of citizens are now actively solicited. Cities have a high concentration of well-educated and middle-class people in possession of qualities favourable for organising collective actions to influence public policies: many of them are well-informed of the policy issues concerned and are able to contribute meaningful input. The connections of some urban dwellers with local or even national leaders enable them to shape policies. Many urban dwellers are often property owners, and therefore have great incentive to influence the public policies that affect their properties' values. State-led citizen participation in the policy-making process is becoming more frequent, but the degree, scope and impact of participation are limited by a range of factors. Many of these factors can be traced to the conflict of citizen participation with the institutions buttressing the authoritarian regime and the command-and-control work style.

Chapter 3 analyses the way the government improves its policy capacity through reforming its taxation system and increasing its resource-extracting ability. This chapter discusses how the fiscal reform in 1994 led to fiscal problems in lower-level governments and effectiveness of the remedial measures in addressing these fiscal problems. The fiscal problems caused by the 1994 tax-sharing reform have affected local governments' ability to undertake the mandates from central government, forced local governments to be more predatory in fundraising, and affected the quality of public goods at local levels. In recent years, central government has centralised some expenditure assignments from local governments to lessen their fiscal stress. It increased its transfer payment to local governments on local education, health care and social security. These measures may help to alleviate problems. The sustainability of these measures requires a more institutionalised transfer-payment mechanism that provides a higher degree of certainty to local governments over the future stream of payments, so that they have higher incentive to spend the transfer payment on budgeted use. A mechanism to ensure the distribution of transfer payment strictly according to designated purposes should be improved.

Chapters 4–6 discuss the improvement of administrative capacity. Chapter 4 examines the reform of spending control. Spending control is an important aspect of governing capacity. Appropriate control of public spending ensures the distribution of public resources strictly according to policy priorities which are reflected in state budgets. This chapter evaluates how far the state budget has been made to reflect the national agendas and how the actual expenditure has been aligned with the budgeted one. This chapter will conclude that while some positive results have been achieved on economising the use of public resources and curbing rent-seeking behaviour, the structural features in the local political landscape reduce the incentive for local leaders to pursue further reform. Some institutional weaknesses – such as failure to constrain local leaders' power and detect the exercise of their discretionary power – enable local officials to circumvent the laws and regulations on expenditure control.

Chapter 5 concerns civil-service reform. This chapter analyses the establishment of the civil-service system and the implementation of the reform of staff appointment, compensation policies and staff development. It points out that the reform has achieved modest success in improving the efficiency, capacity and integrity of government officials. Further success of the reform has been held back by the ambiguities of the reform and the consequential latitude of local leaders to manipulate the reform for protecting their vested interests (namely their abilities to build patronage through appointment and promotion, their authority to use public funds for civil servants' fringe benefits and their desire for maintaining organisational harmony).

Chapter 6 focuses on market regulation and evaluates the capacity of the central government to consistently implement central policies and enforce central laws. An important dimension of administrative capacity is the capacity to efficiently deliver public goods and follow market regulation. A case study of administrative-licensing reform will be used to illustrate this type of reform. Administrative-licensing reform is aimed at improving the business environment of the private sector which is increasingly relied upon for further economic growth and social stability through job creation. Central to the implementation of the Administrative Licensing Law is the questioning of the capacity of the central government to oblige local agents to exercise their authority of market regulation within the central framework. The governing capacity of the Chinese government has been negatively affected by its excessive involvement in economic and social affairs, exemplified by an overly complicated licensing system and resultant corruption. This chapter outlines the reform of the licensing system marked by deregulation. Since the reform is a commitment in the World Trade Organisation (WTO) accession, the deregulation will be evaluated on the basis of the WTO frameworks in addition to the goals of the reform laid out by policy elites. The effort in spurring market deregulation, however, was held back by local governments' missions to boost the domestic economy and the consequential need for protecting local enterprises through licensing systems. The potential of issuing licenses for generating revenue acts as an incentive for local governments to defend the existing licensing system. Chapter 7 is the concluding chapter.

2　Citizen participation in the policy process

In his '25th June' address to the Central Party School in 2007, General Secretary Hu Jintao highlighted the significance of engaging citizens in decision-making processes of public policies. He said:

> The political reform of our country must be steered towards a correct political direction, must be in line with the socioeconomic development, and must satisfy the desire of our people in political participation ... [We] must expand the orderly *citizen participation* in order to improve the democratic system, enrich the means of realising democracy and expand the channels of democracy; implement scientific and democratic decision-making in order to improve the information collection in decision-making, and develop grassroots democracy in order to guarantee that people can exercise their democratic rights according to law.
>
> ('Jintao zai' 23 August 2007; emphasis added)

Hu's speech signifies that the CCP leaders acknowledged the limitations of the top-down authoritarian approach in policy processes and appreciated the contribution of citizens towards policy success. This chapter evaluates the effort of the Chinese government to institutionalise the channels of citizen participation. Although some existing literature provides in-depth analysis on citizen participation in urban China (Shi 1997; Read 2000; Walder 1986),[1] the topic has received much less attention than rural citizen participation. A major reason for the imbalance is that the Chinese government uses village elections as a showcase for the international community about China's democratisation. At the same time, some international donors have sponsored many rural community-development projects which encourage villagers to participate in project design, implementation and monitoring. The efforts of both Chinese governments and outside stakeholders in publicising citizen participation in rural China have attracted much attention from academic communities (Benewick *et al.* 2004: 12).

In fact, citizen participation in urban China also has significant implications with respect to policy advice. Cities are the focal point of economic activities and national and regional politics. The influence of public policies made in cities is more likely to extend beyond small communities and have greater impact on national and regional development than the policies of rural governments. An improvement in the policy-making process in cities is therefore more likely to spill over to other regions. Cities have a strong middle-class presence. They are better educated and informed about public policies. They have different sorts of expertise and social capital that contributes to the improvement of the policy-making process. Wider citizen participation in cities makes it easier to tap their expertise and social capitals, and therefore to improve the processes of policy making and implementation. Therefore more investigations on citizen participation in urban China are necessary.

The scope of study of this chapter investigates the effort of the Chinese government to institutionalise citizen participation in governance, and will exclude the discussion on the participatory activities resulting from the passivity of the state in blocking public participation, as well as the illegitimate modes of citizen participation such as bribery and riots. The rise of cyberspace and the Internet is regarded as the latest channel of citizen participation. Nevertheless, such kinds of participation are also excluded from analysis because of their self-initiation, which has little to do with the intentional efforts of government. Last but not least, this chapter focuses on citizen involvement, one of the four categories of participatory activities proposed by Langton (1978; the other three are electoral participation, obligatory participation and citizen actions).[2] Since this book examines the effort of the Chinese government to reform the policy-making process, citizen actions characteristic of citizen-initiated activities are excluded from analysis. Electoral participation and obligatory participation are government-initiated. However, the former category has only symbolic meaning in China and does little to improve the policy-making process or the legitimacy of the government. The latter category, which includes such activities as jury duty, is of little relevance owing to their absence in China.

This chapter first outlines the contours of the institutional settings and gives an overview of different forms of citizen participation in urban China during the reform era. It is argued that the retreat of the state from the economic and social spheres and the expansion of civil society have reduced the role of work units as major channels of citizen participation. Citizens have shifted their activities beyond their work units to influence the policy process. In comparison to work units, the new vehicles of citizen participation are impersonal and group-based, once regarded as subversive and forbidden by the CCP. The changing context and the consequential new institutional settings have created an environment that instils wider citizen participation. The CCP still maintains a tight control on the scope and depth of citizen participation and precludes extensive, well-organised bottom-up participation. Participatory activities are limited, localised and non-confrontational. They are solicited by the state/local governments to improve public-policy processes rather than engineered by citizens to advance their basic rights. Any activities considered beyond the orbit of state control are vulnerable to state suppression.

Citizen participation: an introduction

Citizen participation refers to the government-initiated activities encouraging individuals and groups to influence administrative decision making and managerial processes (Yang and Callahan 2007: 250). Several decades of an uneasy appraisal of Western democracy have proven that democracy through the ballot box is insufficient to empower citizens to effectively influence decision makers, experts, industrial associations and labour unions who dominate policy choices and sacrifice individual choices. The dismay with the ballot box has led to the distrust of traditional channels of political participation and suspicion of expert-led decision making. Thus in the post-Second World War era, Western democracies have witnessed an expansion of the scope of citizen participation in response to salient external stakeholders who push for participation for the sake of better protecting their basic rights. These external stakeholders include powerful politicians, knowledgeable citizens, other government agencies, legal entities and professional organisations (Yang and Callahan 2007; Hira *et al.* 2005: 53–5). A high degree of citizen involvement, characterised by the participation of citizen representatives in various stages of the policy cycle over an indefinite period, can generate the necessary political will to take effective action on pressing problems. With more participation and more effort at consensus formation, government processes can be made more transparent and democratic. Policy makers can easily understand the needs of the societal groups affected by their decisions. All these contribute to making fairer policy processes and attaining policy outcomes compatible with the general interest (Leach *et al.* 2002: 646–7; Stiglitz 1999).

In the field of comparative politics, a popular concept similar to citizen participation is political participation. A significant difference between these two concepts lies in the level of politics in which participatory activities take place. Politics may be divided into two levels: high politics and low politics. High politics refers to the sphere of activities revolving around principal political issues, abstract ideas and the language of politics, and a political leadership's decisions and actions. The participatory activities that influence high politics are known as political participation. Usually the participatory activities are in the form of selecting political representatives, campaigning and voting. They occur more frequently during election seasons as citizens seek to influence the legislative level and political officials who are held responsible to an elected legislature or directly to citizens (Wang and Wart 2007: 267). Citizen participation takes place at a level of low politics, a sphere involving decisions of implementing the policies formulated by policy elites. The participatory activities concern influencing administrative decision making and seek to influence the executive level. Unlike political participation which peaks during election seasons, citizen participation takes places on a continual basis.

The existing literature about participatory activities in China has not distinguished the two concepts. Some of the literature highlights that during both the Maoist and post-Mao eras, participatory activities in low politics are more effective at influencing policy outcome than in high politics. The reason is that participation in high politics is exclusively the domain of political elites. The participatory activities of average citizens – voting in the election of deputies to people's congresses at various levels – merely play a ceremonial role of legitimating the authoritarian regime. Election is subject to state manipulation. Voters are pressured to vote. Therefore these activities do not live up to a democratic style of participation that permits individuals to abstain from political activities. In the meantime, these activities fail to serve participation's fundamental purpose of affecting the policy process and realising citizen efficacy (Shi 1997; Burns 1988). On the contrary, participatory activities in low politics have the potential of influencing the decisions of low-level cadres who have leverage over programme design and resource distribution. As a result, this form of participation is popular among citizens.[3]

The CCP's concept of citizen participation

In China, where the state monopolises political lives, the CCP's concept of citizen participation shapes the institutional context, forms and degree of citizen participation. The CCP insists that the ultimate aim of citizen participation is to support a supreme, unified national interest defined solely by the Party. Forming organisations and initiating the collective actions outside the orbit of CCP control are forbidden. Citizens were encouraged to work with mass organisations (sometimes known as government-organised non-governmental organisations, or GONGOs), such as the All-China Federation of Trade Unions (ACFTU), the All-China Women's Federation, and the Communist Youth League to influence policies that affected sectional interests, such as labour, women and youth. These mass organisations set up branches in work units, neighbourhoods and schools (Townsend 1969: 3, 172, 173; Lü and Perry 1997). During the post-Mao era, restrictions on the formation of autonomous organisations have relaxed. But as explained below, the concept that citizen participation must be kept strictly under the parameter of the Party-state has not changed in the post-Mao era.

In contrast with liberal democracy's concept of channelling popular influence into administrative decisions, defending citizens against state encroachment on their civic rights and expanding the scope of consumers' rights, citizen participation (better known as mass mobilisation in the Maoist era) in China was considered a policy instrument for executing Party policies. The involvement of people from all walks of life in the 1958 Great Leap Forward for rapid economic development and the Cultural Revolution between 1966 and 1976 for rectifying the Party and the state apparatus were prime examples (Townsend 1969: 3). After reviewing green activism in post-Mao China, Ho argues that citizen participation in post-Mao China is aimed at mobilising people to contribute to the state rather to enable individuals to protect themselves against the state. In face of possible harassment from the state, green activists portray themselves as partners, not opponents of the authorities. Therefore they keep a distance from certain sensitive environmental questions, such as nuclear energy and agricultural biotechnology which the authorities are unlikely to make concessions on, and they avoid any connotation with broad, popular movements, for example, by under-reporting membership numbers to authorities (Ho 2007).

The CCP's mass line principle has shaped the form of citizen participation. Under this principle, cadres are required to maintain direct contact with the masses so that political leaders can be kept informed of citizens' demands. During the Maoist era, work units were places where cadres frequently encountered the masses. In work units, cadres and the masses had an interesting reciprocity. Cadres were influential on the well-being of work units' members because they had extensive authority and controlled abundant resources, such as access to promotion, bonuses, economic benefits, work points, job assignments, education and military service. But at the same time, cadres required members' cooperation to fulfil production targets and enjoyed good ratings in democratic appraisals. Through the reciprocal relationships, citizens found it easier to influence policy outcome in their favour. The impact of such institutional context on participatory behaviour was two-fold. First, cultivation of reciprocal relationships required close personal contacts and particular treatment. As a result, individual-based participatory activities were encouraged, whereas group-based activities were deemed ineffective. Second, reciprocity cultivates organisational harmony and a non-adversarial mode of participation. More confrontational acts like demonstration, strikes, litigation and open debate were frowned upon (Shi 1997; Walder 1986: 1–27).

Institutional context of citizen participation in the reform era

During the reform era, the retreat of state control from the socioeconomic sphere has opened a window for a change in the institutional context and led to the emergence of new forms of citizen participation. To direct more resources to economic reform, China cut its unwieldy and expensive administration costs, as well as expenses on enterprises through market, enterprise and administrative reforms. Some of the economic ministries were transformed into government-owned non-governmental organisations to serve the intermediary role between the state and society. Many state-owned enterprises have gone bankrupt and their associated work units have been dissolved (Chan and Drewry 2001; Liou 1998). At the same time, more and more people work in private enterprises. Unlike government departments and state-owned and collective enterprises responsible for executing certain state policies, private enterprises concentrate on economic production. Workers in these enterprises can hardly influence the implementation of public policies through their workplaces.

In the pre-reform era, people were defined as a social class representing the total unity of one class's interests instead of various social classes with diverse interests. Therefore, once the CCP, which claimed to represent all the 'people', was there, other groups were unnecessary (Ogden 2002: 273–4). To concentrate on economic development and social stability, the Chinese government abandoned the politics-in-command mentality and the notion of class struggle between the enemy and the people. The decline of dogmatic communist doctrine and the stress on pragmatism have opened a window for the formation of non-governmental organisations (NGOs) to represent societal interests which are increasingly diverse with the advent of the market economy. In 2006, the number of registered NGOs under civil affairs bureaux at various levels was over 346,000, up 8 per cent from the previous year (Xiong 2007). The figure excludes the estimated two million unregistered NGOs by the end of 2004 (Yuan 2006: 44). The ideological change and increasing number of NGOs have made group-based participatory activities more likely.

Meanwhile, the retreat of the state in meeting the welfare needs of citizens has changed the personal and non-confrontational approach of citizen partici-pation. The state sector was once the major welfare provider through work units of governments and state-owned enterprises. Tied down by the obligation of welfare provision, state-owned enterprises are less competitive than collect-ive and private enterprises. The state gives more autonomy to state-owned enterprises in unloading their welfare function. Hospitals, colleges and schools are required to raise their fees substantially to make up funding shortfalls. No consensus has been reached about whether enterprises have successfully reduced their responsibility of welfare provision. For example, Gu (2001) gave an affirmative answer to the question while Dittmer and Lü (1996) did not. What is certain is that the emphasis on efficiency value over equity value has forced more ordinary citizens to meet their welfare needs through the market. The associated impact is two-fold. First of all, many people have fallen into distress. The abilities of families and kinship networks to look after vulnerable people have been weakened by such social changes as large-scale migration and the rise of nuclear families. Local governments can hardly take over the role partly due to the fiscal and taxation reforms in the 1990s which deprived them of reliable sources of revenue (see discussion in Chapter 3 for details). Thus new NGOs have emerged to fill the gap of providing human and financial resources for welfare provision (Shang *et al.* 2005). Lots of these NGOs are government-sanctioned; they receive the state's financial and manpower support. But many others are more autonomous and able to mobilise citizen participation in the design and implementation of public programmes, such as the autonomous labour organisations studied by Chen which proactively repre-sented migrant workers in private enterprises and protected their labour rights (Chen, F. 2003: 1024). If government finds these autonomous organisations useful, these autonomous organisations, including those unregistered, may emerge from underground and openly conduct their businesses, provide welfare to the underprivileged and engage in policy advocacy (Shang *et al.* 2005: 122; Yang 2005: 55).

The second impact of the emphasis on efficiency over equity values lies in the greater responsibility the average citizens bear in terms of their welfare cost. People have to purchase their own housing, take charge of property manage-ment, pay the tuition fees of their children and settle their medical bills. The citizens who support their welfare needs by their own means become less dependent on the state. They are therefore more ready to protest against the government if they are dissatisfied with public services and administrative decisions. In a survey undertaken in six cities in 2000, 89.2 per cent of 2,001 respondents stated that they should express their grievances to government departments, and 79 per cent believed that mass media was an appropriate channel for them to do this (Yang and Zhang 2001: 31). In 2001, the Guangzhou city of Guangdong province received 3,181 calls from the public complaining about the city's public security officers ('Jingwu tousu' 7 March 2002). Chinese people also display the same desire for participating in public affairs. Drawing from the data of the World Values Survey, Wang reported that 36 per cent of the respondents in China listed 'giving people more say in important government decisions' as the top two national priorities, with 54 per cent belonging to the post-reform population (born after 1977) and 34 per cent to the pre-reform population (born in 1977 and before) (Wang, Z. 2007: 576). In their survey of 750 residents in Wuhan city of Hubei province, Yu and Li reported that 96.9 per cent of the residents with Wuhan households and 67.6 per cent without households expressed an interest in participating in community affairs and activities (Yu and Li 2006: 14–16). This increasing independence and assertiveness of Chinese citizens signifies their readiness to use more impersonal and confrontational approaches to influence public affairs.

New forms of citizen participation

Citizen participation in post-Mao China still displays a traditional orientation centred on hierarchical culture and an imperative of conformity. Contact with grassroots cadres and individual-based activities remain the most popular forms of citizen participation today. According to a survey of over 1,460 citizens who had experience in taking action to affect government decisions in four cities (Beijing, Haerbin, Wuhan and Guangzhou), 53 per cent approached the government individually, as opposed to 14 per cent approaching the government collectively (Cai 2004: 430). Nevertheless, the changing socioeconomic context has opened up new channels of participation. The state's relaxation of its social control has given rise to NGOs. In Western liberal democracies, NGOs are believed to be spearheads of citizen participation: They are more resourceful than individual citizens, and capable of overcoming the problems of collective actions which hamper the capacity of average citizens to participate in the public-policy process (Hira *et al.* 2005: 53–4). NGOs in China can play similar roles. In recent years, the Chinese government has taken steps to assist the development of NGOs, such as providing tax incentives for corporate donation to NGOs. In January 2007, the Ministry of Finance and the State Administration of Taxation jointly issued the 'Notice on the Policy and Related Administration Issues Regarding Pre-Tax Deductions of Donations for Public Welfare Undertakings and Relief Efforts'. This notice clarifies the procedure of obtaining tax deductions for corporate donations and expands the number of eligible NGOs. The Ministry of Civil Affairs has also started drafting the Charity Law; this will expand the channels of NGOs to obtain donations (AmCham Shanghai and AmCham-China 2007: 52–4).

Much of the current literature on Chinese NGOs revolves around the theme of NGOs' autonomy. Some provide a state-corporatist analysis and conclude that NGOs in China lack autonomy as the state maintains tight control over NGOs' personnel, capital, logistic support and legal status. In exchange for state control, NGOs are licensed and granted a monopoly within their particular segment of society. Through vertically integrating citizens and discouraging horizontal communication among them to form nationwide organisations, the state can prevent civil society from challenging its supremacy (Frolic 1997; Unger and Chan 1995; Chan 1993; Goldman and MacFarquhar 1999; Shue 1994). Others argue that the state control of NGOs is sometimes nominal. NGOs may use their revenue-generating capacity and their contribution to the state organs patronising them to negotiate for more autonomy. Meanwhile, many of the officially organised NGOs are led by reliable cadres appointed by state organs, and thus these NGOs are trusted and allowed a high level of autonomy (Lu 2007; Ma, Q. 2006). To the students who are concerned about governance and state capacity, a more interesting dimension is the ability of NGOs to mobilise societal resources for achieving the stated national objectives and to channel the wishes of their constituencies into public policies. This chapter's discussion of NGOs focuses on public participation in public policy.

Two types of Chinese NGOs can be identified – civilian NGOs and GONGOs. Almost all the documented cases of unregistered NGOs belong to civilian NGOs. With their relatively small numbers and limited resources, the major contribution of civilian NGOs is their vision and strategy of mobilising social capital to influence different stages of the policy process. Ogden pointed out the case of the All-China Lawyers Association, an NGO founded by the Ministry of Justice to advocate protection of the legal rights of lawyers and ordinary citizens from the infringement of government at various levels. The association could dilute the ministry's control by voting out the officials appointed by the Ministry and electing officials more capable of working for the interest of the Association (Ogden 2002: 266). Ma has documented how environmental NGOs successfully convinced the central government to suspend the construction of dams on the Nujiang and Minjiang, two rivers in the south-west (Ma, Q. 2006: 121). The Chinese government's tolerance of bottom-up participation in environmental issues through civilian NGOs signifies the high priority these issues have on the political agenda. China's rapidly growing economy and a surge in heavy industry has catapulted it uncomfortably into the centre of the global climate-change debate. In 2007, China overtook the United States as the world's largest annual emitter of greenhouse gases. Chinese often argued that China was still a developing country and that strict conservation criteria should not be imposed so that its economic growth would continue. But this did not stop criticism from developed countries. To deflect criticism and pacify domestic discontent with environmental problems, China announced the national programme on climate change in June 2007 to encourage energy conservation and promote the use of new technology to trap greenhouse gases. Solely relying on environmental protection bureaux is hardly enough to rein in big polluters. A broader political shift that gave citizens a bigger say in environmental issues was necessary. In 2005, the State Environmental Protection Administration used public hearings to consult the public over the renovation of the Old Summer Palace in Beijing. In addition, the Administration increased the transparency of environmental issues by being the first government agency to announce its own detailed rules to implement the Regulations on Open Government Information which came into effect in May 2008. The rules required officials to disclose information about air and water quality, pollution spills and the names and misdeeds of violators ('China to release action plan' 2 June 2007: 39).

The strategies of NGOs used to represent their members' interests and channel their efforts into policy process include:

1   bargaining, influencing or resisting political constraints through an alliance with mass media;
2   developing independent sources of revenue;
3   expanding their sphere of activities through the use of the Internet;
4   appealing to the public and the international community through the prestige and social networks of organisational entrepreneurs;
5   tapping the expertise of international NGOs;
6   influencing government officials' attitude through research dissemination, the demonstration of alternative models and training courses for government leaders; and
7   legal mobilisation (Yang 2005).

Because bureaucrats usually have to deal with a range of issues while NGOs work on single issues, some NGOs in China may have an advantage over the state with certain kinds of expertise and capacity that are essential for tackling new social problems. As suggested by Howell, the China AIDS Network and the Yunnan Reproductive Health Association have contributed to the design and delivery of certain medical policies (Howell 2004). Green River, an environmental NGO, offered suggestions on protecting the migration route of Tibetan antelopes based on scientific research. These ideas were adopted by the authorities (Yang 2005: 64). Han Dongfang – a leader of the Federation of Beijing Autonomous Labour Unions who had escaped arrest following his involvement in the 1989 Tiananmen Square incident and founded the *China Labour Bulletin* – said that he and other supporters had won the majority of the 30 labour-rights cases that they brought to Chinese courts. In one case, they represented jewellery workers who were sacked after developing silicosis, a lung disease contracted by breathing mineral dust. The court ruled the employer had to pay a record high compensation of 500,000 *yuan* to each worker (Pocha 2007). Han's experience reveals that workers and their representatives are able to negotiate in an autonomous sphere to act independently from the Party-state if they pursue a legitimate cause and avoid confrontation with the authorities.

With the technological advancement of the Internet and text messaging, mobilising the public to press for policy changes is possible even if an organisation in a conventional sense does not exist. The 2007 case of halting a chemical plant project in Xiamen city of Fujian province illuminates this point. The project, situated at the sea coast 16 km from the downtown of the city, was a joint project by a local enterprise and a Taiwan company. After completion, the 10.8 billion *yuan* plant was expected to pump out 800,000 tonnes of p-Xylene, a petrochemical that goes into polyester and fabrics, every year. The project had received all the required approvals and construction was ready to start. Fearful of illnesses such as skin irritation, headaches and breathing problems caused by exposure to the chemical, Zhao Yulen, a prominent scientist in the city, led the opposition to the project, spearheading one million mobile phone text messages urging people to protest. In the face of mass discontent, the city government in May 2007 announced a delay to the project and undertook another environmental assessment. But the public was still dissatisfied. On 1 June 2007, about 7,000 protesters wearing gas masks and holding banners marched through the city to demand the project's cancellation. The following day, a protest of about 2,000 participants took place. In the face of mounting pressure, Mayor Liu Cigui suggested the plant be relocated away from the city. The demonstrations are noteworthy as previous ones of comparable scale took place in villages, not in cities. Unlike the previous protests over the issues of livelihood, this was the first time in China that people took to the streets in the name of environmental protection. A tip-off suggested that some of the protesters were actually hired for 100 *yuan* a day by the property developers whose real worry was the impact of the project on the sale price of their properties (Chua 2007: 31, 33). If this tip-off was true, it suggests that citizens have become more sophisticated in using NGOs and social issues to affect government policies. They understand how to use a legitimate cause to cover up their selfish motives which are more prone to official suppression.

But the authorities own all the means to suppress these actions. As suggested by Huntington, established one-party states cannot stop the emergence of informal groups representing diverse and conflicting interests, and these groups do restrict the ruling party's supremacy (Huntington 1970). Consequently, the Chinese government is not hesitant to rein in these collective actions when necessary. After the two demonstrations, Mayor Liu Cigui accused the protesters of not having voiced their concerns through normal channels, such as the mayor's hotline, and had gone ahead with marches after the government had temporarily halted the projects. He warned that some participants would be punished as they had taken advantage of people's concern about environmental protection to take inappropriate and illegal actions. In July, Li Yiqiang, a Diaoyu Island activist and suspected ringleader behind the June protests, was arrested ('Citizen power' 31 May 2007: 13; 'Xiamen protesters' 2 June 2007: 8; Wang, J. 2007: A6; 'Activists held' 19 July 2007). The arrest of environmental activists is not unprecedented. Wu Lihong, a salesman turned environmentalist, was arrested in April after he reported the worsening pollution at Lake Tai, which was covered by a thick green algae, cutting off water to the city of Wuxi of Jiangsu province in May 2007. The various charges included one that claimed he extorted 55,000 *yuan* from enterprises by threatening to expose how they were polluting the environment. The arrest was believed by some environmentalists to be an act of revenge by polluters collaborating with local officials ('Trial' 9 June 2007: 13).

Collective actions considered subversive or embarrassing to the authorities are subject to suppression. Between 2003 and 2004, Li Dan, an AIDS activist working in Shanqiu city of Henan province, opened an orphanage for children who had lost their parents to AIDS. Without the approval of local authorities, his orphanage remained illegal and no schools were willing to admit the orphans. Li then started his own school called the Dongzhen School for AIDS Orphans. His work drew the attention of the national media and attracted donations to the project. However, he was later told by local officials that his project was illegal and must be closed down. Li refused, and later he and his volunteers were beaten by the police. The school was shut and the orphans were sent to a state orphanage. The true reason for the school's closure and Li's harassment was the unwanted attention drawn by the project to the AIDS epidemic in these locales (Pan 14 September 2004: A01). Even though the work of some NGOs does not conflict with state policies or the parameter laid by central government, local governments may shun it if they feel the work goes against their interests. All the reported arrests of activists only involved the leaders of the collective actions; other participants were set free. Such a strategy is similar to the government's attitude towards industrial actions seeking to resolve strikes but not to offend the participants whose complaints about the violation of labour rights are often legitimate (Cai 2006).

Realising the risk involved in policy advocacy, NGOs push their causes cautiously and seek protection from local authorities whenever possible. Shang has studied the orphanage Home of Dawn (*Liming zhijia*), established by a Catholic church in a Hebei province village. It relied heavily on donations of their followers and the voluntary work of the church's sisters. It remains unregistered because according to Chinese law, only local governments are able to run orphanages. Without legal status, the orphanage cannot apply for medical subsidies and urban social securities, nor can it hold any fundraising events. Legal restrictions can be circumvented. The orphanage is allowed to operate and receive government financial support and preferential treatment. At the time of its establishment, the Hebei provincial civil affairs bureau gave it several one-off grants for sums of 10,000 *yuan*, 2,000 *yuan* and 800 *yuan*. Before 2000, it had no 'collective household' (*jiti hukou*) status, but the orphans could still be exempted from the 'fee of borrowing school place' (*jiedu fei*) – a fee charged on the students without local households. Support from local authorities for unregistered NGOs illustrates the utilitarian attitude of the government towards NGOs. The government tolerates NGOs as long as they do not pose a challenge to the Party-state supremacy and help fulfil local agendas (Shang 2007).

The further development of civilian NGOs is held back by heavy state influence. All NGOs have to register with the Ministry of Civil Affairs or its local bureaux. A prerequisite for registration approval is that the NGOs must have the support of their sponsoring government departments, or be registered as members of a registered umbrella NGO. Unless the NGOs are useful to government departments, usually government departments are reluctant to sponsor them as department directors are worried that they will be implicated in any wrongdoing or complications caused by the NGOs. If NGOs remain unregistered and have no legal status, companies are reluctant to donate funds for fear of being implicated in any illegal activities. It was estimated that over 53 per cent of the funding of NGOs in China is derived from the state coffers (Wang 2002: 1–18). A national survey of NGOs undertaken by Jia and Pan revealed that 56 per cent of the respondents thought their NGOs lacked capital and 43 per cent thought they lacked expertise. The geographical distribution of NGOs is uneven and concentrated in the coastal cities; villages are underserved by them. The same survey found that among the six categories of people, social elites – who usually live in cities – are the most represented by NGOs, followed by women, national minorities and religious followers. Peasants and poor people are underrepresented (Jia and Pan 2006). Most Chinese are peasants and the poor urban migrant workers in cities. The failure of NGOs to penetrate these groups of people may deter them from representing and mobilising the constituency for the purpose of policy making and implementation.

Even though some NGOs have legal status and are financially independent, the state has a free hand to meddle in NGOs' internal affairs. Among the respondents in a national survey with NGOs' leaders conducted in 2005–7, 8 per cent of them thought that the state frequently intervened with civil society 'inappropriately'. Another 30 per cent believed inappropriate intervention sometimes happened (Jia and Pan 2006). The bans on *China Development Brief* and *Minjian* (Civil Society) from publication in July 2007 illuminate the vulnerability of China's non-governmental forces. Both bulletins were largely financially independent. The subscribers and funders of *China Development Brief* included the Asian Development Bank, the United Nations Development Programme, the British Council, the Save the Children Fund and dozens of foreign universities and media organisations. Both bulletins received funding from Partnership for Community Development – a Hong Kong-based fund aimed at mobilising social capital for developmental purposes. Since their respective launches in 1996 and 2005, these two bulletins have widely reported the news of China's NGOs and the appeals of NGOs advocating human-rights protection. *China Development Brief* once published an open letter from 12 organisations calling for a fair trial for the jailed environmental activist Wu Lihong (Young 2007). It has worked closely with Chinese government departments and state-sanctioned organisations such as the provincial environment protection bureau, the education bureau, the women's federation and China Association for NGOs on issues of consultancy and staff development. The patron of *Minjian* is the Civil and Social Development Research Centre of Sun Yat-sen University, a key-point university in

Guangdong province ('Feizhengfu zuzhi' 13 August 2007). Without adequate institutional protection against state encroachment, the participation of NGOs in public policies is difficult to institutionalise.

Cultural factors further affect NGOs in China, namely a high level of trust in the government and a low level trust in NGOs, and inadequate voluntarism. In a survey by Jia and Pan (2006), over 75 per cent of respondents expressed their trust with respect to the army, police, government, political leaders and media, all of which are part of the administration. When it comes to trusting temples, churches, labour unions, democratic parties and enterprises that are distant from the authorities, over 50 per cent answered 'don't know' or gave no answer. Almost half of the respondents answered 'don't know' or gave no answer in response to the question about whether the respondents participated in NGOs more or less often in comparison to 1998. Jia and Pan also measured the degree of voluntarism from three dimensions: voluntary donation, voluntary participation in charitable causes and voluntary participation. The degree of voluntarism is further divided into the width and depth of voluntarism. The width of voluntarism refers to whether Chinese people are willing to participate in many voluntary services. The depth refers to whether they are willing to intensively participate in any voluntary services. Scores were assigned by an expert focus group. It was found that out of the full score of three, the degree of voluntarism in China was not high (see Table 2.1).

The second type of NGO is GONGO. Except for the traditional mass organisations, most of these GONGOs were established during reform era. Many of them are former government bureaux which were transformed into semi-governmental organisations during the administrative reform in the 1990s. Examples of such organisations include: the Association of Chinese Machine-Making Industry, the Association of Chinese Electric Power Industry and the Chinese Consumer Association. GONGOs are more influential than civilian NGOs in the policy process due to their close connection with political elites. The sponsor of 'Project Hope' (a famous foundation for financing education-improvement projects in poverty-stricken regions) of the China Youth Development Foundation is organisationally dependent on its patron the Communist Youth League. Its dependence on state organs enables it to use the logistical and political support of the regional branches of the Communist Youth League for carrying out its programmes. Partly due to its institutional dependence on the

Table 2.1 Voluntarism in China

	Voluntary donation	*Voluntary participation in charitable causes*	*Voluntary participation in NGOs*
Width of voluntarism	1.4	1.5	0.6
Depth of voluntarism	0.8	0.9	0.8

Source: Jia and Pan (2006).

state, it raised over 936 million *yuan* between 1989 and 2004 (China Youth Development Foundation 2006). The role of GONGOs in the policy process is largely restricted to undertaking some of the economic functions that the government gave up during the transition from a planned to a market economy, and includes implementing state policies and advising the governments at various levels about drafting and revising laws. The Association of Chinese Machine-Making Industry, for example, provides their members with market analysis and advises the State Council on technological development through participating in drafting the 'Ten-Five' and 'Eleven-Five' economic-development plans. It also formulates and takes charge of the accreditation system for new industrial products (Civil Society Management Bureau 2005: 17–24). The National Association of Science and Technology established a code of ethics for publishers (Ogden 2002: 275). Before the Spring Festival of 2002, the State Council commissioned the Chinese Consumer Association, a government-sanctioned consumer association, to select consumer representatives to participate in the public hearing of train fares (Liu and Pang 2003: 289).

Alongside the rise of new GONGOs is the change of traditional mass organisations in their strategies of directing citizen participation. Take the example of the labour movement. Two opposing views are prevalent in evaluating labour unions in China. One of the views is that due to their institutional dependence on the Party-state, labour unions place a higher emphasis on social stability and implementation of Party policies than worker representation (Chen, F. 2003: 1010). Since the chairpersons of the firm branches and local levels of the ACFTU were appointed by the Party committees at corresponding levels, they risked being sacked or persecuted if they confronted the management of the firms or local governments on behalf of workers.[4] Citizen participation through the ACFTU is indirect. Under the Labour Contract Law, workers can only engage in collective bargaining for pay raises through the representation of branches of the ACFTU. In enterprises where the AFCTU has not established a branch (and this includes the great majority of enterprises in the private sector), workers may elect their own representatives to negotiate a collective contract with management, but only under the direction or guidance (*zhidao*) of the ACFTU ('National People's Congress' 28 July 2007). Decisions through mediation and arbitration are usually reached by representatives of the labour bureau administration, branches of the ACFTU and the economic administrative organs (representing employers). The aggrieved workers are not permitted to participate. Autonomous labour unions are still prohibited. Legal mobilisation by Chinese trade unions is essentially reactive rather than proactive, aimed at correcting the infringements of rights already stipulated in law rather than pursuing new rights claims (Chen 2004: 29).

Another view towards labour unions is more positive. The ACFTU's institutional dependence on the Party-state does not necessarily rule out its participatory function. It is true that a majority of workers choose not to join labour unions and many industrial disputes have led to mass protests and riots. But three points about ACFTU are noteworthy: First, the decrease in union membership is a worldwide phenomenon. It has been taking place in many Western democracies for more than two decades. The decrease in membership may not be caused by the weaknesses of unions, but by such factors as the increasing mobility of capital and the relative ease that white-collar workers have in terms of job mobility, as well as their numbers in proportion to the total workforce. Second, mass protests and riots are considered detrimental to social stability. The ACFTU and its local branches which are instrumental in maintaining social stability have a high incentive to mediate with management on workers' behalf. Their ability to represent workers determines their credibility and acceptability to those they represent. Third, the ACFTU and its local branches have the task of defending workers' rights. Their ability to advocate on behalf of workers depends on the capacity of the grassroots union, namely the membership numbers and firm-level unions. To recruit members and encourage workers to set up firm-level unions, they must show the workers that they can represent them and fight for their benefits.

Labour protests and riots have increased pressure on the state to make the ACFTU a true labour representative. In April 2006, the State Council's Office of Research released a report on migrant workers in China. According to the report, only 47.78 per cent per cent of migrant workers were able to draw their salary on time and over 76 per cent of them work more than eight hours a day. Over 70 per cent of migrant workers received no fringe benefits. About 80 per cent of the female workers who had taken maternity leave took unpaid leave. These labour-rights violations resulted in a rise in arbitration of labour disputes and wide-spread industrial action. In 2005, 31,400 labour disputes went to arbitration, an increase of 20.5 per cent over the previous year. In 2004, there were over 70,000 group actions and in 2005 there were 87,000 involving 100 people and above. It was estimated that of these group incidents, over 30 per cent were actions involving the defence of migrant workers' rights, and more than 20 per cent were industrial actions in which migrant workers were involved. These actions sometimes involved thousands of people. For example, to protest against arbitrary dismissals, several thousand workers at the Chongqing Special Iron and Steel Plant blockaded the roadway in August 2005. In November 2005, several thousand workers from four state-owned construction companies took to the streets, and on 29 November 2005, a few thousand sacked workers blockaded the office building of the Shengli Oil Field Management Bureau. In February 2006, over 1,000 workers from Heze Textiles in Shandong went on strike for a pay rise. In the past, people participating in collective action fighting for workers' rights were primarily the migrant workers unable to obtain urban residence rights. Most of the city-based workers were reluctant to participate in industrial action for fear that they would be sacked and lose all welfare benefits provided by their employers. In recent years, they have become more militant because after the restructuring of state-owned enterprises, the compensation packages for town- and city-based workers have been lowered to nearly the level of migrant workers'. Workers have little to lose if sacked (Cai 2007).

To deal with the challenges, the ACFTU felt a pressing need to defend workers' rights. In December 2006, Wang Zhaoguo, the Chairperson of the

ACFTU and Politburo member of the CCP, called for the development of 'the socialist view with Chinese characteristics of labour unions in defending workers' rights'. Under this socialist view, the ACFTU had to support economic reform and educate workers to identify with the reform and defend the 'lawful rights of workers'. When talking about the establishment of new unions and membership recruitment, Wang (3 October 2007) said:

> [We] have to enhance the establishment of grassroots unions in order to implement union policy ... [We] have to focus on establishing unions in non-state enterprises, particularly foreign-invested enterprises and recruit rural migrant workers ... [We] have to organise workers, mobilise workers, depend on workers, serve workers and increase unions' appeals to workers.

Since the ACFTU has a mission to defend workers' rights and strengthen its institutional construction, its organisational dependence on the Party-state does not rule out the possibility of local branches negotiating for more freedom in order to be more responsive to their constituencies. This was true even in the early 1990s when the tense political atmosphere in the post-Tiananmen incident period disallowed societal organisations high autonomy from state control. Unger and Chan documented how the Shanghai branch of the ACFTU tried to escape the close scrutiny of the central government by creating a research association and charging the research association with advocating workers' rights – a cause that state-sanctioned labour unions were prohibited from pursuing at that time (Unger and Chan 1996: 116). In July 2007, the Shanghai branch pioneered to become the first trade union in China to sign an agreement of cooperation with a US trade union – the Los Angeles County Labour Federation, AFL-CIO. Under the agreement, the two trade unions shared research about the multinational corporations which operated in both countries, and shared information about workplaces and the companies in which labour unions were organised already, or would be organised (Rojas 2007). By this means, the Shanghai branch can bypass the central authorities to obtain more knowledge and expand its network for achieving its organisational objectives.

Unions adopt several strategies to defend workers' rights and may also help to supervise the enforcement of pro-labour policies, like the Labour Contract Law made effective in 2008. Under this law, employees who have worked for the same company for more than ten consecutive years or who served more than two consecutive contract terms are entitled to the status of permanent employees. In fear of higher labour costs, telecommunications hardware giant Huawei attempted to persuade thousands of long-serving employees to resign ahead of the effective date of the law (1 January 2008). Huawei's proposal caused uproar across the country. The ACFTU then stepped in and forced Huawei to withdraw the proposal (Chow 2007). In June 2007, Xie Liangmin, a senior official of the ACFTU, threatened to oust the four Olympic-licensed goods-producing companies accused of labour abuse, such as hiring children as young as 12, forcing overtime and violating minimum-wage rules. In face of the pressure, the Beijing

Organising Committee for the Olympic Games revoked contracts with these companies ('China punishes' 12 June 2007).

Other forms include participating in the drafting of pro-labour legislation, such as the Employment Promotion Law and the Social Security Law and representing individual workers in labour disputes. Besides that, the ACFTU has actively coordinated with business associations over the issue of staff relations. Since 1989, the ACFTU and its local branches have taken part in over 6,600 joint management–staff groups formed in various levels of governments. Composed of union representatives, business associations, local governments and government departments, these joint management–staff groups meet once or twice a year to discuss matters of common interest, such as the impact of enterprise reform and social development on workers' rights, in addition to investigating controversial labour disputes and providing policy advice to government (*China Labour Bulletin* 29 July 2007). Unlike the labour-management councils in Nordic countries, the decisions of these groups are non-binding with the government and thus their impact on government policies is limited. The role of the ACFTU in protecting workers' rights is expected to be enhanced by the promulgation of the Labour Contract Law. This law would transform labour unions from suppliers of social welfare to defenders of labour rights over the issues of collective bargaining on wages, working hours, workplace safety and layoffs. Employers are required by this law to provide written contracts for their workers and give them a higher degree of job security through a more restrictive use of temporary workers (Kahn and Baroza 2007).

Large membership contributes to workers' rights protection, so the ACFTU aggressively increases its firm-level unions and membership. It has successfully formed trade unions in such multi-national corporations as Wal-Mart, McDonald's and Kentucky Fried Chicken, whose US workers are not unionised. Within 14 months of the establishment of the first labour union in China's Wal-Mart, 77 out of the 84 branches of Wal-Mart have labour unions. These labour unions have 21,000 members, or more than half of the employees (Yu 2007). Despite reports accusing the unions in multi-national corporations of having more interest in collecting membership fees than protecting workers' rights, other reports indicated that these unions had successfully advocated for workers' rights. The Wal-Mart unions in Fuzhou city of Fujian province were said to have successfully persuaded the management to raise part-time workers' wages to 6 *yuan* per hour, above the minimum wage of 5.5 *yuan*, and to abolish the probation period for part-time workers. Migrant workers are another target of unionisation. Though China's trade unions helped 2.8 million migrant workers claim 1.3 billion *yuan* in unpaid wages, the ACFTU realised that the low level of unionisation made it difficult to stop exploitation of workers – only 41 million out of the total 200 million (or 20.5 per cent) migrant workers across the country were union members by the end of 2006. As a result, the ACFTU stepped up its recruitment drive among migrant workers and increased membership from migrant workers by ten million in 2007 (Fu 2007: 6). In view of the emergence of small private enterprises which may be too small to have enough employees interested in forming unions, the ACFTU adopted a new approach for union establishment. Two or more enterprises situated in the same region with fewer than 25 employees in the same industry may form one union. If unions cannot be formed because of the small number of employees, workers' groups may be formed and affiliated with the union at the immediate higher administrative level. Union leaders from the state sector may be deployed to large and private foreign-invested enterprises to assist in forming unions or stand in the election of the leaders of these newly formed unions (*China Labour Bulletin* 29 July 2007). The official website of the ACFTU maintains a special column '*zuzhi qilai*' (Organise) featuring the achievements of its local branches in union building and propagating the successful experience to union officials nationwide.

Another group-based mode of participatory activity is participation through residents' committees. Residents' committees played an important role in mobilising masses to take part in political campaigns and scrutinising counter-revolutionaries in the pre-reform era (Read 2000; Lin 2003a). During the reform era, their primary responsibilities are to mediate disputes among residents in the same neighbourhood, manage housing property, work on community hygiene and provide recreation and welfare to retired residents who cannot receive welfare from previous work units due to the bankruptcy of work units. In addition, they assist the state in policing neighbourhoods, such as reporting Falungong activities to the police and implementing the 'strike hard' campaign (like killing stray dogs considered virus carriers during the SARS outbreak in 2003).[5]

In theory, residents' committees are desirable laboratories for grassroots democracy. They are designated by the state as autonomous organisations run by residents. Their responsibilities are related to soft issues that have little relevance to state secrets and security, important decisions on personnel and finance, economic development or countrywide issues. It is easy for the state to contain the problems arising from failed experiments. In practice, the state uses residents' committees to micro-manage: The staff members and finance of residents' committees are managed by street offices – the lowest level of government apparatus in cities. As a result, residents generally regard these committees as the authorities' executive arms and have little incentive to participate. In a 1999 survey, 20 per cent of the respondents believed that residents' committees were part of the administration; 70.9 per cent thought residents' committees were autonomous organisations under the guidance of street offices. Only 1.8 per cent said residents' committees were completely autonomous organisations (Xu 1999: 87). A survey in two residents' committees in Shanghai municipality found that over 80 per cent of the residents preferred to authorise the representatives of a grouping of households (*jumin xiaozhu*) to vote rather than to use the one-person-one-vote system in the election of residents' committees (Lin 2003b: 74). In another Shanghai residents' committee, the average age of the seven elected cadres was 52. One of them was over 60. Only one of them was male and two were non-Party members. Young people opted out from the election (Li, G. 2004: 20). A survey on the residents' committees in Wuhan city of Hubei province suggested that residents usually participated in residents' committees for recreational, security and charitable purposes. Decision making and discussion about community affairs were the least popular spheres of participation (Yan 2005).

With community affairs becoming more relevant to residents' interests, there are hopes that residents' committees will become popular vehicles of citizen participation. In the wake of mid-1980s housing reform, more citizens purchase their own housing. Unlike the people in the pre-reform era who lived in state-allocated apartments and cared little about housing management, property owners are much more concerned with the quality of housing management which obviously affects the value of their own property. Nevertheless, many property-management companies cannot provide the kind of service that property owners want. The disputes between property-management companies and property owners require strong mediators to settle (Read 2000; Chen, C. 2003). In addition, new social phenomena such as unemployment and migrant workers have forced a large segment of the population out of the protection of the social security net centred on work units and household registration. The emphasis on efficient over egalitarian values in the reform era has forced state-owned enterprises and government departments to shed its welfare functions. Some local governments are left with the welfare functions which they are either reluctant or unable to afford, so they try to unload these functions on residents' committees. Shenyang was one of three cities in Liaoning province selected to experiment with the re-employment programme under the management of residents' committees. The programme was designed to organise neighbourhoods and enterprises, and to develop preferential policies to encourage laid-off workers to set up businesses and to spur firms to employ sizable numbers of these workers, while spreading propaganda about self-reliance (Solinger 2004).

In addition, the 1990 Urban Residents' Committees Law was revised (but had not been approved when this chapter was written) to oblige local governments to allocate extra funding to residents' committees. More funding from local governments may improve the financial situation of residents' committees, relieving them of the duties of revenue generation, and enabling them to concentrate on decision making. To prevent election rigging which undermines the true representation of a residents' committee, the draft version of the new Urban Residents' Committees Law enfranchises new migrants to the communities so that residents' committees will be made more representative. The Law also prohibits any organisations or people from designating, appointing and recalling the members of residents' committees. All the candidates will be nominated by residents with voting rights. The provision, if implemented, will reduce the chance of local leaders' elbowing out the candidates nominated by residents who are unreliable in the eyes of local leaders. Meanwhile, residents' committees are delegated with more authority and autonomy. Trial schemes have been carried out in Beijing, Kunming city of Yunnan province, Guangzhou and Shenzhen cities of Guangdong province, Xiamen city of Fujian province and Qingdao city of Shandong province. Under the trial schemes, residents' committees are responsible for making decisions about community affairs. Its decisions, together with other tasks assigned by street offices, are implemented by community offices (*shequ gongzuo zhan*). Guiyang city of Guizhou province, Qingdao city of Shandong province and Beijing municipality have experimented with not establishing street offices in newly developed neighbourhoods in order to insulate residents' committees from intervention by local authorities. Nanjing city of Jiangsu province abolished some street offices in old districts. Jianghan district of Wuhan city in Hubei province authorised residents' committees to participate in an annual performance appraisal of nine offices under district governments, 13 street offices, over 400 civil servants and more than 1,300 community workers (Zhao 2007; Li 2007; 'Zhongguo juweihui' 23 September 2007; Chen, W. 2003: 72–3, 84–5). With higher authority and greater autonomy, residents' committees are expected to become more prestigious and appealing to the participation-oriented young and better-educated residents.

On top of the revitalisation of old group-based participatory activities is the newly institutionalised individual-based ones, such as a public hearing. The first public hearing in China was held in Shenzhen city of Guangdong province in 1993. Public hearings in China have two major characteristics: First, they are aimed at giving feedback about the decision-making processes and policy proposals, but not at developing performance indicators to evaluate government performance. Second, they have the potential to depoliticise politically charged issues. Price hikes on public utilities, for example, may trigger popular unrest. By putting the price-hike proposal on the agenda of public hearings, the authorities can shift the decisions on price hikes to an administrative process under their control. Public hearings are legally based in around 120 pieces of legislation. Some examples include the 2002 Environmental Impact Assessment Law which obliges property developers to hold open forums and secure opinions from experts and the affected public on environmental-impact assessments ('Zhonghua renmin gongheguo wanjing yingxian pingjia fa' 12 April 2005). The 1996 Administrative Punishment Law allows people with declined or revoked business licenses to seek redress through public hearings ('Xinzhen chufeng fa' 12 April 2005). Under the Price Law, the governments at various levels have to hold public hearings before they determine the price level of public utilities, social services and commodities and services provided by monopolistic suppliers ('Zhonghua renmin gongheguo jiagefa' 2005). By the end of 2001, over ten provinces and directly administered cities, such the provinces of Shaanxi, Heilongjiang, Anhui and Jiangsu, and the municipalities of Beijing and Tianjin have established public-hearing systems on price setting. They held around 200 evidentiary hearings, with agendas focusing on water charges, power charges, gas charges, public transport fares, entrance tickets to tourist attractions, university tuition fees and telecommunication service charges (Han and Zhao 2002).

Public hearings on legislation started at the turn of the twenty-first century. Guangdong province pioneered experimentation with public hearings on drafting the Regulations of Construction Tendering in 1999. In 2000, public hearings on legislation were institutionalised by the Legislation Law. Article 34 of the law stipulates that public hearings and public consultation may be used in the law drafting process ('Zhonghua renmin gongheguo lifa fa' 12 April 2005). By the end of 2004, 24 standing committees of the provincial People's Congress held public hearings on the drafting of 39 laws (Shi 2006). The first public hearing on national legislation was held in 2005, concerning the controversial Property Rights Law. In the same year, National People's Congress held another public hearing to collect public opinion over the revised Individual Income Tax Law (Shen 2006). The system of public hearings opens up a window for activists to reformulate policies. Qiao Zhangxiang, a Beijing-based lawyer and one of the most zealous proponents of public hearings of price hikes, sued the Ministry of Railways in 2001 for not holding a public hearing on train fares at the time of the Spring Festival. Though he eventually lost the case, the State Development Planning Commission (the predecessor of National Development and Reform Commission) worked out a provisional measure which obliges all central ministries to hold public hearings before raising the price of water, electricity, coal, telecommunications and railway tickets ('Public hearings system' 2004).

The impact of public hearings on policy outcome is mixed. In the wake of the 2002 public hearing over the national train-fare hike, the State Council decided that before the Spring Festival, economy-class train fares could rise by 15 per cent, far below the proposed range of 20–30 per cent. To accommodate the wishes of relatively well-off passengers who preferred good service to low fares, the deluxe-class fare hike was set at 35 per cent, far above the proposed 20–30 per cent rise (Liu and Pang 2003: 294). Another public hearing in Beijing municipality received strong protests against the proposal of raising university tuition fees. The protest successfully delayed the fee hike by half a year (Pang *et al.* 2004: 73). The first legislative public hearing in Shijiazhuang city of Hebei province in 2000 produced 29 amendments to a draft bill on river management (Paler 2005: 316). Some surveys suggested otherwise, however. Zhang (2005: 32) cited two surveys, and both suggested that the public was becoming more and more dissatisfied with public hearings due to their formality. Three questions have to be answered to evaluate the impact of public hearings on the policy process and its success in bringing about a high degree of citizen participation:

1   Do public hearings function alongside other participatory institutions, such as citizen committees or courts, councils of information, citizen advisory councils, neighbourhood councils, citizen courts, referenda and initiatives?
2   Is the administration transparent enough that the citizenry are well-informed of the matters in consultation?
3   Are the participants of public hearings representative of a broad spectrum of general public? (Yang 2003: 507)

The answers to all three questions are negative. Societal groups are denied strong institutional positions in the policy process. The NGOs focused on the issues in question and the residents' committees cannot take part in public hearings if they are not officially invited. The authorities maintain a tight grip on the selection of participants in public hearings. Participants are often selected from local people's congresses and people's political consultative commissions, residents' committees, mass media, mass organisations or the Chinese Consumer Association. Sometimes the authorities have reached a consensus with the participants before public hearings begin in order to avoid controversy. In 2007, Hefei city of Anhui province held a public hearing on the rise of water-treatment fees. The authorities refused to disclose the identity of the eight participants in the public hearing, and the public could not offer their opinions to the participants. Moreover, the media were disallowed from broadcasting the proceedings of the public hearing. The public had no idea whether the participants reflect the public's or their own independent, personal opinions (Gao 2007; 'Bullet time' 19–25 May 2007: 68).

Legal actions challenging the legality of government decisions over public hearings have limited impact. Courts are dependent on the Party-state. Their finances are controlled by the Party committees at corresponding level. Their judges are appointed for fixed terms by the Party committees at higher levels while the Party committees at corresponding level can affect the candidates nominated to the higher-level Party committees. Thus the government has full discretion to selectively use public hearings rather than strictly follow laws and regulations. In April 2007, China introduced the first of its 280 bullet trains as part of a scheme that would eventually raise passenger capacity by 18 per cent and freight capacity by 12 per cent. To cover the higher operating costs, the railway ministry decided to raise ticket prices by 50–100 per cent. According to the Price Law, the ministry was supposed to consult with consumers over pricing and apply for approval from the State Council. The ministry claimed that the rules did not apply in this case and refused to hold public hearings (Gao 2007; 'Bullet time' 19–25 May 2007: 68).

The flow of information is far from free, and therefore the citizenry are not well-informed of the issues under consultation. The implementation of opening information up for public scrutiny is contingent on a legal framework effective in reining in an administration which refuses to live up to its legal obligations on transparency issues. An open law that releases national information is non-existent. Before the promulgation of the Regulations on Publicising Government Information in 2007, local-information open decrees were issued by some provincial and prefectural-level governments such as the municipalities of Shanghai and Chongqing, the provinces of Jilin and Hubei, and in the cities of Jiaxing in Zhejiang province, Datong in Shanxi province, Wuhan in Hubei province, Kunming in Yunan province, Hangzhou in Zhejiang province and Chengdu in Xichuan province. The regulations could not rule out the higher discretionary authority of local authorities over the degree of transparency. In June 2006, a journalist referred to Shanghai City Information Open Regulations to sue a government department of Shanghai for its refusal to give interviews. The court refused to hear the case ('Gongkai shi yuanze' 2007: 1). Due to the Regulations on Publicising Government Information, a right to access government-held information has been introduced. Presently, a system centred on the General Office of the State Council is set up for controlling and publicising certain categories of public records. The information involving ill-defined state secrets, national security, public order, economic security and social stability cannot be made readily available ('Zhongguo chengli' 2007: 26). The definition of state secret is so vague that much of the information essential for public consultation may be classified as a state secret and then prohibited from being disclosed. A Shanghai-based lawyer, Zheng Enchong, who had been involved in the defence of economic and social rights of those displaced by urban development projects was sentenced to three years' imprisonment in 2003 for releasing state secrets to New York-based NGO China's Human Rights. In this case, the state secret released was a report on the forced demolition of residences. The reporters were beaten by hooligans suspected to have connections with the property developers behind the forced demolition. This was documented in an internal reference (*neibu canbian*) compiled by the New China News Agency. The report was classified as a state secret because according to the State Secret Law, a state secret is information circulated among a limited number of officials within a limited period of time. When an internal reference is circulated among senior officials, it is classified as a state secret (Deng 2007).

Moreover, participation is neither broad nor representative. Before August 2001, only Qingdao city of Shandong province publicly announced the date of public hearings and welcomed all citizens to attend. Almost all the public hearings are held behind closed doors and restricted to a few participants (Pang, Xue and Shen 2004: 33). A technical reason for that is the financial burden involved in public hearings. The cost involved in genuine open public hearings includes publicity, recruitment of participants, the rental of the venue holding public hearings, and transportation for participants. A public hearing over a draft law in Shenzhen city of Guangdong province in 1999 may cost up to 50,000 *yuan* (Pang, Xue, Jin and Shen 2004: 139). Guiyang city of Guizhou province spent up to 30,000 *yuan* per hour for television coverage of its hearings and thousands of *yuan* for miscellaneous expenses (Paler 2005: 317). The high administrative costs involved are prohibitive for some local governments to hold truly open public hearings. To reduce the administrative costs and to draw more participants, Chongqing municipality pioneered online public hearings in 2005 to consult the public on the supervision of law enforcers. The two-hour public-hearing session drew over 300 people to give their opinions online and over 80,000 clicks on this event were recorded (Fang 2006: 42–3).

The unenthusiastic local authorities are another weakness. After investigating the cases in the United States, Yang and Callahan concluded that the value public managers place on participation is the most important factor in affecting the decisions of citizen involvement. The attitude of public managers can be influenced by the expectations and pressures of salient external stakeholders. Public managers will respond more positively to salient groups such as elected officials, the business community and nonprofit organisations because of their perceived power and relationship with the administration. In addition, the skill level of public managers in engaging citizens has much impact on the outcome of public hearings (Yang and Callahan 2007: 260–1). Wang surveyed local government administrators about citizen input in various management and service functions in the local communities of the United States. He found that citizen participation in decision making and priority setting was very limited. The opportunities for citizen participation are under the control of local government administrators (Wang 2001). China is no different. In an authoritarian regime, no salient external stakeholders have strong institutionalised positions. Therefore they are too weak to pressure government officials to be responsive to their expectations. In 2004, Zhengzhou city of Henan province held a public hearing on water charges. The food industry was a salient external stakeholder, but was not invited to attend the public hearing. A January 2002 public hearing on train fares did not allow the participants enough time to exchange views with other train passengers and survey their own opinions before the public hearing was held (Liu 2007).

Conclusion

In the discussion of China's policy agenda setting, Wang identified six models of policy agenda setting within two dimensions: the initiator of policy agendas (decision makers, advisers and citizens) and the degree of public participation. He refuted the assertions in some Western literature that no political reform had taken place in China. Due to an array of factors such as a general suspicion of the 'efficient-first' economic reform, increasing consciousness and assertiveness of stakeholders, associational revolutions, the changing role of the mass media and the rise of the Internet, Wang argued that citizens have many opportunities to be the initiators of policy agendas and enjoy a high degree of public participation (Wang 2008). His argument underlines that the participatory activities in the post-Mao era are not planned by the state but spontaneously emerge. In response, the state introduces new modes and rejuvenates old modes of participation to channel the participatory activities without compromising the party's supremacy.

By using the OECD's framework of three-level citizen participation,[6] we may conclude that in China, access to information (the lowest level of participation) is easier, but still lacks institutional protection. The Regulations on Publicising Government Information issued in 2007 are not aimed at expanding access to information but standardising the bureaucracy in controlling information. The example of a Shanghai journalist suing the government for refusing to give interviews illustrates that legal action is still ineffective in ensuring the right of accessing information.

The system of consultation – the second level of participation – has improved. Residents' committees have been revitalised and granted more autonomy and financial support. With the advancement of technology in Internet and telecommunications, the activism of NGOs has become more common and the authorities have shown a high degree of tolerance as long as the activities of NGOs are related to issues of high priority. Public hearings on the price of utilities, environmental issues and legislation enable the authorities to solicit public opinion on issues closely related to people's livelihood. Without fair and contested elections in residents' committees, as well as institutionalised positions of NGOs in the policy process, however, the participants in consultation are vetted and controlled by the authorities. The command-and-control approach precludes a broad and representative participation.

There is no evidence supporting the notion that the Chinese government seeks active participation from the public and forms partnership with its citizens in the policy process, which would be the highest level of participation. The CCP has not given up its claim as the representatives of the people and their ability to act in the best interests of the state. With this basic belief unchanged, the CCP has little desire to involve citizens deeply in the decision-making process at all stages. The impact of public hearings on public policies is undermined by the nature of its advisory role. Usually the authorities do not vote and make binding decisions in public hearings. Whether the authorities accept the opinions collected depends heavily on the goodwill of the authorities. Launching a public hearing follows a top-down approach. Government departments and GONGOs, not the citizens, initiate public hearings and consultations. The government's monopoly over the initiation of public hearings denies citizens the right to set agendas. Prioritising political agendas remains the domain of the government. Charitable NGOs help to fill the gaps for welfare provision that governments at various levels are either unable or unwilling to shoulder. However, the role of NGOs is that of a service provider, not as a part of the administration. Without legal status, many of these NGOs are vulnerable to state intervention and have difficulty gaining the autonomy necessary for their foundation and existence as true partners with the administration. By and large, NGOs' role in policy making is confined to the stage of policy implementation and evaluation. The appointment of some NGO leaders to the National People's Congress, the Chinese People Political Consultative Conference and their local congresses does not give them much leverage with policy initiation and formulation. None of them except the chairperson of ACFTU are members of the Politburo, the apex of decision making in China. The chairperson is regarded as a representative of the CCP to oversee unions' activities rather than the workers' top representative, and serves as a partner of the central government over labour issues.

3   Taxation reform

The existing literature on China's fiscal policies presents a contrasting picture of the government's fiscal situation. Some literature suggests that the Chinese government is fiscally sound. The ratio of government debt to GDP is low. Central government is able and willing to increase its fiscal transfer to local governments and its budgetary appropriation to fundamental education and health care – policy areas which are mainly financed by local governments in both China and many other countries. It spends handsomely on the Western Development Project to reduce regional disparities, and abolishes agricultural taxes to reduce the peasants' tax burden. Other literature suggests that local officials are predatory; they violate regulations on fee and tax collection and impose exorbitant fees on peasants. The reasons for the problems are plentiful: corruption and the personal greed of individual local leaders, the lack of effective democratic control and the local governments' need to balance their budgets, service their debts, support unfunded mandates and meet the payroll bill for the unwieldy bureaucracy.

The chapter will focus on these questions: What happens in the fiscal policies that yield such contradictory views? Has the fiscal reform progressed to desirable targets? This chapter will review some basics of the fiscal process and will focus on taxation reform since the 1980s. Then this chapter will evaluate major fiscal reform measures, pointing out that the reform has reflected the political elites' high priority of raising central revenue as opposed to allocating adequate revenue to local governments and dividing expenditure assignments between the centre and localities equitably. The reform has increased central revenue and its share in the gross government revenue at the expense of local governments' revenue adequacy. To deal with fiscal stress, many local governments had increasingly to rely on extra-budgetary revenue, imposing a heavy burden on the average citizen. In response, central government centralised some expenditure assignments and increased the fiscal transfer to local governments. While the burden on average citizens has been lightened, the sustainability of the policy is uncertain given that the fiscal transfer has not been institutionalised. In the face of uncertain central allocation, it is unclear whether local governments will fund projects that require long-term financial commitments.

Background of taxation reform

Taxation is an important means that states use to extract necessary resources for directing national development. In the pre-reform era, the Chinese government extracted resources by three ways: (1) fixed and low labour costs which created bloated profits for many industries; (2) state ownership of industry and restricted entry; and (3) compulsory procurement of agricultural products and mandated trade among producers at plan prices (Wong 1997: 27–8). In addition, disposal of fiscal resources was highly centralised and redistributive. Local governments had to hand over all their budgetary revenue to central government. Central government then redistributed the revenue according to its agenda and the level of economic development of different provinces. Since local governments had little autonomy and incentive to hide their revenue, the monitoring cost of central government over local governments was low. The flip side was that local governments had little incentive to generate tax revenue, and therefore the resource-extraction capacity was much affected.

The resource-extractive mechanism broke down following the emergence of the market economy. Local governments were granted higher autonomy in revenue generation and retention to increase their incentive to extract resources. The gains of the local governments were the losses of central government; central government could no longer command a substantial amount of revenue from local governments. To reformulate the system of sharing the revenue between central and provincial-level governments, the central government introduced a fiscal contracting system known as 'eating from separate stoves' (*fenzao chifan*). Under this system, tax was first collected by the provincial-level governments. Some of the tax revenue was remitted to central treasury and the rest was retained for local use. There were several ways to share tax revenue. The methods used were contingent on the negotiation power and economic situation of provincial-level governments.[1]

The major disadvantage of this system was that it encouraged provincial-level governments to hide revenues from the central government. The discretion of local governments in granting tax exemptions also affected central revenue: many local governments offered incentives such as tax exemptions and deductions to entice new enterprises. In return, these enterprises were required to donate to the local governments or provide local public services (such as roads and bridge building). These financial manoeuvres benefited both local governments and enterprises, but caused heavy losses for the central treasury. The proportion of tax revenue under the central government's control dwindled; the taxation system became less redistributive. Meanwhile, the negotiations between central and provincial-level governments were prolonged and complicated. This way of tax sharing lacked the transparency and certainty necessary for forecasting and long-term planning (Zhang 2006: 459).

Tax-sharing reform in 1994

Under this background, a tax-sharing reform was introduced in 1994 in order to simplify the tax structure, replace the product tax and business tax in many services. Taxes were classified into three major categories: central taxes, local taxes and shared taxes (the part of revenue shared between central and provincial-level governments).[2] With a clear formula, tax assignment became more transparent and institutionalised. The sharing of tax revenue was no longer subject to negotiation. Both central and provincial-level governments had greater certainty about their future tax revenues. Long-term fiscal planning was then easier.

The 1994 tax-sharing reform moved Chinese tax administration closer to international standards. Provincial-level governments were assigned several taxes on immobile (or scarcely mobile) factors and goods such as urban land-use taxes, urban construction and maintenance taxes and taxes on land-based resources. This allowed provincial-level governments enough stable sources of revenue that they did not need to compete with each other for goods and other factors through lowering the tax rate. Local governments which bore the costs of processing handling licences and providing public service for users were fully compensated (Brosio 1995: 179). The central tax office was set up to collect central revenue that was partially shared with provincial-level governments. The performance of the central tax office was evaluated on the amount of revenue collected. This tax-collection system corrected the over-reliance on the local tax offices that had incentive to hide tax revenue for local treasuries.

Brosio suggested taxes such as personal income tax which lead to wealth redistribution should be assigned to the central government. To discourage competition among local governments for factors of production through lowering the tax rate and undermining gross tax revenue, the central government should be assigned the responsibility for the customs tax, corporate income tax, taxes on mobile factors and goods, and the value-added tax on manufacturing. Sales taxes levied at the retail stage (or consumption taxes) can be given to local governments in so far as it is possible to restrict the tax to residents and interjurisdiction mobility of production factors is not the concern. Brosio (1995: 179) further pointed out that China does not strictly follow these practices. Personal income tax is assigned to provincial-level governments. Consumption tax is collected by central government. The corporation income tax generated by central enterprises and banks and non-bank financial intermediaries was assigned to central government while provinces retained the corporation income tax generated by other enterprises. The value-added tax on manufacturing was shared between central and provincial governments at a fixed rate of 75 per cent for the central government and 25 per cent for local governments. A single province in China is as big as many countries, undertaking the policies of wealth redistribution within individual provinces through the leverage of personal income tax may reduce administrative bottlenecks and increase efficiency. Furthermore, the worries of interjurisdictional competition for factors of production and the consequential loss of tax revenue through tax reduction and concession are nonexistent in

China: the taxation reform prohibited local governments from determining the tax rate and granting tax breaks. This underlies the reform leaders' strong emphasis on the central government's role over major taxation decisions.

The aftermath of tax-sharing reform

Tax-sharing reform has successfully improved the resource-extractive capacity of central government. The revenue of central treasuries as a proportion of gross tax revenue rose from 22 per cent in 1993 to 55.7 per cent in 1994 and remained between 48.9 per cent and 55 per cent throughout the post-1994 period. In contrast with the pre-1994 period, central revenue exceeded expenditure (see Figure 3.1). The fiscal health of central government has improved, from a budgetary deficit of 35.46 billion *yuan* in 1993 to surplus of 777.26 billion *yuan* in 2005 (see Figure 3.2). Central tax revenue rocketed from 87.44 billion in 1993 to 283.08 billion in 1994 and continues to increase.

Table 3.1 suggests a gloomier picture. While the share of central tax in both total tax revenue and GDP also rose substantially, the resource-extractive capacity of the state (measured in terms of proportion of the total tax revenue in GDP) dropped slightly from 12.04 per cent in 1993 to 10.64 per cent in 1994 shortly after the introduction of tax sharing. Though the rate later increased and peaked at 15.72 per cent in 2005, it did not go significantly higher than 13.73 per cent in 1991.

The 1994 tax-sharing reform achieved revenue adequacy for the central government at the expense of local governments' resource-extractive capacity. The types of tax created after 1993 (consumption tax and VAT on imports, consumption tax, personal income tax, vehicle purchase tax and cargo tax) benefited the central government much more than local governments. The abolition of several taxes hurt local governments more than the central government. The most noteworthy one was product tax – the third most important source of tax to local

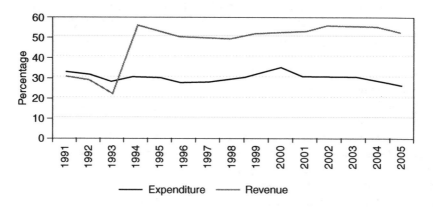

Figure 3.1 Proportion of central revenue and expenditure as the gross government revenue and expenditure (source: National Bureau of Statistics (2006: 286)).

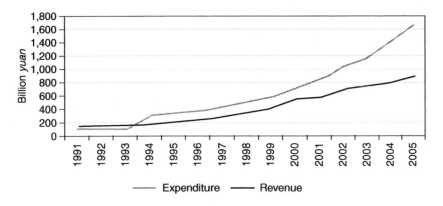

Figure 3.2 Central revenue and expenditure, 1991–2005 (source: National Bureau of Statistics (2006: 286)).

government in 1993 (see Table 3.2). The agricultural tax – the seventh most important source of tax – was abolished in 2006 to lessen peasants' burden. Local governments' share of value-added tax – the most important source of revenue for local governments – was drastically reduced from 88.2 per cent in 1993 to 26.5 per cent in 2005. Its share of the stamp tax on the security exchange dropped from 100 per cent in 1993 to 2.9 per cent in 2005. The change in the tax

Table 3.1 Tax revenue and GDP

Year	Central tax revenue (billion yuan)	Central tax as a proportion in total tax revenue (%)	Central tax as a proportion in GDP (%)	Total tax as a proportion in GDP (%)
1991	78.06	26.10	3.58	13.73
1992	84.36	27.02	3.31	12.25
1993	87.44	21.65	2.47	12.04
1994	283.08	58.11	5.87	10.64
1995	320.26	55.82	5.27	9.93
1996	345.77	50.04	4.86	9.71
1997	422.87	51.36	5.35	10.43
1998	482.44	52.08	5.72	10.97
1999	574.77	53.80	6.41	11.91
2000	689.27	54.78	6.95	12.68
2001	833.86	54.50	7.60	13.95
2002	1,023.03	58.01	8.50	14.66
2003	1,160.40	57.90	8.54	14.74
2004	1,416.61	58.62	8.86	15.11
2005	1,605.18	55.78	8.77	15.72

Sources: Calculated from Finance Yearbook of China Editorial Committee (ed.), *Zhongguo caizheng nianjian* (Finance Yearbook of China) (various years); National Bureau of Statistics, *China Statistical Yearbook* (various years).

Table 3.2 A breakdown of tax types, 1993 and 2005 (billion *yuan*)

Types of tax	1993		2005	
	Central	Local	Central	Local
Consumption tax and VAT on imports	N/A	N/A	421.18 (100%)*	0 (0%)
Consumption tax	N/A	N/A	163.38 (100%)	0 (0%)
Personal income tax	N/A	N/A	125.69 (61%)	83.80 (39%)
Vehicle purchase tax	N/A	N/A	58.33 (100%)	0 (0%)
Cargo tax	N/A	N/A	1.38 (100%)	0 (0%)
Product tax	18.28 (22%)	63.86 (78%)	N/A	N/A
Other tax on industry and business	0 (0%)	29.43 (100%)	N/A	N/A
Fixed assets investment adjustment	0 (0%)	3.84 (100%)	N/A	N/A
Salt tax	0 (0%)	0.79 (100%)	N/A	N/A
Special consumption tax	1.35 (100%)	0 (0%)	N/A	N/A
Special petrol tax	0.16 (100%)	0 (0%)	N/A	N/A
Value-added tax	12.76 (12%)	95.39 (88%)	793.13 (73%)	286.08 (27%)
Stamp duty on security exchange	0 (0%)	3.51 (100%)	6.65 (97%)	0.20 (3%)
Business tax	7.50 (8%)	89.11 (92%)	12.96 (3%)	410.28 (97%)
Resource tax	0.28 (11%)	2.28 (89%)	0 (0%)	14.22 (100%)
Company income tax	46.96	21.02	320.40	213.99
Urban land-using tax	1.51 (50%)	1.51 (50%)	0 (0%)	13.73 (100%)
Urban maintenance and construction tax	0.21 (12%)	1.51 (88%)	0.47 (1%)	79.1 (99%)
Tariffs	25.65 (100%)	0 (0%)	106.61 (100%)	0 (0%)
Tax on the use of cultivated land	0.75 (26%)	2.19 (74%)	0 (0%)	14.19 (100%)
Agricultural tax	0 (0%)	29.89 (100%)	0 (0%)	5.94 (100%)
Tax rebate for foreign trade company	−29.97 (100%)	0 (0%)	−404.89 (100%)	0 (0%)
Other taxes	2.96 (100%)	0 (0%)	0 (0%)	151.11 (100%)

Sources: Finance Yearbook of China Editorial Committee (ed.), *Zhongguo caizheng nianjian 2001* (Finance Yearbook of China 2001), p. 381; Finance Yearbook of China Editorial Committee (ed.), *Zhongguo caizheng nianjian 2006* (Finance Yearbook of China 2006), p. 403.

Note
* As a proportion of the total amount of that tax type.

composition pushed local governments' budgetary deficit from 6.78 billion *yuan* in 1992 to 172.66 billion in 1994 and 1,005.35 billion in 2005. The deficit as a percentage of budgetary revenue rose from 2.71 per cent in 1992 to 74.69 per cent in 1994, despite dropping mildly since then (see Table 3.3).

Another problem of tax-sharing reform was the removal of several important sources of local revenue without the corresponding removal of local expenditure assignments. In 1999, local governments at various levels financed 90 per cent

Table 3.3 Revenue and expenditure of provincial-level governments

Year	Revenue (billion yuan)	Expenditure (billion yuan)	Deficit (billion yuan)	Deficit as a percentage of revenue (%)
1989	184.24	193.50	9.26	5.03
1990	194.47	207.91	13.44	6.08
1991	221.12	229.58	8.46	3.83
1992	250.39	257.18	6.78	2.71
1993	339.14	333.02	−6.12	N/A
1994	231.16	403.82	172.66	74.69
1995	298.56	482.83	184.27	61.72
1996	374.69	578.63	203.94	54.43
1997	442.42	670.11	227.69	51.46
1998	498.40	767.26	268.86	53.94
1999	559.49	903.53	344.04	61.49
2000	640.61	1,036.67	396.06	61.83
2001	780.33	1,313.46	533.13	68.32
2002	851.50	1,528.15	676.65	79.47
2003	985.00	1,722.99	737.99	74.92
2004	1,189.34	2,059.28	869.94	73.14
2005	1,510.08	2,515.43	1,005.35	66.58

Source: National Bureau of Statistics (2006: 286).

of the expenditure on social services (education, health, culture and science). County and township-level governments had to be responsible for 70 per cent of the budgetary expenditure on education and 55 per cent on health care. Prefectural and county-level governments were made responsible for 100 per cent of the expenditure on unemployment benefits and social security (Huang and Di 2003: 59, 72). In the cases reviewed by Pei, including both developing and developed countries, central governments assumed around 50–96 per cent of total education expenditure (Pei 2008: 171).

In theory, local responsibility for primary education and preventive health care may be advantageous and result in better quality due to local supervision and more opportunities for communities to express their preferences and priorities. Tertiary education, research and development, as well as hospitals, have economies of scale that benefit more than one jurisdiction. In such cases, higher levels of administration or finance may be needed (Ahmad 1995: 78). The principle of expenditure assignment works only when local governments demonstrate a sound fiscal condition. This is not the case in China. Having local governments finance education and health care in many liberal democracies ensures that local governments are accountable to local constituencies. This consideration was not seriously practised in China. The current assignment of expenditure responsibilities goes against a principle of expenditure division: Central/federal governments or provincial/state governments are responsible for the expenditure aimed at promoting egalitarian values and redistributing income.

To cover their budgetary deficits, provincial-level governments have become increasingly reliant on central fiscal transfers. Fiscal transfer as a percentage of the total local governments' expenditure jumped from 13.84 per cent in 1993 to 50 per cent in 1994. After dropping slightly in the mid-1990s, the percentage rose again in late 1990s. The amount of fiscal transfer has multiplied by 18 times in 12 years. In contrast, central government became less dependent on the local governments' transfer (see Table 3.4).

While almost all countries give their local governments control over at least one tax rate, in China, local governments are not authorised to establish new tax categories or adjust tax rates. Often when local governments have some control over tax rates, they will have fiscal policies that are more responsive to the needs and wishes of the local population (Heady 1997: 66). Without such control over tax rates, taxation reform badly affected the fiscal health of sub-provincial governments. One estimate suggests that sub-provincial governments employed 67 per cent of all public employees across the country but only took 15 per cent of total tax revenue (Huang 2007: 46–7). The fiscal stress of sub-provincial governments was further dampened by three factors. First, intra-provincial fiscal transfer is inequitable. Fiscal transfer from the centre is composed of two parts: (1) funds distributed on the basis of the fiscal strength of local governments (*cailixing zhuanyi zhifu*, originally called *yibanxing zhuangyi zhifu*), and (2) earmarked funds (*zhuanxiang zhuanyi zhifu*). Funds distributed on fiscal strength are aimed at reducing the disparity among different provinces. Local governments are

Table 3.4 Fiscal transfer, 1992–2004

Year	Fiscal transfer from central to local governments (billion yuan)	Fiscal transfer as a percentage of local governments' expenditure (%)	Fiscal transfer from local to central governments (billion yuan)	Fiscal transfer as a percentage of central governments' expenditure (%)
1992	59.65	19.06	55.86	23.14
1993	54.47	13.84	60.03	24.00
1994	238.91	50.08	57.01	13.76
1995	253.41	45.91	61.00	13.47
1996	272.25	42.08	60.39	12.39
1997	285.67	39.11	60.38	11.20
1998	332.15	40.17	59.71	9.26
1999	408.66	42.42	59.81	7.26
2000	466.53	42.54	59.91	5.89
2001	600.20	43.73	59.10	4.28
2002	735.18	46.18	63.80	4.52
2003	826.14	46.29	61.86	3.94
2004	1,040.80	49.09	60.72	3.32

Source: Calculated from Finance Yearbook of China Editorial Committee, *Zhongguo caizheng nianjian* (Finance Yearbook of China) (various years).

authorised to decide how to distribute the funds. This only accounts for around 20 per cent of the total fiscal transfer in 1994, though the percentage has risen to over 50 per cent in recent years (see Table 3.5). Earmarked funds are allocated for specific purposes such as capital investment, expansion of voluntary education in rural education and debt servicing. Different from funds distributed on fiscal strength, local governments have little autonomy over using the earmarked funds. In the past, much of the transfer payment was earmarked for subsidies on food and other consumer products for urban residents. In more recent years, capital investment, social security, agriculture and education have received most of the transfer payments. Earmarked funds are often given in the form of matching funds. Only local governments with sufficient fiscal reserves can allocate extra public monies to obtain the matching funds. Thus earmarked funds can hardly address regional disparities or improve the local governments' fiscal strength (Zhang 2007: 52–3).

The second factor is that there is no clear formula to share the revenue between provincial-level and sub-provincial governments. Consequently, sub-provincial governments are unsure of their future revenue. In response, some provinces have tried to institutionalise intra-provincial tax sharing. In January 2003, Liaoning province singled out five types of taxes for sharing: value-added tax, business tax, income tax, personal income tax and property taxes. The provincial government retained 10 per cent of value-added taxes, 30 per cent of business taxes, 20 per cent of income taxes, 15 per cent of personal income taxes and 50 per cent of property taxes. Cities retained 75 per cent of value-added taxes, 0 per cent of business taxes, 60 per cent of personal income tax, and 0 per cent of property taxes. County and township-level governments reaped the rest

Table 3.5 Gross fiscal transfer, 1994–2005

Year	% of the fund distributed on fiscal strength in the gross fiscal transfer	% of earmarked fund in the gross fiscal transfer	Total amount of fiscal transfer (billion yuan)
1994	21.52	78.48	46.0
1995	26.18	73.82	50.8
1996	24.77	75.23	65.0
1997	27.75	72.25	71.7
1998	19.30	80.70	108.8
1999	20.36	79.64	178.8
2000	27.77	72.23	223.3
2001	34.83	65.17	337.6
2002	40.33	59.67	402.4
2003	42.42	57.58	451.2
2004	43.21	56.79	602.8
2005	51.93	48.03	734.1

Source: B. Zhang (2007: 52–3).

of the tax revenue. To raise the incentive of sub-provincial governments to generate tax, Liaoning rebated them a portion of the tax revenue in excess of the planned level, and rebated all to the 40 relatively poor counties. Such a clear delineation of intra-province tax sharing, however, is not practised widely in China. Sometimes, the sharing was based on a formula unfavourable to lower-level governments. In Linzhang county of Hebei province, for instance, the more lucrative sources of taxes (that is, business tax, value-added tax, local product tax, agricultural land-use tax and agricultural tax) are assigned to county governments. The local product tax and agricultural land-use tax are used for paying the salary of township-level government employees. Township-level governments can only retain administrative fees, penalties, land-deed taxes and water-resource taxes. Allocation of revenue and fiscal transfer to sub-provincial governments depends more on local leaders' political skills and negotiation power than the level of economic development in different localities. This fiscal arrangement undermines the redistributive impact of the fiscal system (Song *et al.* 2004: 56–8, 212–14; Bing 2005: 12–14; Zhou 2005: 17–18).

Third, the lower-level governments may be imposed upon to help out unfunded or partially funded mandates – central policies without extra or sufficient central funding. These mandates were very diverse in nature, aimed at realising central policies. For example, central government might get loans from provincial governments when needed but never pay them back. Provincial-level governments may be instructed to purchase a certain amount of national bonds. The central government may also decree to offer pay hikes to civil servants and recruit more public employees to alleviate the unemployment problem but require local governments to foot the bill. These mandates may be construed as a strategy of upper-level governments to squeeze out lower-level governments' hidden extra-budgetary funds (Holzer and Zhang 2004: 32; Jin and Zhang 2006: 61). These mandates may be extremely burdensome. In February 1993, the State Council decreed the speeding up of the development of collective enterprises in the central and western regions. In response, Jiangxi province set an annual industrial growth target of 45 per cent, with a 300 per cent rise in industrial output in six years. The growth targets were distributed to township-level governments and included as performance indicators of township leaders. If township leaders failed to meet these targets, their overall performance would be vetoed. To fulfil the targets, a township government with annual budgetary revenue of less than one million *yuan* had to incur a debt of over two million *yuan* (Song *et al.* 2004: 63–5).

Owing to fiscal stress, many sub-provincial governments ran into debt. It was estimated that over 60 per cent of the counties across the country were in the red (Yep 2004: 56). In 2003, the combined debts of governments at county, township and village levels were estimated at one trillion *yuan*, or 8.3 per cent of China's total GDP (Ong 2006: 381). A study of three township-level governments (see Table 3.6) revealed that in 2000, the debt level of a township-level government in Jiangxi province may be more than twice its annual budgetary revenue. The debt level per capita of a township-level government in Jiangsu province rose by 16 times between 1996 and 2002.

Table 3.6 Debts of three township-level governments, 1996–2002

Debt level as a proportion of annual budgetary revenue (%)	1996	1997	1998	1999	2000	2001	2002
A township in Jiangxi province	45.8	37.3	79.5	201.4	254.2	165.1	86.6
A township in Hebei province	2.6	22.4	50.4	93.5	94.4	N/A	N/A
A town in Jiangsu province	6.9	6.3	5.0	15.1	30.3	14.8	23.2
Debt level per capita (yuan)							
A township in Jiangxi province	20.1	24.1	65.7	87.4	96.3	79.9	80.7
A township in Hebei province	36.7	37.2	125	226.6	236.9	231	N/A
A town in Jiangsu province	37.6	38.0	38.1	131.6	291.6	297.0	604.3

Source: H. Song *et al.* (2004: 63–5).

Table 3.7 is a breakdown of the use of the debt raised by four township-level governments. Much of the debt was spent on payroll, government office blocks and tax remission to upper-level governments – all of which are incapable of generating a future stream of income for debt repayment. Thus these township-level governments have found it nearly impossible to repay the debt by themselves.

To make ends meet, local governments had to increase various taxes, charges, fees and fines. These taxes and fees were numerous and included: agricultural tax and surcharge, special products tax, slaughter tax, farmland-utilisation tax, contract tax, animal husbandry tax and education surcharge. In a Heilongjiang village (see Table 3.8), the tax and fee burden rose from 6.81 per cent of household income in 1993 to 12.92 per cent in 1995 and 14.80 per cent in 1996. Much of the taxes and fees collected were transferred to upper-level government. The peasants' burden was lighter in more affluent regions where the vibrant commercial and industrial activities generated much revenue for villages and the villages did not need to depend on collecting fees from peasants. Even so, the peasants' burden has become heavier since the introduction of tax-sharing reform (see Table 3.9).

User charges were also raised to cover the shortfall in revenue. Brosio (1995: 189) argued that user charges may improve the quality of public-service delivery because charges and fees stimulate consumers to express their dissatisfaction by looking for alternative providers in the private sector, moving out of the community, or voting out the politicians in office. There is also a global trend for local finance to be more reliant on user charges. But such channels that allow for the expression of dissatisfaction are unavailable to most Chinese people who can hardly afford education and health-care services from private providers.

Table 3.7 The composition of debt of four townships, 1996–2001

Use of debt	Debt level and percentage of total debt	A township in Jiangxi province	A township in Hebei province	A town in Jiangsu province	A township in Heilongjiang province
Running collective enterprises	Debt (thousand *yuan*)	2,616	0	0	890
	Percentage (%)	35.3	0	0	15.8
Developing agriculture	Debt (thousand *yuan*)	3,142	121	0	0
	Percentage (%)	42.4	2.8	0	0
Infrastructure construction	Debt (thousand *yuan*)	941	0	0	4,740
	Percentage (%)	12.7	0	0	84.2
Government office blocks construction	Debt (thousand *yuan*)	44	400	3,450	0
	Percentage (%)	0.6	9.2	46.3	0
Payroll	Debt (thousand *yuan*)	440	1,100	4,001	0
	Percentage (%)	5.9	25.2	53.7	0
Tax remittance	Debt (thousand *yuan*)	0	1,812	0	0
	Percentage (%)	0	41.5	0	0
Others	Amount (thousand *yuan*)	227	931	0	0
	Percentage (%)	3.1	21.3	0	0
Total amount (thousand *yuan*)		7,410	4,364	7,451	5,630

Source: H. Song *et al.* (2004: 56).

Table 3.8 Tax-and-fee burden in a Heilongjiang Province village

Year	Income per household (yuan)	Tax and fee burden per household (yuan)	Tax and fee/ income per household (%)	Revenue remitted to upper-level government per household (yuan)	Remitted revenue/ income per household (%)
1986	2,022	44	2.18	34	1.70
1987	1,962	50	2.55	39	1.99
1988	2,487	60	2.41	46	1.85
1989	2,789	80	2.87	65	2.33
1990	3,101	80	2.58	66	2.13
1991	3,203	77	2.40	62	1.94
1993	5,240	357	6.81	290	5.53
1995	8,095	1,046	12.92	939	11.60
1996	7,208	1,067	14.80	912	12.65
1997	8,393	1,006	11.99	826	9.84
1998	9,939	665	6.69	503	5.06
1999	8,257	811	9.82	653	7.91
2000	8,935	744	8.32	612	6.85
2001	8,071	731	9.06	585	7.25

Source: Calculated from H. Song *et al.* (2004: 157–8).

Migration from one city to another is not a viable option, given that migration implies the loss of welfare entitlement attached to an urban household residence. The authoritarian nature of the regime also precludes the possibility of voting out under-performing local leaders.

In 1991, governments at various levels were responsible for over 95 per cent of all education expenditure. The rest was shouldered by students' families in the

Table 3.9 Tax-and-fee burden in a Jiangsu Province village

Year	Income per household (yuan)	Tax and fee burden per household (yuan)	Tax and fee/ income per household (%)	Revenue remitted to upper-level government per household (yuan)	Remitted revenue/ income per household (%)
1993	9,286	140	1.51	58	0.62
1996	14,137	561	3.97	166	1.17
1997	14,204	751	5.29	522	3.68
1998	14,209	649	4.57	389	2.74
1999	13,909	618	4.44	362	2.60
2000	15,889	297	1.87	136	0.86
2001	16,522	170	1.03	0	0

Source: H. Song *et al.* (2004: 160).

form of tuition and miscellaneous fees. In 2004, the percentage of education expenditure derived from such fees rose to 19 per cent (Ministry of Education 2005: 629). In 1990, medical expenses accounted for 2 per cent of urban residents' private consumption and 5.1 per cent of rural residents' private consumption. In 2005, the percentage rose to 7.6 per cent and 6.6 per cent respectively. Between 1980 and 2004, the total expenditure (by government and household) on health care increased by 52 times, from 14.3 billion *yuan* to 759 billion *yuan*. Household health-care expense increased by 133 times, from 3.04 billion *yuan* to 407.1 billion *yuan*. The proportion of health-care expenses to gross household expenditure increased from 2.5 per cent to 7.4 per cent (for urban households) and from 2.4 per cent to 6 per cent (for rural households) (Ministry of Health 2006: 89). In 1991, expenditure on education and health care accounted for 18.24 per cent and 2.55 per cent of the gross budgetary expenditure respectively. The percentage dropped to 15.68 per cent and 1.66 per cent in 2004 (see Table 3.10).

Rural areas were discriminated against in fiscal distribution. In 2002, only 43 per cent of health expenditure was spent on the rural population, or 60 per cent of the total population. Worst of all, almost all health expenditure was allocated to the payroll of 'personnel within establishment' (*bianzhi nei renyuan* – personnel who are recruited with the approval of upper-level governments). As most of the personnel in township and village clinics are outside the establishment, these clinics receive very little public funds (Wang, X. 2006: 45). In the face of expensive health care, many patients cannot receive timely treatment. In 2003, 48.9 per cent of the patients could not afford medical treatment, a substantial rise

Table 3.10 Expenditure for education and health care

Year	Gross budgetary expenditure (billion yuan)	Expenditure for education (billion yuan)	Education expenditure/ gross budgetary expenditure (%)	Expenditure for health care (billion yuan)	Health-care expenditure/ gross budgetary expenditure (%)
1991	338.67	61.78	18.24	8.64	2.55
1992	374.22	72.88	19.48	9.61	2.57
1993	464.23	86.78	18.69	10.79	2.32
1994	579.26	117.47	20.28	14.70	2.54
1995	682.37	141.15	20.69	16.33	2.39
1996	793.76	167.17	21.06	18.76	2.36
1997	923.36	186.25	20.17	20.92	2.27
1998	1,079.82	203.25	18.82	22.51	2.08
1999	1,318.77	228.72	17.34	24.79	1.88
2000	1,588.65	256.26	16.13	27.22	1.71
2001	1,890.26	305.70	16.17	31.35	1.66
2002	2,205.32	349.14	15.83	35.04	1.59
2003	2,465.00	385.06	15.62	43.93	1.78
2004	2,848.69	446.59	15.68	47.42	1.66

Sources: Ministry of Education (2005: 629); Ministry of Health (2006: 87).

from 36.4 per cent in 1993. In 1998, 21.6 per cent of poor peasants sank into poverty due to previous expenses on health care. In 2003, the figure rose to 33.4 per cent (Wang and Zhang 2007: 26–7).

Another strategy for coping with local fiscal problems is to make full use of the tax sources. Many local governments encourage infrastructure projects and property development to increase the tax revenue from local sources, including urban land tax, urban construction and maintenance tax and real-estate tax. According to a survey in Zhejiang province by the Development Research Centre of the State Council, the tax revenue related to infrastructure construction and property development accounted for 37 per cent of the gross tax revenue of several affluent cities and counties in the province. In addition to tax revenue, property developers in Zhejiang province had to pay local governments special fees for using the land. These fees may amount to 70 per cent of the extra-budgetary revenue of several cities in Zhejiang province. Owing to the significance of land development to the local coffers, the property markets in many localities have become overheated. The excessive land development has also engendered problems such as the mandatory displacement of villagers and the under-compensation for these displaced villagers and the loss of their agricultural land (Huang 2007: 46–7).

Coping strategies for the challenges of tax sharing

Major measures of dealing with the fiscal burden include cost cutting, more fiscal transfer and tax reduction. To cut costs, some township governments were merged and the bureaucracy was downsized (see the discussion in Chapter 5). In 2000, the central government launched the Western Development Programme (WDP). Until 2005, the accumulated fiscal transfer from the central government to the western regions under WDP amounted to over 500 billion *yuan*. One-third of the long-term national debt was spent on western development (Western Development Office 2008). Even though WDP has faded after Hu Jintao became General Secretary of the CCP in 2003, central fiscal transfer continues to be skewed towards the western and central regions under Hu's guiding principles of establishing a 'harmonious society' and pursuing a 'scientific view of development' (see Table 3.11).

Meanwhile, tax-for-fee reform has been phased in since the late 1990s. Many of the fees imposed on peasants were abolished. The agricultural tax rate was

Table 3.11 Distribution of fiscal transfer in 2005, by regions

Regions	Earmarked fund (%)	Gross fiscal transfer (%)
Western regions	41	42.7
Central regions	42.9	45.1
Coastal regions	16.1	12.2

Source: Li and Xu (2006: 34–5).

abolished in 2006. Fee collection was more strictly regulated. Sub-provincial governments were prohibited from imposing surcharges which were not stipulated in the 2004 Administrative Licensing Law – a law regulating the government's authority over charging licence fees. Fees approved and collected at the provincial level had to be reported to the Ministry of Finance and the National Development and Reform Commission (Chou 2007; OECD 2006: 143). At the same time, several types of taxes and surcharges collected in rural areas were abolished altogether, including husbandry taxes, special product taxes (except the tobacco tax), surcharges for township-level governments, education surcharges, administrative fees (*xingzheng shiye xing shoufei*) and labour services. The tax-for-fee reform and abolition of the agricultural tax saved peasants a tax burden of 125 billion *yuan* (Ministry of Finance 2005: 8).

The relief of the peasants' burden, however, came with a high price tag for local governments. While peasants' tax burden was reduced by 125 billion *yuan* every year, the compensation from central government to local governments in 2005 was only 66.2 billion *yuan* (Jin 2006: 51). Since local governments had to make up for the shortfall, their fiscal situations were further strained. Before the tax-for-fee reform and abolition of the agricultural tax, the township-level governments under Wanrong county of Shanxi province managed an annual operating fund of over 10 million *yuan*. After the reform, the annual operating fund was slashed by 70 per cent. Many township-level governments face more serious fiscal problems and have to request that officials take a no-pay leave to save money. To increase operating funds, some government officials diverted earmarked funds and payroll expenditures for unauthorised uses. In Guangdong province, the fiscal situation of 80 per cent of the township-level governments deteriorated; 10 per cent failed to pay their employees on time (He 2006: 10; Xue *et al*. 2005: 41–2).

Meanwhile, lower-level governments were given more fiscal transfer and greater autonomy in their use of the fiscal transfer. The earmarked funds which used to account for more than 70 per cent of the gross fiscal transfer have declined as a proportion of the gross fiscal transfer. The fund distributed on the fiscal strength of local governments – over which lower-level governments have wider discretion in spending – has increased in amount and significance (see Table 3.12). The fund is composed of the following: general fiscal transfer (*yibanxing zhuanyi zhifu*), aimed at narrowing regional disparities. Local governments are authorised to decide how to use the monies. The growth of general fiscal transfer is the fastest among the different types of fiscal transfer. Introduced in 1995, when the amount was only 2.1 billion *yuan*, general fiscal transfer increased by over 50-fold to 112 billion *yuan* within ten years. Subsidies of public employees' salary (*tiaozheng gongzi zhuanyi zhifu*) aid local governments which cannot afford the public employees' pay hike mandated by the central government. Fiscal transfer for tax-for-fee reform (*nongcun shuifei gaige zhuanyi zhifu*) is used to compensate the local governments whose revenue is affected by tax-for-fee reform. Subsidies to the autonomous regions and prefectures (*minzu diqu zhuanyi zhifu*) are distributed to the five autonomous regions

Table 3.12 A breakdown of gross fiscal transfer, 1994–2005

Year	Fund distributed on fiscal strength (billion yuan)							Earmarked fund (billion yuan)	
	General fiscal transfer	Subsidies to the autonomous regions and prefectures	Subsidies on public employees' salary	Fiscal transfer for tax-for-fee reform	Fiscal transfer to counties and townships	Other fiscal transfer	% of the fund in the gross fiscal transfer	Earmarked fund	% of the fund in the gross fiscal transfer
1994	–	–	–	–	–	9.9	21.52	36.1	78.48
1995	2.1	–	–	–	–	11.2	26.18	37.5	73.82
1996	3.5	–	–	–	–	12.6	24.77	48.9	75.23
1997	5.0	–	–	–	–	14.9	27.75	51.8	72.25
1998	6.1	–	–	–	–	14.9	19.30	87.8	80.70
1999	7.5	–	10.8	–	–	18.1	20.36	142.4	79.64
2000	8.5	2.5	21.7	6.8	–	22.5	27.77	161.3	72.23
2001	13.8	3.3	63.4	8.0	3.3	25.8	34.83	220.0	65.17
2002	27.9	3.9	81.7	24.5	3.3	21.0	40.33	240.1	59.67
2003	38.0	5.5	90.1	30.6	3.3	23.9	42.42	259.8	57.58
2004	74.5	7.7	99.4	52.3	–	26.6	43.21	342.3	56.79
2005	112.0	15.9	147.6	66.1	15.0	24.6	51.93	352.9	48.03

Source: B. Zhang (2007: 52–3).

(Tibet, Xinjiang, Ningxia, Guangxi and Inner Mongolia) and the autonomous prefectures in other provinces. Despite being a relatively small sum, the amount of this subsidy has increased by six times from 2000 to 2005. Usually, the regions with a strong presence of ethnic minorities are less developed economically.

Fiscal transfer to counties and townships (*xianxiang jiangbu zhuangyi zhifu*) provides fiscal support for lower-level governments mainly to implement the 'three-award-one-subsidy' policy (*sanjiang yibu*). Introduced in 2005, this policy was aimed at encouraging lower-level governments to downsize the bureaucracy. Under the policy, the central government awarded 500,000 *yuan* to county-level governments for every township that they abolished, and 4,000 *yuan* for every public employee that county and township-level governments laid off. Extra subsidies were allocated to the provincial and prefectural-level governments which increased their fiscal transfer to county governments. There are variations among different provinces in implementing the policies. For example, if the counties in Shandong province could generate 15 per cent more than their targeted revenue, the provincial government would allocate them a subsidy equivalent to 20 per cent of the extra revenue. Under the policy, the central government transferred 15 billion *yuan* and 23.5 billion *yuan* in 2005 and 2006 respectively to the counties designated as 'poor' (counties which fail to meet their 'basic expenditure'). Provincial and prefectural-level governments increased their fiscal transfer by 22.1 billion *yuan*. Counties generated extra revenue amounting to 6.7 billion *yuan*. Thanks to the policy, the number of poor counties was reduced from 791 in 2003 to 29 in 2005 (Jin 2007: 10–18; Zhang 2006: 20; Department of Finance, Shandong Province 2006: 21; Budget Bureau, Ministry of Finance 2006: 17–20). In 2004, Liaoning province transferred five billion *yuan* to county and township-level governments, or a 31.2 per cent increase from 2003 (Bing 2005: 12–14).

Education and health care are the two major sectors benefiting from the transfer. In 2004, central government earmarked 59.32 billion *yuan* for rural education. Most funds were spent on central and western regions: western regions received 26.75 billion *yuan*, central regions 27.23 billion *yuan* and coastal regions the rest. The fiscal transfer accounted for 68.2 per cent, 58.8 per cent and 11.3 per cent of the budgetary funds on rural education in the three regions, a remarkable improvement over the several years since it began. It was estimated that the fiscal transfer increased the proportion of budgetary funds in rural education expenditure from 61.8 per cent in 1999 to 80.6 per cent in 2004 (Department of Finance, Zhejiang Province 2006: 17; Ding 2006: 9–11). To extend the coverage of free education, the central government was responsible for 80 per cent of the funds required in western regions and 60 per cent in coastal regions. With extra central funds, free fundamental education could be provided in the western rural regions in 2006, and extended to all rural regions across the country in 2007. In addition, the central government earmarked 1.43 billion *yuan* to provide free textbooks and subsidised boarding places to 34 million students in rural primary and high schools. It shared with local governments in a 50:50

ratio the expenditure for improving campus facilities (Lin 2007: 16; 'Guowuyuan guanyu shenhua' 2007). For a higher commitment from local leadership to education, central government required local governments to fully implement the policy of eradicating tuition and miscellaneous school fees in rural areas by 2007. Local leaders would be evaluated on their abilities to enforce this policy (Murphy 2007: 90).

The impact of the central transfer is often watered down by misappropriation. In 2003 the central government launched a plan to provide free or subsidised vocational training for rural people who were either preparing to migrate or who had already migrated to the cities. This plan was financed by funds from the central and local governments. In 2004, the central government allocated 300 million *yuan* to this project. Yet many agricultural counties diverted the funds to alleviate their fiscal shortages (Murphy 2007: 86–7). To prevent lower-level governments from misappropriating education funds, Jiangxi province instructed county governments to set aside a budgetary education fund of 20 *yuan* for every primary school student and 30 *yuan* for every junior high school student. For the schools in poor regions, Jiangxi earmarked 10 *yuan* for every student, or 23.47 million *yuan* on aggregate. In 2004, the earmarked fund from the provincial government increased by 5 *yuan*. In 2005, the budgetary education funds from county governments were raised to 40 *yuan* and 60 *yuan* for every primary and junior high school student respectively. For the schools in poor regions, the education fund per primary school student and per junior high school student was 60 *yuan* and 80 *yuan* respectively. In addition, the provincial government earmarked 3.61 billion *yuan* for the teachers' payroll (Zhao and Yang 2006: 15).

Another weakness of central transfer is that earmarked funds from the central government are usually spent on capital investment, such as improving the quality of campuses, but not on operating costs such as the teachers' payroll and the schools' operating funds – the largest expenditure items of education (Cai 2005: 16). As a consequence, the central allocation may be able to alleviate peasants' financial burden, but not improve the quality of rank-and-file of teachers; many rural governments can only afford teachers' basic salary but not the statutory subsidies which account for 30–40 per cent of their compensation packages (Zhang 2007: 17–18). Furthermore, fund allocation is not institutionalised. The amount of funds allocated is not worked out on the basis of a formula, but on the fiscal situation of the central and provincial-level governments. To save for rainy days, lower-level governments may hold back the spending of the fiscal transfer. In 2000, only 75.44 per cent of the central subsidy of public employees' salary worth 21.7 billion *yuan* was spent. In 2001, the subsidy grew to 89.2 billion, but only 59.19 per cent was used (Research Team on Improving the Mechanism of Financing Rural Voluntary Education 2005: 7). In 2006, the increase in the central fiscal reserve helped to push up the fiscal revenue of Tibet by 26.4 per cent, but the spending on education fell by 8.7 per cent (Li 2008). The huge unspent fiscal transfer diluted the impact of the fiscal transfer.

With regard to health care, the Ministry of Health relieved the burden of township-level governments in 2002 by instructing county governments to finance township health care (Wang, X. 2006: 44). In 2003, a rural health-insurance scheme was kicked off. The scheme set up health-care funds contributed by individual peasants and the governments at central, provincial and county levels.[3] Peasants may freely choose to participate in the scheme. The central and provincial governments each contribute 10 *yuan* each to the account of every participant. Later on, the contribution of the central government was raised to 20 *yuan* for every participant. In 2006, the amount contributed by the central government was 4.73 billion *yuan* (Ministry of Finance 2005: 13). The exact share contributed by different parties varies across the country. The trend shows that the peasants' share is shrinking. In Hainan province, peasants were responsible for 30 per cent of the total contribution between 2003 and 2005. In 2006, the share went down to 25 per cent. The central government's contribution was maintained at around 12.5 per cent. The shares of cities and counties decreased dramatically from almost 35 per cent to 18 per cent. The province has become the main contributor (44 per cent, or 63.17 million *yuan*). The shift of the expenditure assignment from sub-provincial to provincial-level governments is a sensible move, given the fact that the system was implemented together with tax-for-fee reform and the abolition of agricultural tax. These two policies have cut the revenue of sub-provincial governments. Meanwhile, the health-care fund grows quickly: the total amount of the health-care fund in 2006 was more than twice as much as the amount collected between 2003 and 2005. In 2006, the system covered 51 per cent of the counties and 410 million peasants, or 46 per cent of all peasants in China. The plan was to cover all peasants by 2010 (Yao and Hao 2007: 27).

With more funds, the Xinjiang autonomous region was able to cut the average minimum medical consultation fee by 50 per cent, and raise the maximum subsidy on each consultation by three times to 15,000 *yuan* (Zheng and Su 2007: 29). But the coverage of the health-insurance scheme was uneven. The health-insurance scheme in the provinces of Shaanxi, Gansu, Ningxia, Qinghai and Xinjiang covers less than half of the employees, and almost none of the elderly, children and self-employed. In 2007, there were still over 250 million people (or 20 per cent of the population) uncovered by any public health-insurance scheme (Mao and Yang 2007: 62–3). Besides that, rural residents still fail to enjoy health-care service that is on a par with their city counterparts. In 2003, rural participants in the scheme had to be responsible for 79 per cent of their own consultation fees. The national average was 70.3 per cent, and 45 per cent in cities (Wang, X. 2006: 45).

The central government has also taken over much of the expenditure assignment over social security – an expenditure item which is classified as a local expenditure assignment in many countries. Between 2001 and 2005, the central government shouldered 70 per cent of the expenditure on disaster relief and 81 per cent of the expenditure on 'Two Ensure' and the 'Minimum Ensure' (allowance for basic pension insurance, allowance for basic livelihood insurance for laid-off employees from state-owned enterprises, and allowance for minimum living standards).

Table 3.13 Expenditure on social security, 2001–5

Item	Expenditure by central government (in billion yuan)	Expenditure by local governments (in billion yuan)
1 Expenditure on "Two Ensure" and the "Minimum Ensure"	336.62 (81%)*	76.52 (19%)
2 Expenditure on disaster relief	17.40 (70%)	7.33 (30%)

Source: Finance Yearbook of China Editorial Committee (2006: 415).

Note
* The percentage as the total expenditure.

Conclusion

The reform of fiscal policy may be construed as a coping strategy employed by the central government overwhelmed by steering national development and controlling local governments due to the decentralisation of resource-extractive capacity in the 1980s. Through tax-sharing reform in 1994, the central government successfully improved its resource-extractive capacity at the expense of local governments'. Since then, all provincial-level governments have faced a budget deficit. To make up for the shortfall of funds, provincial-level governments took over some of the tax bases of sub-provincial governments. In the face of dwindling revenues, township-level governments had to compromise the quality of public service and run into huge debts. Heavy taxes, fees and fines were imposed on peasants. This raised the peasants' burden and aroused rural popular discontent.

As a result, addressing the grievances of peasants and alleviating the fiscal difficulties of lower-level governments were placed high on the political agenda. Since the late 1990s, the Chinese government has phased out the agricultural tax and allocated more fiscal transfer to lower-level governments. Certain expenditure assignments over rural education and health care have been shifted to the central and provincial levels. It was evident that the peasants' burden was relieved. The sustainability of these policies depends on three factors:

1   the ability and willingness of people-in-the-street to contribute a fair share for financing public services;
2   the fiscal situations and commitment of central and provincial-level governments; and
3   The incentive of the governments at all levels in economising the use of public resources and spending the earmarked funds on designated purposes.

The first factor is likely that the average household income is rising and the coverage of the health-insurance scheme is expanding. The question is that without even regional development and an effective mechanism to redistribute fiscal resources, the rise in the average household income of those in less-developed regions will continue to lag behind. This will widen the quality gap of public service among different regions. To correct the rural–urban imbalance of education quality, a series of documents released in 2006 ruled that an increased educational budget was to be used mainly for rural education (Murphy 2007: 90).

Similar logic may be applied in evaluating the second factor. After Hu Jintao and the fourth generation took over political leadership in 2002, the central government reversed its past strategy of developing the economy at all costs and ignoring a lower priority on the well-being of those who failed to benefit from the economic development. The new leadership proposed the guiding principles of a 'scientific view of development' and a 'harmonious society'. Under these guiding principles are policies designed to correct regional imbalance and improve the livelihoods of disadvantaged people. Given that the vibrant economy is growing at breakneck speed, both central and local governments will have more fiscal revenue to improve public services. Nevertheless, uneven regional development implies that the lower-level governments from the less-developed regions may not be able to generate enough revenue to deal with the expenditure responsibilities. Whether the central and local governments have strong commitment to the improvement of public service is also unknown. Despite the rhetoric of increasing the central appropriations on fundamental education, the central government provided less than 10 per cent of the budgetary education expenditure worth 579.6 billion *yuan* in 2006. In the same year, spending on education only accounted for 3.01 per cent of GDP, short of the internationally accepted 4 per cent target for developing countries. The growth rate of spending on education in 12 provinces and autonomous regions was slower than growth in fiscal revenues. This was an infraction of the Education Law. Inadequate budgetary appropriation forced many schools to pay teachers' salary by loan. In 2006, the debt incurred by schools was estimated to be 200 billion *yuan* (Li 2008).

The third factor is harder to tell. The distribution of fiscal transfer was not well-institutionalised. Who could get how much was not contingent on a pre-determined formula or local governments' fiscal situations, but on the bargaining power of different parties involved in the allocation of the fiscal transfer. Political motives are another factor affecting the funding levels. The regions with a high concentration of ethnic minorities, for example, receive extra funding out of fear of social unrest. Meanwhile, the sharing of expenditure assignments among different levels of government is not institutionalised. Upper-level governments may liberally impose unfunded mandates on lower-level governments. Without adequate certainty about future streams of income and expenditure assignments, local governments have incentive to hold back any extra funds rather than spend it on pre-determined purposes. As indicated by Auditor-General Li Jinhua, provincial governments are supposed to be responsible for the largest share of expenditure on improving the structural safety of dangerous buildings in high schools and primary schools. In reality, however, provincial governments covered 22 per cent of the expenditure item. Township-level governments, village committees and schools had to shoulder 31.5 per cent of the expenditure whereas the rest was covered by central-level (25 per cent), city-level (4.5 per cent) and county-level (17 per cent) governments (Li, J. 2006: 59).

The Organic Law of Village Committees and village elections are useful for motivating local officials to use public spending efficiently, and collect taxes and fees strictly according to state budgets. Kennedy argued that in the towns and townships where the village election and nomination process are free from the intervention of government officials, the elected village officials were accountable to the villagers and had greater incentive to resist unpopular policies such as illicit collection of taxes and fees by towns and township governments (Kennedy 2007). Due to higher dependence on transfer payments and the lack of proper democratic control, local governments in less-developed regions are unlikely to be accountable to local constituencies and spend the public monies sensibly. Under these circumstances, increasing the amount of transfers may only result in more political competition for the transfers, further expansion of local bureaucracies, and rent-seeking behaviour. Unless there is an effective mechanism of spending control to ensure that the fiscal transfer is spent on budgeted items in an efficient manner, the increase in the fiscal transfer can do little to improve the quality of public goods, relieve the fiscal stress of lower-level governments and, above all, achieve the central agenda.

Currently, effective laws and regulations in controlling the use of earmarked funds are insufficient. In 2005, the earmarked funds were worth 351.7 billion *yuan*, or 31 per cent of the gross fiscal transfer. The spending of 70.59 billion *yuan* – or 20 per cent of the earmarked fund – is done without any regulation (National Audit Office 2006). In the aftermath of the 2003 earthquake, central government allocated 120 million *yuan* to Datao county of Yunnan province for rescue and relief purpose. Some 41.11 million *yuan* (or 34 per cent) were either misappropriated or diverted to other purposes. It was reported that 20 per cent of budgetary grants earmarked for poverty relief were deployed without full compliance with the relevant regulations, of which 31 per cent was used for financing other public expenditures and 29 per cent was used for balancing the local budget (Yep 2008: 239). Local officials have strong incentives to direct earmarked funds to industrial projects; such projects might generate more fiscal resources. Also, local officials face a performance-appraisal system in which the output and profit of township and village enterprises are major performance indicators. Central leaders have noticed the logic and therefore stepped up spending control to alleviate the problems. Chapter 4 provides an analysis and evaluation of this reform.

4   Reform of spending control

Without effective control on public spending, political leaders are unclear whether public monies are efficiently used and allocated in accordance with government priorities. Ensuring fiscal discipline and administrative honesty is difficult. This chapter portrays the contour of the measures of the Chinese government aimed at bridging the information gap over spending control. Such measures address how to increase the incentive of local officials and department directors to implement the reform and underline the desire of reform leaders to address technical issues rather than tackle the political challenges arising from spending control. Accordingly, the structural weaknesses and bureaucratic politics that have impeded effective control of public spending remain intact.

The background of reforming public-spending control

In China, three types of public spending can be identified: (1) the expenditure covered by budgetary and extra-budgetary funds; (2) the expenditure incurred by state-owned enterprises and public-service units; and (3) non-performance loans owed by state-owned and collective enterprises. Under the agenda, the Chinese government's second and third types of expenditure fall under the scope of reforming enterprises, public-service units and banks; thus the analysis of this chapter focuses on the control of the first kind of public spending. This entails two stages: budget preparation and budget execution. Budget preparation sets the gross amount of public monies that can be spent and distributes public monies among different policy areas and functional departments. It is a process of setting a benchmark for spending control according to the government's policy priorities. Budget execution ensures that public spending is only – and exactly – on budgeted targets. Overspending and spending on unbudgeted targets are regarded as problematic and in need of correction.

The functional bureaucracy responsible for coordinating budget preparation is the central budgeting agency (CBA, or Ministry of Finance in China). There is no common institutional composition of the CBA across countries, and the range of functions of CBAs may differ from time to time and from nation to nation. In continental Europe and Scandinavia, CBAs usually have a narrower role of bookkeeping. Individual line ministers may have great high autonomy in budget preparation. In contrast, the CBAs in such countries as the United Kingdom, Canada, Australia and New Zealand are regarded as all-powerful central agencies able to exert policy influence (Wanna 2003: xxvi). Governments with effective budgetary control are characterised by strong and coherent leadership in the budgeting process. Cabinets first outline the spending priorities, set the overall spending levels and decide the distribution of budgetary expenditure among major policy areas on the basis of the budgetary requests from spending ministries. With reference to the cabinets' decisions on spending priorities, CBAs prepare a budget specifying the amount allocated to spending ministries. Spending ministries cannot dispute the allocated amount and may only decide the allocation of the funds among their various programmes (Diamond 2006: 23).

Apparently, the leadership of budgeting preparation in China is incoherent. The Ministry of Finance cannot effectively direct the budget planning and supervise the budget execution of other ministries. In preparation for state budgets, the Ministry of Finance has to share authority with the National Development and Reform Commission (over new investment projects) and the Government Offices Administration of the State Council and Ministry of Human Resources and Social Security (over new positions and payroll level). These commissions and ministries are not obliged to consult the Ministry of Finance or consider the implications of their proposed projects on the subsequent operating costs. Once they approve funding applications, the Ministry of Finance can barely challenge any decisions and must approve the request for covering the operating costs every year (Cheung 2003: 218). As a functional bureaucracy, the Ministry of Finance is not powerful; its representativeness is absent from the Party Centre's central leading group for economics and finance, the leading group reporting to the CCP Politburo on financial issues. In contrast, the National Development and Reform Commission has its representative in the leadership group.

Furthermore, the Ministry of Finance cannot dictate to other spending ministries and allocate funds according to the State Council's policy priorities. Instead, the Ministry of Finance must react to the spending proposals from ministries.

Table 4.1 Central leading group for economics and finance, 2006

Position in the leading group	Name
Group Leader	Hu Jintao (General Secretary of the CCP)
Deputy Group Leader	Wen Jiabao (Premier)
Deputy General Secretary and Director of the Executive Office	Wang Chunzheng (Vice Minister of National Development and Reform Commission)
Deputy Director of the Executive Office	Wei Liqun (Director of State Council Research Office), Chen Xiwen (Director of the Executive Office, Central Rural Affairs Leading Group), Yang Linglong, Liu He

Source: *China Directory 2007*, pp. 31–2.

The vast majority of the central government's fiscal expenditures are dispersed among the ministries of the State Council. The ministers, not the Ministry of Finance or the Premier of the State Council, have real control over fiscal resources. Provincial governors have to go to different ministries to negotiate for budgetary funds for their own provinces and therefore the decision-making process of geographical distribution of budgetary funds is prolonged (Wang and Hu 1999: 264). Local governments also lack coherent leadership in preparing their own budgets (Ma, J. 2006: 484, 490). As a result of the incoherent process of preparing budgets and the ongoing negotiations for fund allocation after budgets are prepared, state budgets hardly reflect the true policy priorities of the central government.

The function of state budgets as benchmarks of spending control is weakened by several factors. First, state budgets cannot put a cap on overall expenditure. Spending ministries may apply for additional funding after state budgets are approved. Second, the budget cycle is irrational. State budgets are approved by the National People's Congress in March, three months after the start of the budget year. This renders the approval symbolic and fails to hold the administration accountable to the legislature over budgetary issues. Local budgets cannot be approved before the approval of the budgets of the immediate higher-level governments. The budgetary plans of the lowest-level governments may not be approved until near the end of a budgetary year. To ensure the operation of local governments even without approved budgets, local governments are still permitted to use public funds as long as the amount of public funds does not exceed particular thresholds. Third, budget is compiled on functional (such as education, health care and administration) but not departmental bases. No single ministers or department directors can be held answerable for budgetary expenditure. Fourth, much of the fiscal transfer from the central to local governments is excluded from local budgets and the scrutiny of the local people's congresses. In 2005, for example, 15 central ministries bypassed the provincial people's congresses and allocated subsidies of 38.37 billion *yuan* to their provincial branches. Only 44.5 per cent (or 344.43 billion *yuan*) of the tax rebate and subsides worth 773.37 billion *yuan* were included in provincial budgets (Huang and Di 2003: 136). In view of that, the Ministry of Finance required provincial governments to include an estimated amount of the tax rebate and subsidies in their budgets in 2005. The actual amount of tax rebate and subsidies spent in the previous year was used for estimation. Nevertheless, the estimated amount was usually under-reported as the provincial people's governments usually only spent around half the total amount and saved the rest for such purposes as funding spontaneous projects and qualifying for matching funds from the central government (National Audit Office 2006).

The fiscal decentralisation since the 1980s further weakened the ability of the government to control spending. Governments at various levels have greater leverage in generating extra-budgetary funds. The extra-budgetary revenue is part of the government revenue excluded from the planned revenue, such as officially sanctioned levies beyond the narrowly defined state budgets. Extra-budgetary

Table 4.2 Extra-budgetary revenues of central and local governments

Year	Total amount (billion yuan)	Collected by central government (billion yuan)	Collected by local governments (billion yuan)
1992	385.49	170.77	214.72
1993	143.25	24.59	118.66
1994	186.25	28.33	157.92
1995	240.65	31.76	208.89
1996	389.33	94.77	294.56
1997	282.60	14.51	268.09
1998	308.23	16.42	291.81
1999	338.52	23.05	315.47
2000	382.64	24.76	357.88
2001	430.00	34.70	395.30
2002	447.90	44.00	403.90
2003	456.68	37.94	418.74
2004	469.92	35.07	434.85

Source: National Bureau of Statistics (2006: 299).

funds are less transparent and more vulnerable to misuse because they are usually kept by spending departments in secret bank accounts which finance bureaux can rarely scrutinise. A rough estimate of the OECD suggested that the expenditure from extra-budgetary funds rose from 2 per cent of GDP in the mid-1990s to around 4 per cent of GDP in the early 2000s (OECD 2006: 20–1). Because of chronic problems with the local budgetary deficit, extra-budgetary funds are more significant to local governments than the central government. The amount of extra-budgetary revenue collected by the central government dropped from 170.77 billion *yuan* in 1992 to 24.59 billion in 1993, and from 94.77 *yuan* in 1996 to 14.51 billion *yuan* in 1998. Since then, the amount remained at a moderate level. However, the fiscal stress in the wake of 1994 tax-sharing reform has forced local governments to rely more on extra-budgetary funds, rising from 214.72 billion *yuan* in 1992 to 434.85 billion *yuan* in 2004 (see Table 4.2).

Reform measures

In 1999, the Chinese government initiated a series of budgeting reform measures aimed at narrowing the information gap for budget planning and control. Transparency of the budget preparation has been increased. In Article 10 of the Regulations on Publicising Government Information issued by the State Council in April 2007, all the governments at the county level and above are required to make public their budgets and reports of budget execution. Article 12 requires township-level governments to disclose their actual revenue and expenditure and the allocation of earmarked fund.[1] In some cities, bureau directors are required to disclose the gross payroll expenditure and monetise public employees' fringe benefits in kind (for example, housing, cars and mobile phones) for the ease of public scrutiny (Chou 2008: 65). The invitation of citizens to participate in the budgeting process converges with the current trend of Western democratic countries. Through a higher degree of citizen participation, the plans of resource allocation are more likely to reflect citizens' wishes. This is conducive to enhancing trust, building a sense of community and, above all, gaining support for proposed budgets (Ebdon and Franklin 2006).

Some provinces experimented to specify budget items more clearly, supply more budgetary information for scrutiny and provide a more coherent leadership over the budgeting process. Hubei province, for instance, instructed its departments to structure their budgetary expenditure in three broad items: personnel, operating and programme expenditures. Spending departments had to consolidate all their revenue and expenditure into bank accounts supervised by finance departments at corresponding levels. Expenditures had to be approved and dispensed by finance departments restructured to strengthen their monitoring function and improve the coherence in budgeting process. Budgeting offices and treasury offices were created to separate the functions of budget compilation and execution. Specialised agencies were set up; each agency was responsible for examining the budgetary requests of a grouping of spending departments. By this means, spending departments only needed to deal with one instead of several agencies (Ma, J. 2006).

The central government endorsed certain local experiments to reform the preparation of the state budgets. From January 2007, central ministries were required to organise their financial reports in three parts: revenue, expenditure under an economic classification (*zhichu jingji fenlei*) and expenditure under a functional classification (*zhichu gonglen fenlei*). Expenditure under an economic classification was the old type of expenditure classification in which expenditure items were organised on a functional basis. Expenditure under a functional classification was a ministry-based classification (see Table 4.3). Beneath the three parts of financial reports were broad categories (*lei*) and standard categories (*kuan*). In the parts of revenue and expenditure under functional classification, standard categories were specified into sub-categories (*xiang*). Sub-categories were further divided into items (*mu*) in the revenue part. A major weakness of this new classification is its failure to single out the payroll expenditure from the budget. The directors of spending departments have the independence to divert operating expenditure to personnel expenditure and slowed the efforts of stepping up spending control (Yin 2007: 26–7).

To provide a strong and coherent leadership over the budget execution, the Ministry of Finance was given the authority of revenue collection and spending on behalf of functional ministries. In 2001, six central ministries were selected for a pilot test which charged the Ministry of Finance with dispensing payroll, settling payment of capital spending and procuring on behalf of these six central ministries. In 2005, the authority of the Ministry of Finance over revenue collection and spending was extended to all central ministries. Around 90 per cent of the State Council-approved fees were scrutinised by the Ministry of Finance. At

Table 4.3 Revenue and expenditure classification

Parts in Financial Report	Broad categories	Standard categories
Revenue	1 Tax revenue	Value-added tax, consumption tax, business tax, enterprise income tax, personal income tax, resource tax, fixed-capital tax, urban-construction tax, property tax, stamp duty, urban land-use tax, land value-added tax, tax on vehicle licences, anchorage tax, tax on vehicle purchases, custom duty, tax on agricultural land, tax on deeds, other taxes
	2 Social security revenue	Contributions to retirement schemes, unemployment insurance, fundamental health care, industrial accident insurance, birth insurance, other insurance
	3 Non-tax revenue	Revenue of government foundation, earmarked revenue, lottery revenue, administrative revenue, fines, revenue from state-owned enterprises, revenue for renting out state-owned resources and capital, other revenue
	4 Loan repayment	Domestic loan repayment, foreign loan repayment, domestic indirect loan repayment, foreign indirect loan repayment
	5 Debt	Domestic debt, foreign debt
	6 Transfer payment	Remitted funds, funds distributed on the basis of fiscal strength fund (cailixing zhuanyi zhifu), earmarked funds, transfer payment in government foundation, transfer payment in lottery charitable foundation, transfer payment in extra-budgetary fund, transfer payment among government agencies, balanced surplus from previous budgetary year, transfer-in capital
Expenditure under economic classification	1 Wage and fringe benefit	Fundamental wage, subsidy, bonus, housing provident fund, rental subsidy, home-purchase subsidy, society security contribution, meal expenditure, meal allowance, others
	2 Commodity and printing	General administration, printing, consultation, administrative fee, water charge, electricity fee, postal fee, air conditioning, property-management fee, transportation fee, business trip, overseas trip, maintenance fee, rent, conference, training, reception, material and supplies, equipment procurement, construction, warfare, petroleum for military use, maintenance fee on military equipment, weapon procurement, special-use petroleum, labour wage, fee for project commission, labour union fee, fringe benefit, others
	3 Subsidy on individuals and households	Semi-retirement (lixiu), retirement, demobilisation, relief for families of deceased, living subsidy, poverty relief, health care, education grant, scholarship, production subsidy, others

continued

Table 4.3 Continued

Parts in Financial Report	Broad categories	Standard categories
	4 Subsidy on enterprises and public-service units	Subsidy on enterprises, subsidy on public-service units, subsidy on interest payment, others
	5 Transfer payment	Transfer payment among different levels of governments, transfer payment among same levels of government, transfer payment among government agencies of different ranks, transfer payment among government agencies of the same ranks
	6 Gift	Domestic gift, overseas gift
	7 Interest of debt servicing	Bond, debt from national bank, debt from other financial institutions, debt from foreign governments, debt from international organisations, others
	8 Repayment of principal	Domestic debt, foreign debt
	9 Construction	Housing, office equipment, specialised equipment, vehicle, infrastructure, large-scale repair, IT network, storage, others
	10 Indirect loan and share acquisition	Domestic loan repayment, foreign loan repayment, domestic indirect loan repayment, foreign indirect loan repayment, share acquisition, others
	11 Others	Funds for preparation, funds in reserve, subsidy on social security funds, unclassified project expenditure, others
Expenditure under functional classification	1 General public service	People's congress, people's political consultative commission, government office, development and reform, statistics, finance, taxation, audit, custom, personnel, discipline inspection and supervision, population and family planning, commerce and trade, intellectual property rights, industry and commerce, food and drug supervision, quality supervision, land resources, oceanic affairs, surveying and mapping, earthquake, meteorological affairs, ethnic affairs, religious affairs, Hong Kong and Macao affairs, archive affairs, Communist Party, democratic parties and Federation of Industry and Commerce, mass organisation, lottery affairs, national debt, others
	2 Diplomacy	General administration, agencies abroad, overseas aid, international organisation, overseas cooperation and exchange, overseas promotion, border control, others
	3 National defence	Army and national reserve, national defence mobilisation, others

Category	Contents
4 Public security	Military police, public security, national security, procuratorate, court, justice, prison, labour education, national secrets, others
5 Education	Education administration, fundamental education, vocational education, adult education, distance education, overseas education, special-needs education, teacher and cadre continuing education, education surcharge, others
6 Science and technology	Science and technology education, fundamental research, applied research, technology research and development, technology service, social sciences, technology popularisation, technology exchange and cooperation, others
7 Culture, sports and media	Culture, relics, sports, broadcast, news press, others
8 Social security and employment	General administration, civic affairs, appropriation to social security foundation, subsidy social security foundation, retirement funds for government and public-service units personnel, subsidy for enterprise bankruptcy, job placement subsidy, relief for families of deceased, demobilisation, social welfare, enterprises for handicapped employees, minimum subsidy for urban residents, other relief for urban residents, relief for rural residents, relief for natural disasters, Red Cross, others
9 Social insurance	Basic retirement, unemployment, fundamental health, industrial accident, birth, others
10 Health care	General administration, health service, community health, health security, disease prevention, health supervision, women and children health care, rural health care, Chinese medicine, others
11 Environmental protection	General administration, environment detection, environment protection, ecology protection, natural forestry protection, reverting agricultural land into forestry, containment of desert, reverting grazing land into grassland, reverting agricultural land into grassland, others
12 Urban and rural community	General administration, planning and management, public facilities, residence, hygiene, street market, government housing fund, expenditure on renting state-owned land, public utilities, others
13 Agriculture and water work	Agriculture, forestry, irrigation, south–north water transferral, poverty relief, agriculture comprehensive exploitation, others
14 Communication	Road and sea transportation, rail transportation, civic aviation, others
15 Industry, commerce and finance	Mining, manufacturing, construction, power generation, information industry tourism, foreign direct investment, crop and oil, commodity circulation, storage, finance, tobacco, production safety, state-owned asset supervision, small and medium enterprises, recyclable energy, energy saving, others
16 Others	Fund for preparation, fund in reserve, others
17 Transfer payment	Remitted fund, fund distributed on the basis of fiscal strength fund (cailixing zhuanyi zhifu), earmarked fund, transfer payment in government foundation, transfer payment in lottery charitable foundation, transfer payment in extra-budgetary fund, transfer payment among government agencies, balanced surplus at the end of budgetary years, transfer-out capital

Source: 'Zhengfu shouzhi fenlei gaige fangan: Caizhengbu yusuan [2006] shisan hao', pp. 62–3.

local levels, over 370 billion *yuan* was spent under the scrutiny of the finance bureaux at various levels. Direct payment to suppliers from finance bureaux at various levels was worth 250 billion *yuan*. But the reform failed to deeply penetrate the administrative hierarchy. Until 2005, fewer than 160 prefectural-level cities adopted this system (Li, J. 2006: 55–6; Wang 2005: 62–3; Li 2003: 53–4; Jin, R. 2006: 8–11).

Scrutiny of the use of extra-budgetary funds was stepped up. More and more extra-budgetary funds were classified into budgetary funds so that finance bureaux could more easily scrutinise the use of such funds. In 2003, 118 types of administrative levies collected by 30 central ministries and departments were classified into budgetary revenue. In 2004, another 62 types of administrative fees collected by 26 ministries were classified into budgetary funds (Ma and Luo 2005: 56). By the end of 2005, the budgetary revenue covered 90 per cent of the State Council-sanctioned administrative fees collected by central ministries (National Audit Office 2006). As a result of the reclassification, the budgetary revenue rose more quickly than extra-budgetary revenue did, with the result that the share of budgetary revenue in gross government revenue has been rising in recent years (see Figure 4.1).

The control over public spending at lower-level governments was also tightened. Quite often, lower-level governments lack expertise in financial management. In a survey of five villages in Huaihua city of Hunan province, the highest education level of the accountants was high school and only two out of the ten accountants attained this level. In the meantime, eight out of the ten accountants had fewer than three years' work experience (Chen *et al.* 2006: 4). The poor quality of public employees mirrors the brain-drain problems in lower-level governments across the country, especially in the economically depressed regions where the well-educated talent flocks to affluent regions for employment. Between 1991 and 1997, the number of public employees leaving seven counties in Guangxi province exceeded the number arriving by 100 per cent (Study Group

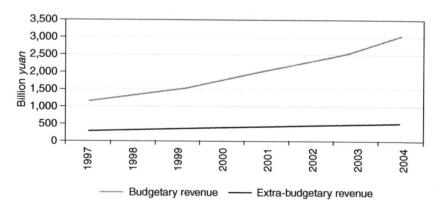

Figure 4.1 Budgetary and extra-budgetary revenue, 1997–2004 (source: National Bureau of Statistics (2006: 286, 298)).

of the Research Office of the Organisation Department of the CCP Central Committee 1999: 294). The number of cadres leaving Tibet and Qinghai between 1980 and 1997 was almost 12 times the number arriving (62,300 versus 5,100) (Study Group of the Organisation Department of the CCP Qinghai Provincial Committee 1999: 389). In Guangxi province, only 38.37 per cent of its technical specialists (*zhuanye jishu renyuan*) had college degrees (*dazhuan*), well below the national average of 45.7 per cent (Study Group of the Organisation Department of the CCP Guangxi Autonomous Region Committee 1999: 347). The lack of expertise in financial management sometimes resulted in violations of the laws and regulations of spending control. For example, the Regulations of Petty Cash Management in Villages stipulated that village cashiers were permitted to keep petty cash of up to only 1,000 *yuan*. However, a cashier of a village in Jingbian county of Shaanxi province was able to draw upon a public fund of 100,000 *yuan* ('You yang' 2006: 4).

In view of the difficulty in recruiting and retaining qualified accountants for governments at the township level, county-level governments were charged with managing the budgets of township-level governments and handling budget preparation, procurement of government supplies, clearance of financial transactions, payroll payment, disbursement of operating funds to village schools and approval of township budgets. For close scrutiny on the use of public funds, the provinces of Zhejiang, Anhui and Gansu integrated township bureaux of finance and land with county bureaux. The management of the personnel and salaries of the two township bureaux was transferred from township governments to county bureaux of finance and land. The reporting relationship between county and township finance bureaux became binding. The townships in Gansu province have no independent budgets. The structural adjustment weakened the pressure from township-level governments on township finance bureaux for circumventing regulations of spending control. In 2006, 18 provincial-level governments centralised the spending authority of all township-level to county-level governments. Another ten provincial-level governments undertook the centralisation in selected regions (Liu and Tao 2007: 175–6; Liu, Q. 2006: 4; Department of Finance, Anhui Province 2006: 23–5).

To reduce bottlenecks in financial scrutiny further, provincial-level governments took over for the authorities and scrutinised the preparation and execution of county budgets from the prefectural-level government. By 2006, 28 provinces had taken over the authorities. From then on, it was provincial finance departments that supervised the counties' financial report, budget execution and debt servicing. Gansu province instructed county-level governments to submit their budgets to provincial government for approval. Hubei province allocated the fiscal transfer directly to county governments. Prefectural-level cities are prohibited from more tax revenue from counties than the amount they collected in 2003 (Budget Bureau, Ministry of Finance 2006: 17–20; Fu 2006: 22–3). Interestingly, both measures violate Article 2 of Budget Law, stating that each level of government is responsible for their budget. To strengthen the supervision of the provincial finances, the Ministry of Finance has set up special offices in provinces and large cities with independent planning status (*jihua danlie shi*). These representative offices are charged with two major functions: supervision of centrally disbursed expenditure to ensure compliance with central spending targets, and supervision of provincial taxation bureaux in conjunction with the State Administration of Taxation and provincial-level governments (Yang 2004: 125).

The control mechanism external to financial bureaucracy has also improved. The number of central state organs audited and the amount of the misused public funds discovered increased (see Table 4.4). In 2003, the National Audit Office published the full text of its annual audit report for the first time in China's history. In 2007, the National Audit Office released an audit report involving 49 ministerial-level organs, alleging the misuse of public monies worth 27 billion *yuan*. Illegal use accounted for 4 per cent of the amount and wastage for another 5 per cent. The increasing transparency through publishing audit reports provides the public with necessary information and allows the public to, in effect, supervise the government. Public outcry over the waste and corruption documented in the audit reports was spread through cyberspace and mass media due to public pressure from the disclosure. According to Auditor-General Li Jinhua, the improvement in the control mechanism was effective in alleviating corruption problems in financial management ('3.6b' 2007: 1).

The audit reports shed light on the spending irregularities of the central ministries. All of the central ministries and bureaux audited by the Office – including the gatekeeper of financial control such as the Ministry of Finance and the People's Bank of China – were reported to have violated financial regulations. In 2005, for example, the Ministry of Finance blurred the division between government revenue and expenditure and transferred tax revenue of ten billion *yuan* from the China National Petroleum Corporation to subsidise the China Petroleum and Chemical Corporation. The People's Bank of China was found to have diverted an operating fund of 126 million *yuan* to employees' bonus and subsidies. It violated relevant regulations in using 1.01 billion *yuan* budgeted for the acquisition of fixed assets, such as keeping the money in commercial bank accounts which were beyond the scrutiny of the Ministry of Finance (National Audit Office 2006). Thanks to the National Audit Office's investigation, a budget fund of 4.16 billion *yuan* was found to have been misappropriated by 38

Table 4.4 Number of central state organs audited and amount of misused funds discovered, 2004–6

Year	2004	2005	2006
The number of central state organs audited	38	48	56
The amount of misused fund (billion yuan)	9.06	5.51	46.88

Source: 'Zhongguo shenji baogao: 2006 niandu zhongyang yusuan zhixing he qita caizheng shouzhi de shenji gongzuo baogao zongshu' (Audit report of China: A working report of execution of central budget and other budgetary revenue and expenditure) (2007: 16).

central ministries. Another 11.76 billion *yuan* was found to have been kept in ministries without being used or reported to the Ministry of Finance. The Party punished 213 officials; 76 were arrested, sued or sentenced by the courts (Li, J. 2006: 55–6).

Three types of spending irregularities can be identified from the audit reports of the National Audit Office. The first type is failure to disclose an extra-budgetary fund in order to keep the funds beyond the scrutiny of the Ministry of Finance. Between 1996 and 2003, the Ministry of Railways transferred a budgetary fund of 3.2 billion *yuan* into two firms under the Ministry. A profit of 685 million *yuan* was generated from the fund. The Ministry kept the profit in the two firms without reporting to the Ministry of Finance. Between March 2002 and June 2005, the Ministry of Education collected 234 million *yuan* from English-proficiency examination fees and kept 47.71 million *yuan* for its own use. The Ministry of Information Industry was found to have secretly kept rental revenues of 142 million *yuan* during the period 2001–5 (National Audit Office 2006).

The second type of spending irregularities is the falsification of financial data for control purposes. In 2005, the National Audit Office revealed that the Ministry of Finance, the State Administration of Taxation and the People's Bank of China substantially under-reported the amount of capital which was spent in violation of regulations (see Table 4.5) (Yue 2005: 16–18).

The third type is the unauthorised use of budgetary expenditure on financing employees' fringe benefits, running businesses or paying debts. A total of 13 central ministries committed this infraction (see Table 4.6). In 2004, the investigation of the National Audit Office resulted in the suing of 1,020 officials suspected of violating financial-control regulations. Eventually, 236 of them were found guilty. Another 1,525 officials were brought to the attention of party disciplinary bodies which handed down disciplinary actions to 457 officials (Yearbook of China Audit Editorial Committee 2005: 780–1).

Table 4.5 Falsifying financial data for control purpose

Central ministries	Amount of capital spent in violation of regulations (from respective central ministries) (billion yuan)	Amount of capital spent in violation of regulations (from National Audit Office) (billion yuan)
Ministry of Finance	1.27	8.66
State Administration of Taxation	2.04	31.2
People's Bank of China	2.24	41.9

Source: Yue (2005: 17).

Table 4.6 Unauthorised use of budgetary expenditure, 2005

Departments	Details
State Development and Reform Commission	9.59 million *yuan* spent on 14 staff quarter units and 2.21 million *yuan* spent on personal insurance policies
Beijing Institute of Technology (under State Commission of Science, Technology and Industry for National Defence)	24.11 million *yuan* spent on staff quarters
Beijing Bureau of Ministry of Railways construction.	164 million *yuan* spent on resort hotel
Ministry of Information Industry	1.59 million *yuan* spent payroll expenditure
China Ethnic Affairs Post (a newspaper under State Ethnic Affairs Commission)	10.3 million *yuan* spent on debt repayment

Source: National Audit Office (2007).

Impact of reforming public-spending control

Measured by the rate of cost saving, it can be cautiously concluded that the reform has achieved a modest success. The reform of government procurement – the second-largest government expenditure item after payroll expenditure – may illuminate this point.[2] The savings rate from government procurement is around 10 per cent of the total procurement fund, far below the international average of 20–40 per cent. The total value of procurement following procuring regulations (less than 2 per cent of GDP) is substantially below the international standard among developing countries (up to 13 per cent) (Chou 2006: 533–49; Domberger *et al.* 1995: 1454–70; World Bank 1994). The objective of cost saving through downsizing the bureaucracy is also missed, as evidenced by rising administrative expenses (see the discussion in Chapter 5).

The reform of spending control has several weaknesses. The reform focuses on technical aspects of budget planning and execution. Irrational budget cycles and the lack of coherent leadership in charge of budget preparation and execution are left unresolved. Senior officials can scarcely be held responsible for spending irregularities. The National Audit Office once discovered that in 2002 and 2003, the central ministries and provinces altogether misappropriated 450 billion *yuan* of central taxes and land-development capital, 285 billion *yuan* of local taxes and 245 billion *yuan* of funds for infrastructure construction, agriculture, irrigation, environmental protection, health care and education. The Central Discipline Inspection Commission proposed publicising the problems through the New China News Agency. The provincial secretaries and governors of Hunan, Shandong, Anhui, Jiangsu, Guangdong and Shanghai opposed the idea, arguing that some Politburo members such as Li Changchun, Wang Ju, Hui Liangyu, Wu Guanzheng and Jia Qinglin were implicated in the misappropriation. They worried that openly publishing the reports would lead to public discontent with the Party Centre (Li, Z. 2004: 14–16).

In 2005, all provinces were discovered to have misappropriated land-development taxes. Then, the National Audit Office proposed the investigation of 12 provincial party secretaries and governors (Guangdong, Fujian, Guangxi, Yunnan, Jiangxi, Hunan, Jiangsu, Liaoning, Shanghai, Shandong, Henan and Heilongjiang) and six ministers (Construction, Communications, Customs, Land and Resources, Information Industry and Taxation). The Director of the Central Organisation Department, He Guoqiang, strongly opposed the investigation, arguing that under the principle of party leadership, investigation into senior officials was the jurisdiction of the Central Discipline Inspection Committee, not the National Audit Office (Luo 2005: 11). Since senior officials are protected from sanctions in their laxity in controlling public spending, state budgets are not always effective in controlling expenditure. In 2003, the central government spent 14.44 billion *yuan* on social security and 4.21 billion *yuan* on the reform of state-owned enterprises. The figures represented 375.9 per cent and 209.2 per cent of the budgeted expenditure respectively (Jin 2004: 24). Many central ministries still keep secret bank accounts despite repeated calls for their abolition. According to the National Audit Office (2006), a research institute under the Ministry of Public Security kept foreign currency equivalent to 6.43 million *yuan* in secret accounts. The Ministry of Civic Affairs sold a piece of land for 18.09 million *yuan* without advance authorisation from the Government Offices Administration of the State Council. The land-sale revenue was kept in secret bank accounts. Between 2003 and 2006, a firm under the Ministry of Land and Resources kept 493,000 *yuan* in a secret bank account and spent 375,000 *yuan*. In 2003, the National Development and Reform Commission were required to hand over a surplus of 43.41 million *yuan* from a subordinate office to the central treasury. In 2005, the Commission kept 16.40 million *yuan* (National Audit Office 2006).

Meanwhile, the reform follows a top-down approach, seeking to collect more information for decision makers to control spending departments through finance bureaux. The classification of extra-budgetary into budgetary funds, centralisation of licensing authority, the strengthening of finance bureaux's oversight of spending departments and the recentralisation of budget management from central ministries to the Ministry of Finance, from county-level governments to provincial-level governments and from township-level governments to county-level governments all share this commonality. Owing to the inevitability of information asymmetry and the divergence between central and local priorities, close supervision cannot rule out the possibility that policy implementers shirk and hide information in order to evade the attention of fault-finding superiors. To prevent local governments raising excessive debts and going against financial prudence, Article 28 of Budget Law prohibited local governments from issuing bonds. However, many township-level governments circumvented the restriction by instructing the directors of the enterprises affiliated with them to borrow capital from banks, and then transferred the capital to the governments (Ong 2006; Yep 2004).

The top-down approach and restrictions on the autonomy of spending departments were divergent from the OECD's bottom-up approach of public-spending control. In OECD countries, the reform may be considered a process of setting up incentive-compatible institutions to align the interests of department managers with the objectives of spending control. Diamond pointed out that 88 per cent of the OECD countries have authorised central ministries to take care of their own procuring activities (operating within certain limits); 26 per cent allow government organisations to receive one appropriation for all of their operating expenditure items instead of separate appropriations for salaries and operating expenditures; 9 per cent do not restrict the transfers between appropriations. In return for the new autonomy, department managers are required to meet the objectives of government policies. Under the more decentralised management models, department managers were found to have more incentive to save costs in budget preparation and execution (Diamond 2006: 1, 5).

The performance-evaluation system of local leaders widens the gap between the reform objectives and the interests of local leaders over the issues of spending control. In the reform era, local governments' authority over capital-investment decisions was drastically expanded while the central government could neither monopolise the investment-allocation process nor the sources of investment funds. The performance-evaluation system is characterised by a heavy stress on economic growth (such as growth of industrial production, growth of GDP and the amount of tax and non-tax revenue), social stability and party building (see the discussion in Chapter 5). The high priority on economic growth has encouraged spending on capital investment. China's capital expenditure as a percentage of total government expenditure was higher than all but one OECD country (Korea). Capital spending relative to GDP was about three times the OECD average and almost double that of the highest OECD country (Korea) (OECD 2006: 69). Local officials have such a high incentive to spend capital investment that many of them continue to spend even though much of the capital investment is either useless or underutilised. Only half of the public infrastructure projects financed by the capital spending have met government standards. Out of the 526 such projects in 28 provinces and municipalities, 26 per cent were incomplete and a further 26 per cent were non-operational, substandard or operated below planned capacity (OECD 2006: 63–9; Japan Bank for International Cooperation 2003). A vivid example was an exhibition centre in Sanya city of Hainan province constructed for Miss World Beauty Pageant and completed in 2003. With a price tag of 122 million *yuan*, the exhibition centre was seriously under-utilised. In one year, it was left unused for 360 days. The lack of revenue and high maintenance cost caused the city such a large financial burden that the local government decided eventually to auction the exhibition centre ('Sanya' 23 May 2007). The position-rotation system magnified the negative impact of the performance-appraisal system over budget execution. Worried that local governors might establish their own patronages and undermine central control, central leaders regularly rotate local governors to different locales. Because of their short terms of office, local governors tend to pursue tasks which help to quickly produce work results at the expense of the localities' long-term benefits. An example of this is overspending on capital investment. Worse still, the excessive capital investment is spent when many local governments are heavily in debt (see Chapter 3).

Conclusion

In contrast with the OECD's bottom-up approach in reforming the control of public spending by delegating power to department managers and providing them with incentives to economise the use of public funds, spending control in China follows a top-down approach. The reform seeks to bridge the information gap and increase the clarity of policy content of spending control in order to strengthen top-down control. Parts of the spending authorities of local bureaux have been moved to the finance bureaux and upper-level governments. The use of public funds has been made more transparent through expanding the coverage of budgetary funds. Budgets are prepared on a departmental instead of a functional basis so that, in theory, it is easier to hold department directors responsible for their spending.

Tackling technical issues is central to the reform of spending control. The political challenges of budgetary control are not addressed. The authority of budget approval remains dispersed among the Ministry of Finance, the National Development and Reform Commission, the Government Offices Administration of the State Council and the Ministry of Personnel. Bridging the information gap cannot rule out information asymmetry. This is especially true in China's administration which is disjointed and fragmented. Many agents are involved in spending control and monopolise some information essential for effective spending control. It is impossible for policy elites to continuously scrutinise their agents. Therefore solely relying on bridging the information gap to save costs has achieved limited success. Though spending departments are repeatedly ordered to cancel their secret bank accounts and deposit their funds into bank accounts managed by the treasury, it is still possible for spending departments to maintain secret bank accounts that impede finance bureaux from effectively supervising the flow of public funds. The current institutions make the interests of these agents incompatible with cost saving: Position rotation and the need to produce tangible achievement encourages local governors to spur economic growth and capital investment at the expense of financial prudence. The very nature of spending control goes against the personal interests of local governors and department directors who remain resistant to reforms of spending control.

5   Civil service reform

Introduction

A competent civil service provides sound policy advice for policy makers, contributes to the reformulation of policies considered too controversial or too ambiguous to implement, and facilitates the collection of information for monitoring policy outcome. This chapter investigates the implementation of civil-service reform since 1993, marked by the promulgation of the Provisional Regulations of State Civil Servants. Special attention will be focused on the four most important areas of the reform: establishment of the civil-service system; staffing reform; reform of staff development; and wage reform. Reform set-ups of the civil service have been established, but some of them exist symbolically. The reason may be traced to the implementation process which has played out as a series of conflicts between central policy makers and local leaders. Central policy makers were more concerned with meeting their desired objectives, whereas local leaders placed more emphasis on coping with the conflicts arising from the reform implementation. To mitigate the conflict, many local leaders compromised the reform by delaying reform programmes and distorting or not implementing others.

Political development and civil-service reform in China

The term 'cadres' has long been used to refer to the managerial and professional staff working in public sectors, including state-owned enterprises, public-service units, mass organisations, and all branches of government (executive, legislative, judiciary and CCP). The more specific term 'civil servants' was first officially adopted in the 1993 Provisional Regulation of State Civil Servants (the blueprint that marked the start of civil-service reform). In the Provisional Regulations, 'civil servants' refers to the employees at managerial level working in executive branches. The definition excludes the temporary workers and support staff (*gongqin renyuan*), together with most health, education and social-service providers who do not execute administrative functions.[1] Effective as of January 2006, the Law of Civil Servants expands the definition to include all employees hired according to the establishment plan (*bianzhi*) and paid by the state treasury.

The new definition includes the manual workers in the executive branch and all employees in the legislative and judicial branches.[2] According to the new definition, civil servants numbered 6.5 million in 2004, with over 90 per cent working in the local governments ('New law' 2004). The sectors of health and education, as well as a wide array of market regulatory bodies such as banking, insurance and securities commissions were excluded from civil service and remain classified as public-service units.

Although the civil-service system has been established for more than a decade at the national level, many departments have not yet singled out the category of civil servants when compiling their statistics. In official statistics and archives, the terms 'cadres' (*ganbu*) and 'officials' (*guanyuan*) are used more frequently than 'civil servants' (*gongwuyuan*). For the convenience of analysis, the discussion below interchangeably uses the phrases 'civil servants', 'cadres', 'public employees' and 'officials'.

Civil-service reform in China is an extension of cadre-management reform – a major capacity reform measure in the 1980s in response to the CCP's desire to build up performance legitimacy through reforming its inefficient administration (Chan and Lam 1996, 1995a, 1995b; Lee 1991; Burns 1994a, 1993, 1989a, 1987). Echoing the desire of post-Mao leaders to build their authority on the basis of institutions, the reform sought to institutionalise the merit principle in the cadre-management system. Civil servants are recruited, deployed and promoted in accordance with their work-related skills and qualifications instead of patronage and *guanxi*. Their performance is evaluated and based on their contribution to organisational missions. The evaluation results are communicated to civil servants themselves for staff development. Training is provided to raise their competence in carrying out their duties. Adequate wages are dispensed to retain the most talented employees. The wage levels and awards are linked to performance levels to ensure that civil servants are fully motivated to display their potential.

The first blueprint of civil-service reform was proposed by former Party Secretary Zhao Ziyang. He suggested moving the authority of managing cadres up to vice-ministerial level from the CCP to the Ministry of Personnel. The leading Party members' groups (*dangzu*) which supervised the implementation of the Party's personnel policies in government departments would be abolished (*Renmin ribao* 1988). By this means, Zhao hoped that the management of most of the leading cadres would be made on merit as opposed to political criteria.

The plan shocked many Party leaders as it undermined the *nomenklatura* system – a list of leading public sector positions under the full control of the CCP. It suffered a setback after Zhao was purged for his supportive attitude towards the 1989 students' movement. The CCP was preoccupied with the quest for stability and feared that civil-service reform would further erode its authority. It reasserted its control of cadres and substantially scaled down civil-service reform. The final version of the reform implemented in 1993 focused on the technical issues of personnel management, such as establishing the civil-service system and reforming the practices of staffing, staff development and wage administration (Xu 1994: 219; Burns 1994b, 1989b). Party committees at all levels maintained their control over the management of all leading officials. The State Council and local governments, under the supervision of *dangzu*, remained as the Party's executive arms to implement the Party's personnel policies (Zhu *et al.* 1996: 235, 402, 403).

Establishment of the civil-service system

The first step of civil-service reform was to set up a civil-service system. This involved 'three determinants' (*sanding*): to determine the missions of each department; to determine departments' organisation structure; and to determine the number of employees that each agency should employ. A mechanism was devised to transfer the qualified cadres into the civil service. Departments and personnel were downsized; the re-expansion of bureaucracy – a bureaucratic pathology since the 1960s (see Figure 5.1) – was prohibited. The several rounds of administrative restructuring cut the number of the central ministries from 41 in 1993 to 30 in 1998, and finally to 28 in 2007 (see Table 5.1).

However, the actual number of central departments exceeds 28. Under the State Council, there are another 18 organisations, one special organisation, four administrative offices, 14 public-service units, 11 administrations and bureaux, and the State Council Office, in addition to the commissions and ministries. Some of these organisations and bureaux were previously ministries but were downgraded during the 1990s. For instance, the Ministry of Forestry, the State Physical Culture and Sports Commission and the Ministry of Radio, Film and Television were downgraded to the State Forestry Administration, the State Sports General Administration and the State Administration of Radio, Film and Television in 1998 respectively. Some of them (State Administration of Foreign Exchange, China Banking Regulatory Commission and China Securities Regulatory Commission) were newly created to take charge of the new economic regulatory functions of central government. At the local level, some township-level

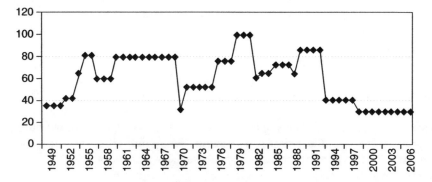

Figure 5.1 Number of departments in state council (source: Z. Liu (2003: 72–83); *China Directory* (various years)).

Table 5.1 State ministries and commissions (selected years)

State ministries/commissions	1993	1998	2003	2007
State Council Office	✓	✓		
Foreign Affairs	✓	✓	✓	✓
National Defence	✓	✓	✓	✓
State Planning Commission (renamed State Development Planning Commission in 1998)	✓	✓		
State Development and Reform Commission			✓	✓
State Economic and Trade Commission	✓	✓		
State Commission for Restructuring Economy	✓			
State Education Commission (renamed Ministry of Education in 1998)	✓	✓	✓	✓
State Science and Technology Commission (renamed Ministry of Science and Technology in 1998)	✓	✓	✓	✓
State Commission of Science, Technology and Industry for National Defence	✓	✓	✓	✓
State Ethnic Affairs Commission	✓	✓	✓	✓
Public Security	✓	✓	✓	✓
State Security	✓	✓	✓	✓
Supervision	✓	✓	✓	✓
Civil Affairs	✓	✓	✓	✓
Justice	✓	✓	✓	✓
Finance	✓	✓	✓	✓
Personnel	✓	✓	✓	✓
Labour (renamed Ministry of Labour and Social Security in 1998)	✓	✓	✓	✓
Geology and Mineral Resources (renamed Ministry of Land and Natural Resources in 1998)	✓	✓	✓	✓
Construction	✓	✓	✓	✓
Power Industry	✓			
Coal Industry	✓			
Machine-Building Industry	✓			
Electronics Industry	✓			
Metallurgical Industry	✓			
Chemical Industry	✓			
Railways	✓	✓	✓	✓

continued

Table 5.1 Continued

State ministries/commissions	1993	1998	2003	2007
Communications	✓	✓	✓	✓
Posts and Telecommunications (renamed Ministry of Information Industry in 1998)	✓	✓	✓	✓
Water Resources	✓	✓	✓	✓
Agriculture	✓	✓	✓	✓
Forestry	✓			
Internal Trade	✓			
Foreign Trade and Economic Cooperation	✓	✓		
Commerce			✓	✓
Culture	✓	✓	✓	✓
Radio, Film and Television	✓			
Public Health	✓	✓	✓	✓
State Physical Culture and Sports Commission	✓			
State Family Planning Commission (renamed State Population and Family Commission in 2003)	✓	✓	✓	✓
People's Bank of China	✓	✓	✓	✓
National Audit Administration	✓	✓	✓	✓
Total number of ministries/commissions	41	30	28	28

Sources: *China Directory 2007*, p. 49; *China Directory 2004*, p. 88; *China Directory 1999*, p. 81; *China Directory 1994*, pp. 48–9.

governments were either merged or abolished to save administrative costs. Certain success has been achieved (see Figure 5.2).

On average, governments at all levels expended 60 per cent of their revenue on wages, with some local governments spending a larger share. In Gansu Province, where three-quarters of the 85 counties depended on subsidies from the provincial government, 80 per cent of the county budgetary expenditure went on personnel costs. The revenue of Lingshui county of Hainan province in 1996 (31.7 million *yuan*) was even smaller than its payroll (40.9 million *yuan*). Even after administrative reform in 1997, the payroll still stood at 26.38 million *yuan*, or 83 per cent of its total revenue. Some impoverished local governments cannot regularly pay their employees (Chou 2003a: 85). A township government in Heilongjiang province had to spend over 53 per cent of its debt on its payroll during the period 1996–2001 (Song 2004: 56). Given that most of the government money is used for covering payroll expenditure, successfully downsizing the personnel can substantially contribute to the state capacity. In 1993, the central

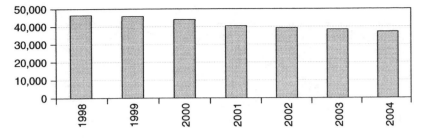

Figure 5.2 The number of township-level governments (source: National Bureau of Statistics (various years)).

government demanded a 20 per cent cut in the personnel of the State Council and a 25 per cent cut across the country. In 1998, the then premier Zhu Rongji demanded a further 47 per cent cut in personnel of the provincial-level governments and a 50 per cent cut across the country. The cut in provincial-level governments ranged from 3.9 per cent (Shanghai city) to 33.7 per cent (Hunan province). The cut for prefecture-level and city governments ranged from 11.6 per cent (Jilin province) to 47.5 per cent (Shanxi province). For county-level governments, the cut ranged from 6.3 per cent (Shanghai city) to 53.8 per cent (Tianjin city), and for township-level governments it ranged from 8.6 per cent (Shanghai city) to 58.3 per cent (Shangdong province) (see Table 5.2).

To maintain staff size within the permitted number, the Ministry of Personnel issued the 1994 Provisional Regulations of the Recruitment and Selection of State Civil Servants, obliging the governments at prefecture level and below to observe provincial establishment plans. Otherwise staffing decisions were void; the responsible officials were subject to disciplinary action.[3] Shandong province instructed its financial bureau not to pay civil servants who were not recruited according to the establishment plan (Yang and Gao 2005: 2).

Despite the downsizing efforts, the total number of civil servants remained steady at around 5.3 million ('New law' 2004). The size of the public sector fell from 109 million (almost 10 per cent of the population) in 1993 to an estimated 62 million people (or 5 per cent of the population) in 2005, but the shrinking of public sector was mostly due to the contraction of state-owned enterprises. Employees in government (*jiguan*) and public-service units (*shiye danwei*) have remained relatively steady in number (see Figure 5.3). All of the provincial-level governments and all but three central ministries hired more employees than permitted. The number of public employees at county level rose from 237,500 in 2002 to 305,000 in 2005 (Tian 2007: 17–18) (also see Table 5.3).

Ironically, downsizing campaigns went against the original intention of cutting back personnel costs and improving efficiency. Persuading redundant employees to resign requires expensive retraining and special allowances. One source reported that the 1998 downsizing campaign cost the central government 70 billion *yuan* (Li, L.C. 2006: 70). To persuade local governments to downsize their administration, Shandong province refrained from cutting the lower-level

Table 5.2 The planned establishment of different regions, 1993

Regions	Planned establishment at provincial-level government	Per cent cut (%)	Planned establishment at prefecture-level government	Per cent cut (%)	Planned establishment at city-level government	Per cent cut (%)	Planned establishment at county-level government	Per cent cut (%)	Planned establishment at township-level government	Per cent cut (%)
Beijing	35,000	15.0	N/A	N/A	N/A	N/A	8,000	50.2	13,640	45.1
Tianjin	34,200	20.0	N/A	N/A	N/A	N/A	5,000	53.8	10,955	29.2
Hebei	6,760	18.0	2,500	33.7	52,388	19.9	65,100	15.7	99,885	37.2
Shanxi	5,900	25.8	5,000	47.5	29,300	24.8	43,770	25.7	50,280	56.1
Inner Mongolia	5,500	25.1	8,000	41.3	23,500	33.3	36,610	33.6	46,305	35.4
Liaoning	6,160	24.9	N/A	N/A	72,000	24.8	20,800	21.5	47,895	52.4
Jilin	5,360	22.4	1,200	26.4	37,650	11.6	15,200	18.6	333,000	23.9
Heilong-jiang	6,300	33.4	2,570	35.2	58,200	20.3	31,800	26.8	47,370	46.8
Shanghai	37,000	3.9	N/A	N/A	N/A	N/A	6,000	6.3	10,050	8.6
Jiangsu	7,300	24.9	N/A	N/A	71,000	20.4	29,150	16.3	85,155	34.4
Zhejiang	6,160	17.1	825	15.7	46,525	25.2	25,600	28.4	65,645	35.6
Anhui	6,160	23.3	5,400	35.5	34,350	26.6	51,937	22.8	64,845	42.8
Fujian	5,650	25.6	3,000	23.2	27,300	20.6	28,600	19.7	36,520	47.8
Jiangxi	5,650	19.1	5,500	36.8	23,350	21.0	43,290	26.6	57,600	44.4
Shandong	7,500	24.4	5,500	46.8	70,100	26.5	48,750	23.8	100,000	58.3
Henan	7,400	21.9	6,200	46.1	49,000	34.5	72,000	30.0	98,200	46.5
Hubei	6,400	17.2	5,600	38.5	52,050	33.4	34,650	37.5	62,550	40.2
Hunan	6,560	33.7	6,000	41.7	38,000	29.6	50,360	21.7	101,460	47.2
Guangdong	7,500	21.8	N/A	N/A	105,000	N/A	36,400	N/A	78,000	N/A
Guangxi	5,900	24.7	7,600	25.9	21,000	32.1	45,178	30.1	52,995	46.2
Hainan	3,850	15.5	N/A	N/A	6,700	23.5	7,300	41.9	10,135	45.6
Sichuan	8,330	17.1	11,700	21.8	65,000	31.0	93,650	18.0	204,099	34.5
Guizhou	5,300	15.4	7,500	24.4	15,600	14.5	36,650	17.9	54,035	40.6
Yunan	5,960	18.8	13,010	27.0	16,700	18.2	56,000	22.2	85,370	36.2
Tibet*	N/A	N/A	N/A	N/A	N/A	N/A	N/A	N/A	N/A	N/A
Shaanxi	6,000	N/A	6,000	N/A	23,300	25.8	42,100	27.4	61,100	55.1
Gansu	5,460	26.0	7,150	28.5	16,000	19.5	29,572	8.5	33,616	30.0
Qinghai	3,660	24.2	2,950	29.4	3,100	21.9	10,100	26.8	9,369	31.2
Ningxia	3,400	22.9	950	20.8	5,300	21.1	6,950	23.0	6,648	491
Xinjiang	5,800	22.9	11,700	19.4	16,500	17.7	31,500	10.9	27,475	23.6

Source: China Local Administration Editorial Committee (1995: 249–451).

Note

* The total establishment across Tibet was 28,017, 5,000 more than the original workforce.

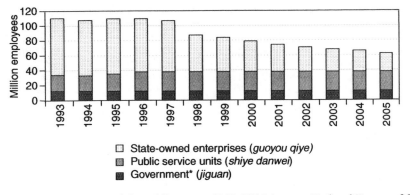

State-owned enterprises (*guoyou qiye*)
Public service units (*shiye danwei*)
Government* (*jiguan*)

Figure 5.3 The size of the public sector, 1993–2005 (source: National Bureau of Statistics (various years)).

Note
* Not all employees in government are civil servants. The above figure includes non-civil servants, such as the employees in political parties (including the CCP and democratic parties (*minzhu dangpai*)), mass organisations (*qunzhong zuzhi*) and religious organisations.

governments' operating fund originally linked with the size of personnel (Department of Finance, Shandong Province 2006: 22). Some local governments turned their departments into industrial associations and public-service units and continued to fund these new organisations. The finance bureau of Hubei province transformed its budget-preparation division into a public-service unit. All the personnel in the division were transferred to the unit. This coping strategy helped the finance bureau to reduce the number of personnel on the establishment plan but did not reduce the payroll expenditure (Huang and Di 2003: 218). Furthermore, the administrative expenses were inflated by the compensation for luring public employees to accept early retirement, the civil servants' pay hike and pension payment. As a consequence, both the amount of administrative expenses and its share were rising (see Table 5.4).

Lower-level governments in less-developed regions are resistant to downsizing because their overstaffing problems are particularly serious. County-level and township-level governments, the two lowest levels of governments,

Table 5.3 Permitted and actual number of public employees, 2006

Rank	Permitted number	Actual number
Provincial/ministerial	228	944
Vice-provincial/ministerial	1,262	12,487
Prefectural/bureau	4,865	11,075
Vice-prefectural/bureau	17,410	86,580

Source: Tian (2007: 18).

Table 5.4 Administrative expenses, 1992–2005

Year	Administrative expenses (billion yuan)	Share of administrative expense in government expenditure (%)	Year	Administrative expenses (billion yuan)	Share of administrative expense in government expenditure (%)
1992	46.34	12.38	1999	202.06	15.32
1993	63.43	13.66	2000	276.82	17.42
1994	84.77	14.63	2001	351.25	18.58
1995	99.65	14.16	2002	410.13	18.60
1996	118.53	14.93	2003	469.13	19.03
1997	138.89	14.72	2004	552.20	19.38
1998	160.03	14.82	2005	651.23	19.19

Source: National Bureau of Statistics (2006: 283).

employed less than 60 per cent of the country's civil servants (Xi 2002: 29). But 85 per cent of the civil servants hired outside the establishment plan (*bianzi wai*) in the country worked in these two levels of governments (Wang 2004: 25). Another report estimated that the actual number of township employees was two or three times as many as the permitted number (Jiao 2004). The resistance was due to local leaders' dilemmas. Many lower-level governments in less-developed regions did not have enough expertise, funds and infrastructure to develop enterprises and absorb manpower. Private sectors were too weak to create enough job opportunities. Given that local leaders had a responsibility to maintain social stability and guarantee job opportunities for demobilised soldiers, they often had to compromise the task of establishment planning and efficiency value (Chou 2003c). Local governments have little incentive to downsize personnel. The number of personnel is sometimes linked with budgetary appropriation and transfer payment from higher-level governments. In some poor regions, increasing personnel is a way to receive more transfer payments (Huang and Di 2003: 140). In view of the local resistance to downsizing, central government announced in 2004 that it would dissolve or incorporate 876 townships to try to slash 86,400 jobs and 864 million *yuan* a year in financial expenditures (Jiao 2004). However, the jobs slashed only accounted for 1.6 per cent of the total number of government posts. The move only marginally contributed to cost-saving.

Staffing reform

Staffing in the pre-reform and early reform eras was plagued by secrecy, nepotism and corruption. Jobs were not allocated by local cadres, but were not competed openly and fairly. Aspirants to government positions had little hope of success if they had neither connections nor good family backgrounds. For staff appointments, political credentials and seniority were more important than work-related abilities and performance level in the decisions of staff appointment. Peasants and workers were considered unqualified for administrative duties and often denied the chance of joining the cadres. As a consequence, the administration was run by cadres with good political qualifications but without commensurable job-related abilities (Liou 1998: 99).

Staffing reform is characterised by the promotion of a higher degree of openness and a greater emphasis on merit in the selection process. The first open recruitment in the post-Mao era took place in 1978. The recruitment drive involved 23 provincial-level governments hiring 34,000 cadres. In the beginning, open recruitment was irregular, infrequent, limited to cadres with urban household (*hukou*) status and fresh university and secondary school graduates. The positions filled through open recruitment were restricted to non-leading positions (*feilingdao zhiwei*) at the section level (*keji*). Later some local governments recruited workers, peasants and citizens without urban households. In 1986, Shenzhen city of Guangdong province and Qingdao city of Shandong province experimented with nationwide recruitment to hire officials up to the bureau level (*juji*) (Li 2000). The State Council extended the application of open recruitment and allowed all permanent Beijing urban residents to take the national civil-service examinations in 1995 ('Civil service exams' 1995), and in 1998 called for the lifting of the ban prohibiting non-permanent residents from taking the civil-service examination. Later, the household restrictions for taking the national examination were entirely removed, implying that the playing field for candidates from different regions was levelled. This helped to expand the pool of candidates and made it easier to recruit candidates of higher calibres ('Civil service recruitment' 2003). Between 1993 and 2000, 29 provincial-level governments filled 350,000 positions by open recruitment (Li 2000). In 2001, the transparency in the civil-service examination was increased by launching online job applications. Qualifications of different positions were made open in the official websites of the Ministry of Human Resource and Social Security (www.mohrss. gov.cn) and local personnel bureaux. Online applications were popular – the number of online job applications surged from 30,000 to over 540,000 between 2001 and 2004 (Huang 2004: 34).

The principles of openness and transparency are also applied to the appointment of civil servants to leading positions (*lingdao zhiwu*). The significance of openly recruiting these civil servants lies in the fact that these civil servants are the major decision makers at various levels of government and are under the tight control of the Party. Openness and transparency implies that the local Party secretaries have to give up some degree of secrecy and flexibility involved in appointment decisions. In July 2002, the Party Centre issued the Regulations on Appointment of Leading Cadres to regulate the appointment of civil servants to leading positions working in governments at county level and above. Chapter 9 of the Regulations stated that open competition may be used for appointing leading officials in local Party committees and government departments. Under open competition, the nature of vacancies, the qualifications required and the procedure of application were made open. By increasing the openness and transparency, recruitment exercises could attract a larger pool of candidates of high calibre. Behind-the-scenes manipulation became more difficult. Furthermore, seniority was no longer important in appointments, so ambitious civil servants had more incentive to improve their work-related knowledge.[4]

Two types of open competition can be identified. The first type was called *gongkai xuanba*. Qualified aspirants working in and outside state organs were allowed to apply for these positions. The second type, known as *jingzheng shanggang*, was restricted to candidates from particular departments or groupings of the functional bureaucracy (*xitong*). Article 38 of the Regulations further increased the transparency of appointments through a public-notification system. After candidates for the leading positions up to prefectural level were selected, selective officials were consulted for the appointment ('Zhonggong zhongyang' 2005). The public-notification system was designed to ensure that the selected candidates were truly qualified. There were cases of the notification invoking popular protest against the selected candidates which resulted in holding back the appointments (Burns 2004: 38).

In 2004, the Organisation Department of CCP Central Committee started to draft 'Provisional Methods in Assessing Local Leaders through a Scientific View of Development'. Two rounds of pilot tests were implemented in 12 provincial-level governments to experiment with the Provisional Methods. After three major revisions, the final version was issued in 2006. A major characteristic of the Provisional Methods is the stipulation that the democratic recommendations (*minzhu tuijian*), democratic test (*minzhu ceping*), democratic polls (*minzhu tiaocha*) and contested elections (*chai e xuanju*) should be used in the selection of candidates considered for leading positions. In 2007, the Party Centre issued a decree of 'Local Leadership Groups Living with a Scientific View of Development' to restate the significance of 'democratic recommendation' and specify the procedures in Chapter 2 ('Tixian kexue' 2007). The decree required local Party committees to consult retired local leaders and the leaders of local state organs before they nominated candidates to local leadership groups (*lingdao banzi*). If consensus on the list of nominees could not be reached, local Party committees could produce the final list of nominees by voting, provided that there were more standing candidates than there are vacancies. Article 10 stipulated that if candidates were nominated to leadership positions in people's governments, the democratic recommendation should include representatives from democratic parties, local branches of the All-China Federation of Industry and Commerce, and significant persons without party affiliations. The wide consultation may help to alleviate the possibility of local Party secretaries manipulating appointment decisions.

The case of Jian city of Jiangxi province in selecting section-level (*keji*) civil servants is illustrative of the recruitment of four leading officials at township level with more openness and transparency. The recruitment office first invited job applications and explicitly stated the requirements for job candidates. A total of 117 people submitted job applications. Then the members of recruiting departments were invited to mass meetings (*qunzhong dahui*) to solicit their opinions on the job applicants. Afterwards, the organisation department of the city Party committee consulted the following people for opinions: directors of county departments; important party members; the deputies of county people's congresses; and the people's political consultation conferences. After that, job candidates were selected for the next round of selection tests by voting. The voters included members of the county Party committees, people's congresses and people's political consultation conferences, the leading officials of people's governments, and all county-level cadres.

After selection tests, the top four job applicants stood for another election round which was in the form of an anonymous vote by the county Party standing committees. Party standing-committee members made decisions based on the results of selection tests, the number of votes cast in the previous election for the job applicants and the opinions collected from a mass meeting. The candidates applying for government offices were then invited to address township people's congresses about their missions and abilities. Those candidates applying for Party offices addressed the Party congresses. The final decisions of appointment were made by people's congresses and Party congresses respectively, through voting. The experience of Jian city has the potential of expanding the pool of job candidates and increasing the openness and transparency in recruitment processes without compromising Party control (Lin and Ren 2007: 44–5).

Since open recruitment has become more common, the civil servant qualifications have improved. In 2001, more than 56 per cent of civil servants had an education level of college and above, a 25 per cent increase since 1993 ('Personnel reforms' 2001). In the 2004 recruitment exercise, 91.7 per cent passing the qualifying stage had university degrees (Zhu 2004: 13). Implementation of open recruitment at the local level was less successful. Between 2000 and 2002, township-level governments hired only 43.26 per cent of their new recruits through open recruitment, as opposed to an average of 62.7 per cent across the country (Zhongzubu 18 July 2004). Initially the central leaders expected to introduce open recruitment in governments at all levels by 1995 (New China News Agency 1996: 140). By the end of 1998, 30 provincial-level governments had introduced open recruitment, but only 18 of them had extended open recruitment to the township level ('Renshi gongzuo' 29 December 2005).

The shortage of qualified candidates may explain the restrictive use of open recruitment in lower-level governments. Because Ganzhou city of Jiangxi province was less developed than the coastal regions, less than one-third of the university graduates were willing to work in their hometown. Some enterprises in the city failed to hire a single employee with suitable professional knowledge for six consecutive years (Chen 1997: 6). In 1995, the Qianan county of Hebei province found that less than 1 per cent of the 62,620 employees working in its 1,546 township and village enterprises had received a high school technical education (*zhongzhuan*), and as many as 25 per cent had only received a primary education. Among the enterprise managers and directors, only 7 per cent had college degrees and 32.6 per cent had an education at the level of junior high school or above (Peng 1995: 48). Between 1980 and 1997, the number of cadres leaving the Tibet autonomous region and Qinghai province was almost 12 times the number transferred in (62,300 vs. 5,100) (Zhao 1997: 34). As talent is unwilling to work in undesirable locations, the non-open recruitment method, along with Party organisations and state-owned enterprises, may be more effective for local governments to bring in personnel with required skills and knowledge.

Reform of staff development

Performance appraisal and training are two major staff-development activities. A good performance appraisal can provide employees with regular feedback on their work and give them opportunities to correct their weaknesses. The feedback and opportunities are essential for raising employees' productivity and channelling their abilities and efforts to fit organisational expectations. Training is necessary to improve employees' work-related attitude, skills and knowledge. Good training programmes help employees to correct their weaknesses (Pynes 1997: 122; Dresang 1999: 181; Klingner and Nalbandian 1998: 275).

The performance-appraisal exercises in the past failed to give employees regular feedback on their performance. In 1989, the CCP decreed an annual mandatory appraisal, but the regular annual appraisal was an exception, not a rule. Only leading officials had to undergo performance appraisal; appraisals of non-leading officials were uncommon (Contemporary China Editorial Committee 1994: 369; China Personnel Yearbook Editorial Board 1991: 98). The laxity in performance-appraisal exercises was due to the exercises' potential to damage personal relationships (*guanxi*). Under the Chinese administrative hierarchy, the reporting line was vertical, and horizontal coordination among the different functional bureaucracies was insufficient. Information and directives across departments had to be conveyed through informal channels buttressed by personal relationships. Personal relationships could only be cultivated in a harmonious work environment in which people avoided the type of conflict that would potentially arise when discussing their colleagues' weaknesses. Hence many local leaders were reluctant to do performance-appraisal exercises (Fewsmith 1996; Takahara 1992: 88).

Another weakness of the past performance-appraisal system was that it prioritised political integrity rather than merits. The major purpose of the past performance-appraisal exercise was to spot 'corrupt cadres', not to improve cadres' performance. A cadre's political stance was the main determinant of his or her rise or fall. In addition, the past performance-appraisal system could neither differentiate between cadres of different performance levels, nor link the performance levels with rewards and disciplinary actions. Accordingly, appraisal activities could not effectively motivate cadres to work towards organisational missions (Harding 1981: 85–6; Lee 1991: 389; Contemporary China Editorial Committee 1994: 372–4).

The promulgation of the Provisional Regulations of State Civil Servant Appraisal in 1994 kicked off the performance-appraisal reform. Department directors were required to appraise all their department members at the end or beginning of every year. At the beginning of the appraisal exercises, departments had to set up appraisal commissions composed of representatives from management, labour side and personnel offices to oversee appraisal exercises. Department members were required to write personal reports of their work performance. Based on these personal reports and their own assessments, department directors rated civil servants according to a four-grade classification: excellent, satisfactory, basically satisfactory and unsatisfactory. In comparison to the three-grade classification adopted in 1993, the four-grade classification was believed to be better able to provide an accurate record of civil servants' performance levels and give them feedback. Appraisal grades are assigned on the basis of five performance areas: political credentials (*de*); ability (*neng*); diligence (*qin*); achievement (*ji*); and integrity (*lian*). The Law of Civil Servants did not clearly specify the performance areas. Some local governments experimented to quantify them in order to work out appraisal grades in a more scientific manner. The local experiments were characterised by a heavier emphasis on work-related skills, knowledge and attitude (*neng, qin, ji* and *lian*) over political credentials. Before the performance grades of civil servants were finalised, department directors had to submit the grade proposals to appraisal commissions for approval so that department directors could find it more difficult to manipulate appraisal grades (Zhu *et al.* 1996: 162–3).

Performance-appraisal reform has made three achievements. First, the reform has institutionalised the regular annual appraisal. Over 97 per cent of all civil servants across the country are evaluated every year. Second, the reform has reversed the past emphasis on political integrity and underscored the importance of civil servants' work performance. Generally speaking, the weighting of political virtue only accounts for 10–40 per cent of the total mark in the annual performance appraisal, while the rest of the marks are distributed according to work performance. Third, the reform links appraisal grades to reward and punishment. Those rated excellent are noted in future promotions while those rated unsatisfactory are not considered. Those rated excellent and satisfactory are entitled to a year-end bonus. If rated either grade in two consecutive years, they can enjoy a grade increment along the civil-service pay scale. Those rated unsatisfactory will be demoted, and dismissed if rated unsatisfactory for two consecutive years (Chou 2005: 45–6). By these means, civil servants have more incentive to improve their work performance for the sake of a good performance report.

Despite this, performance appraisals did not enjoy high credibility among civil servants: only 18.2 per cent of the civil servants believed that performance appraisals were fair and objective (Study Group of Civil Service Examination and Appointment 1995: 17–20). The reform could hardly improve the work incentive of civil servants substantially, given the small amount of merit pay (5 per cent of civil servants' basic salary) awarded (Chou 2003b).[5] Moreover, the impact of the reform was undercut by the egalitarian tendency in appraisal ratings. Generally speaking, more than 80 per cent of civil servants were rated satisfactory and less than 1 per cent rated unsatisfactory.[6] In the meantime, over 99 per cent of them were rated either excellent or satisfactory. Almost all civil servants were therefore entitled to some merit pay and reward. The link between unsatisfactory grades with demotion and dismissal decisions was little more than symbolic. Given that appraisal grades were barely linked with dismissal decisions, only 0.05 per cent of civil servants were sacked between 1996 and 2003 ('Reform civil servants' pay' 2004).

Local leaders are evaluated on a cadre responsibility system which is based on a Soviet practice of industrial management. Under this system, factory managers were appraised according to sets of specific production quota. The performance indicators of local leaders are characterised by a heavy emphasis on economic growth, and to a lesser extent social development and Party building. Specific indicators vary across the country. Common specific indicators are related to the level and growth rate of GDP per capita, the level and growth rate of fiscal revenue per capita, the level and growth rate of residents' income, energy consumption, production safety, fundamental education, urban employment, social security, cultural life, population and family planning, natural resource conservation, environmental protection and scientific development and innovation (see Table 5.5) ('Zhongzubu yinfa' 2007).

Table 5.5 Performance indictors for evaluating the county and city mayors in Liaoning Province

Indicators	Mark
(1) Economic construction GDP and growth rate; gross value and growth rate of agricultural output; gross value and growth rate of industrial output; budgetary revenue (tax revenue, enterprise revenue, bond revenue and other revenue) and growth rate; net income of peasant per capita and growth rate; disposable income of urban resident and growth rate; arable land preservation; amount of major agricultural product produced and growth rate; commercialisation of agriculture; growth rate in gross value of state property; gross value and growth rate of remittance by state-owned and collective enterprises; gross value and growth rate of tax paid by non-state enterprises; gross value of fixed investment; gross value of foreign direct investment; gross value of foreign exchange income	60
(2) Social development Birth rate; number of crime; crime detection rate; satisfaction of the public towards social order; completion rate of voluntary education; proportion of expense on science and technology to budgetary revenue; number of spiritually civilised units; performance in dealing with three main pollutants; forest coverage rate	20
(3) Party building Percentage of leading officials in county/city governments having attained satisfactory results on the political knowledge examination; percentage of rural party branches rated excellent; party member training; percentage of party branches rated excellent in urban enterprises and service units; new party member; public satisfaction with leading cadres	20

Source: Study Group of Organisation Department, Liaoning Province Party Committee (1999: 180).

Local leaders may 'subcontract' the performance indicators to their subordinate department directors, and link the reward, penalty and career advancement of their subordinates to the realisation of these performance targets. In 1997, for example, Guizhou province assigned Puding county a target of 20 per cent revenue growth. To meet this target, the county finance bureau entered performance contracts with its 11 subordinate townships and towns, requiring them to achieve an annual revenue growth (after tax-sharing with the central government) of 15 per cent, 20 per cent and 25 per cent respectively, depending on the fiscal situation of the townships and towns. Those meeting their targets would be given a bonus of 10,000 *yuan*, 20,000 *yuan* and 30,000 *yuan*; the township leaders would receive 3,000 to 5,000 *yuan*. Failure to meet their targets was subject to a penalty of the amounts equal to the rewards (that is, 3,000 to 5,000 *yuan* for township leaders). Additional rewards were given to those meeting their targets three years in a row (Wong 2000: 58).

As a result of the high stakes involved in the result of their performance appraisal, local leaders may pursue the specific targets but sacrifice the good causes which are difficult to specify in performance contracts. The worship of GDP growth at the expense of environmental protection is a typical example. Yunnan province reportedly insisted on carrying out the development project of Dian Chi and turning it into tourist attraction even though the expected annual cost of cleaning up the pollution generated by the project (four billion *yuan*) was higher than the project's expected annual revenue of two billion *yuan*. The reason for green lighting the project was that the total GDP growth generated by the project was worth over six billion *yuan*. The huge financial implication and its positive impact on the appraisal result of provincial leaders produced strong inducements for provincial support (Du 2006: 26–7). The sacrifice of environmental protection is a nationwide phenomenon. Across the country, pollution caused losses of 512 billion *yuan* (or about 3 per cent of the GDP) in 2004. The estimated cost of pollution treatment amounted to 287 billion *yuan* (or about 1.8 per cent of the GDP) ('The greener the better' 2006). The State Environmental Protection Administration estimated the economic losses caused by environmental degradation (2.1–7.7 per cent) and pollution (5–13 per cent) of China's GDP in 2004 (Guo 2006a: 7).

On top of environmental problems, the emphasis on economic growth may undermine state capacity as it encourages local leaders to grant investors tax arrears (known as tax expenditure (*shuishou zhichu*) in China) which adversely affects tax revenue. Though central government prohibited tax arrears, it was widely used as local governments had to compete for investors and achieve good appraisal results. Meanwhile, the information asymmetry made it difficult for audit and finance bureaux to detect this practice (Huang and Di 2003: 145). Furthermore, the performance appraisal gave local leaders much incentive to exaggerate their achievements and downplay their failure. In March 2006, the Central Discipline Investigation Commission sent investigative teams to the municipalities of Beijing and Shanghai and the provinces of Guangdong and Hubei to verify governors' work reports. All the four provincial-level governments were found to have over-reported their achievements and under-reported their weaknesses (see Table 5.6).

Central watchdogs were long aware of the problems of falsifying work reports. In September 2001, the then Secretary of Central Discipline Investigation Commission Wei Jianxing proposed to dismiss the leading officials who seriously falsified their reports. But his ideas were not adopted. Similar ideas were floated again in October 2004 and November 2005 in Central Discipline Investigation Commission, but the fierce resistance from other senior officials killed the ideas (Yue 2006: 16).

The pursuit of a scientific view of development – the general principle of policy making proposed by General Secretary Hu Jintao – opened a window of opportunity to correct the performance-appraisal system. To realise the principle's target for a balanced national development, CCP floated the ideas of the green GDP in 2004 and investigated the possibility of integrating environmental protection into the local leaders' performance appraisals (Tang and Sun 2004). Many local leaders in the western regions also lobbied hard for green GDP

Table 5.6 The reported and actual achievements and weakness of four provincial-level governments

	Very satisfied/satisfied (reported by the provincial-level governments)	Very satisfied/satisfied (verified by Central Discipline Investigation Commission)
Public opinions towards the performance of Party and government departments		
Beijing municipality	55%	37%
Shanghai municipality	62%	22%
Guangdong Province	58%	24%
Hubei Province	58%	26%
The 'affordability' of house prices		
Beijing municipality	45%	20%
Shanghai municipality	50%	14%
Guangdong Province	60%	25%
Hubei Province	70%	35%
City unemployment rate		
Beijing municipality	7.8%	11.5%
Shanghai municipality	6.8%	18.5%
Guangdong Province	8.2%	16.4%
Hubei Province	5.6%	15.8%
Number of demonstration, sit-in protests and appeals		
Beijing municipality	247	377
Shanghai municipality	168	377
Guangdong Province	2,660	7,500
Hubei Province	655	1,650

Source: S. Yue (2006: 17).

test-runs as a green GDP gave them a golden chance to fairly play with the better-developed coastal belt and to get some relief from the intense pressure of GDP growth. The focus of implementing a green GDP died out in 2007 due to opposition from the development-oriented local leaders and central bureaucrats. Then the State Council set up a new system to evaluate the performance of provincial governors and the party secretaries of polluting state-owned enterprises on energy saving and pollution reduction. These officials were assigned targets of energy saving and pollution reduction, and government and enterprises were given a full mark of 100: 60 on energy saving and 40 on pollution reduction. Those who scored below 60 would be dismissed. To assess the performance, the provincial governors and party secretaries would report the achievement of emissions reduction to the State Council. The report was reviewed by assessment teams composed of officials from 17 central ministries, such as the State Environmental Protection Administration, the National Development and Reform Commission, the Ministry of Personnel and the State-Owned Assets Supervision and Administration (Chan 2007).

In addition, other central ministries pushed for further reform of the performance evaluation to realise their missions. The Ministry of Land Resources, for instance, proposed the performance indicators of farmland protection. The Ministry of Civil Affairs argued for evaluating leading officials on how well they supported their parents. The Ministry of Agriculture wanted to incorporate 'timely wage payment to peasant workers'. The Ministry of Culture insisted on 'the preservation of antiques, cultural and historical heritages'. Taking advantage of the State Council's target of providing housing subsidies and low-rent housing to ten million low-income families by 2010, the Ministry of Construction (now called the Ministry of Housing and Urban–Rural Development) advocated a performance indicator of 'the quality of the housing occupied by low-income households' (Wu 2007; Guo 2006b: 6–7). To prevent local leaders from pursuing particular policy areas at the expense of others, the subordinates of local leaders were invited to evaluate local leaders. According to Chapter 3 of the 2007 decree, 'Local Leadership Groups Living up to a Scientific View of Development', the directors of local state organs may participate in the evaluation of local governors when local governors' terms of office came to end. Similar to ordinary civil servants, local governors are evaluated on their political credentials, ability, diligence, achievement and integrity.

The second part of staff development is civil-service training. Civil-servant training is aimed at enhancing administration efficiency and capacity by raising the civil servants' job-related knowledge and skill level. Political training – once the most important form of training – has lost much of its appeal since the 1990s. In 1999, 39,151 civil servants in Beijing city participated in civil-service training. Among them, 14,031 participated in refresher courses, 10,863 in professional training and 10,216 in programmes for raising their educational level. Only 1,568 participated in political training (Beijing Local History Editorial Committee 2000: 173).

Civil-service training is characterised by its non-elitist model. According to a training compendium issued by the State Council in early 2007, China plans to put all civil servants through training courses in the next five years (Feng 2007). Civil servants are provided with professional training in the later stage of their careers, in contrast with French and British systems which arrange prestigious training for potential high-flyers early in their careers. Civil-service training institutes were set up at various levels of government to take charge of training. At the apex of the hierarchy of the training institutes were the Central Party School and the National Institute of Administration. The Institute was responsible for training civil servants at bureau level (*siju ji*) and above. In 1996, it was authorised to offer master's degrees and doctoral degrees in management studies and admit new university graduates and young civil servants. The graduate of these programmes may be appointed directly to the civil service (Law Committee 1994). Some local governments further institutionalised civil-service training by listing a good record of training participation as a prerequisite for career promotion (Organization Department of CCP Shanxi Provincial Committee 1999: 44; 'Quanfangwei' 2000: 12).

The substantial growth of training expenses illustrates the significance of civil-service training on the capacity-building agenda. The average training expenditure on each civil servant in the State Council rose from 157 *yuan* in 1994 to 295 *yuan* in 1998, an average increase of 17 per cent increase a year (Wen *et al.* 2001: 6). There is no consensus on the exact amount of training expenses. One report indicates that the actual amount on civil-service training in 2002 was US$35 billion. A spokesman of the Ministry of Finance denied the figure, pointing out that the central and local governments spent 1.1 billion *yuan* and 1.8 *yuan* respectively on civil-service training in 2004 (Cui *et al.* 2006). In 2004, Guangzhou city of Guangdong province decided to partially finance civil servants' continuing education. The financial support would range from 30 per cent to 50 per cent of tuition fees, capped at a ceiling of 30,000 *yuan*. Meanwhile, civil servants would be entitled to 12 days off each year to attend training courses (Zheng 2004). In Shanghai municipality, all civil servants at bureau level are required to take refresher courses every three to five years. The training expense on each civil servant was about 6,000 *yuan*, a handsome amount in comparison to the municipality's GDP per capita of 50,000 *yuan* (Tran 2003: 35). The effectiveness and efficiency of these training activities have raised public concern as many of them involved overseas excursions and lavish spending, and the actual expenditure often substantially exceeded budgetary expenditure (see Table 5.7).

Table 5.7 Budgetary and actual expenditure on civil service training

Year	Budgetary expenditure (US$)	Actual expenditure (US$)
1998	5.2 billion	28 billion
2000	7 billion	32 billion

Source: Cui *et al.* (2006).

Wage reform

A good wage system, argued Dresang, should display three characteristics. First, the wage level should be comparable to the market price in order to attract the most competent people and to retain the most talented employees. Second, it should be able to motivate employees to apply their full talents and energy to their work. Third, it must be affordable to employers (Dresang 1999).

The first characteristic scarcely existed in the pre-1993 wage system. For the purpose of higher staff motivation, central leaders reinstated bonus payments to employees in state-owned enterprises in 1977 (Cao *et al.* 1994: 212). The bonus distribution widened the pay gap with their counterparts working in government. In 1993, the wage level of managers in state-owned enterprises on average was 26 per cent higher than government cadres' at comparable ranks (National Bureau of Statistics 1995: 123). Poor pay demoralised government officials. In a 1988 survey, 70 per cent of government cadres revealed their intention to transfer to enterprises or public-service units (Lu 1997: 187).

Motivational benefits – the second characteristic of a good compensation system – were inadequate. A motivational wage system should have the power to cultivate a belief among employees that a positive correlation exists between their performance and desirable rewards (Dresang 1999: 28; OECD 1997: 1, 41, 44). This trait, however, conflicted with the Chinese managerial practice of egalitarian distribution of extra pay. Before 1985, officials of the same rank received the same pay, regardless of their performance and complexity of duties. The egalitarian distribution of fringe benefits further blunted the motivational function of the past wage system. Fringe benefits were made up of a wide range of items, like apartments, sedan cars and subsidies on air-conditioning, transportation and other daily necessities. In 1978, a bonus (excluding housing welfare and other subsidies in kind) roughly accounted for 14.3 per cent of the total money income of an official. It rose to 27.6 per cent in 1980, 34.1 per cent in 1986 and 42 per cent in 1991 (Contemporary China Editorial Committee 1994: 159). Though the 1985 wage reform widened the officials' pay level according to their performance and complexity of duties, the pay difference was too small to motivate the officials (Cheung and Poon 2001; Ministry of Personnel 1994: 89).

The aims of wage reform were, first, to offer merit pay to good performers in order to introduce greater motivational factors. Second, a mechanism of regular pay increments was installed so that civil-service pay could catch up with the non-state sector's pay trend. Third, the reform was to reduce the egalitarian fringe benefits as a proportion of the whole compensation package (Ministry of Personnel 1994: 89–92, 182; 'China's civil servants' 2001). The reform diverged from the egalitarian tendency of the wage system in Mao's era. The inter-rank pay difference was widened by increasing the eight wage grades in 1985 to 15 in 1993 and 27 in 2006. The intra-rank pay difference was also widened from 3–7 steps in 1985 (Chou 2003a: 204–32) to 6–14 steps in 2006 (see Table 5.8a and b). Moving upwards along the grade wages and responsibility wages depends on civil servants' performance levels. As the discussions on performance appraisal

Table 5.8a Composition of 2006 wage system (grade wages (yuan))

Grade (Jibie)	Sub-grade (Dangci)													
	1	2	3	4	5	6	7	8	9	10	11	12	13	14
1	3,024	3,180	3,340	3,500	3,660	3,820	—	—	—	—	—	—	—	—
2	2,770	2,915	3,060	3,205	3,350	3,495	3,640	—	—	—	—	—	—	—
3	2,530	2,670	2,810	2,950	3,090	3,230	3,370	3,510	—	—	—	—	—	—
4	2,290	2,426	2,562	2,698	2,834	2,970	3,106	3,242	3,378	—	—	—	—	—
5	2,070	2,202	2,334	2,466	2,598	2,730	2,862	2,994	3,126	3,258	—	—	—	—
6	1,870	1,996	2,122	2,248	2,374	2,500	2,626	2,752	2,878	3,004	3,130	—	—	—
7	1,700	1,818	1,936	2,054	2,172	2,290	2,408	2,526	2,644	2,762	2,880	—	—	—
8	1,560	1,669	1,778	1,887	1,996	2,105	2,214	2,323	2,432	2,541	2,650	—	—	—
9	1,438	1,538	1,638	1,738	1,838	1,938	2,038	2,138	2,238	2,338	2,438	—	—	—
10	1,324	1,416	1,508	1,600	1,692	1,784	1,876	1,968	2,060	2,152	2,244	—	—	—
11	1,217	1,302	1,387	1,472	1,557	1,642	1,727	1,812	1,897	1,982	2,067	2,152	—	—
12	1,117	1,196	1,275	1,387	1,472	1,557	1,642	1,670	1,749	1,828	1,907	1,986	2,065	—
13	1,024	1,098	1,172	1,246	1,320	1,394	1,468	1,542	1,616	1,690	1,764	1,838	1,912	1,986
14	938	1,007	1,076	1,145	1,214	1,283	1,352	1,421	1,490	1,559	1,628	1,697	1,766	1,835
15	859	924	989	1,054	1,119	1,184	1,249	1,314	1,379	1,444	1,509	1,574	1,639	1,704
16	786	847	908	969	1,030	1,091	1,152	1,213	1,274	1,335	1,396	1,457	1,518	1,579
17	719	776	833	890	947	1,004	1,061	1,118	1,175	1,232	1,289	1,346	1,403	—
18	658	711	764	817	870	923	976	1,029	1,082	1,135	1,188	1,241	1,294	—
19	602	651	700	749	798	847	896	945	994	1,043	1,092	1,141	—	—
20	551	596	641	686	731	776	821	866	911	956	1,001	—	—	—
21	504	545	586	627	668	709	750	791	832	873	—	—	—	—
22	461	498	535	572	609	646	683	720	757	—	—	—	—	—
23	422	455	488	521	554	587	620	653	—	—	—	—	—	—
24	386	416	446	476	506	536	566	596	—	—	—	—	—	—
25	352	380	408	436	464	492	520	—	—	—	—	—	—	—
26	320	347	374	401	428	455	—	—	—	—	—	—	—	—
27	290	316	342	368	394	420	—	—	—	—	—	—	—	—

Table 5.8b Composition of 2006 wage system (responsibility wages (*zhiwu gongzi*))

Rank *(zhiwu)*	Grade	Wage of leading positions *(lingdao zhiwu) (yuan)*	Wage of non-leading positions *(fei* lingdao zhiwu*) (yuan)*
State level	1	4,000	–
Deputy state level	2–4	3,200	–
Provincial/ministerial level	4–8	2,510	–
Deputy provincial/ministerial level	6–10	1,900	–
Bureau level	8–13	1,410	1,290
Deputy bureau level	10–15	1,080	990
County/division level	12–18	830	760
Deputy county/division level	14–20	640	590
Township/section level	16–23	510	480
Deputy township/section level	17–24	430	410
Section member	18–26	–	380
Office clerk	19–27	–	340

Source: 'Guojia gongwuyuan gongzi gaige taobiao' (Civil service wage reform).

suggested, the difficulty in differentiating the performance level of civil servants undermines the achievement of the first objective of wage reform of introducing greater motivational factors.

Successive pay increases since the mid-1990s were indicative of the successful institutionalisation of regular pay hikes. A report by the research office of the CCP Central Committee and the State Council Research Office pointed out that the basic salary of public employees (*gongzhi renyuan*) increased by 7–11 times between the mid-1980s and 2003. If all the benefits and subsidies were added up, the whole compensation package increased by 10–50 times. In Shanghai municipality and the provinces of Guangdong, Jiangsu and Zhejiang, the basic salary and bonus of the public employees at section level (*keji*) ranged from 1,320 to 1,440 *yuan* a year in the mid-1980s. In 2003, the total amount rose by 57–83 times (75,000 to 120,000 *yuan* a year) (Luo 2004: 11–12). The substantial rise in salary has raised the concern of paying civil servants out of departments' secret bank accounts and the possible breach of financial regulations (see the discussion on secret bank accounts in Chapter 4).

Lower-level governments are believed to be more likely to violate the regulations on civil servants' fringe benefits and subsidies. A former civil servant from Shanghai city pointed out that many civil servants preferred to work in district governments rather than in city governments despite the latter's prestige and job-promotion opportunities. The main reason was that district governments were administratively further away from the scrutiny of the central government as opposed to the city governments. District governments were less vigorous in enforcing the spending control on salary and subsidies, and thus more generous in disbursing subsidies.[7] Another study echoed this notion: in order to step up the monitoring of the securities industry, the Central Securities Commission integrated with the Shanghai Securities Commission which was previously funded by and responsible to Shanghai municipality. As the Shanghai Securities Commission was under closer scrutiny from central government, the officials in the Commission could no longer enjoy semi-legal subsidies (Heilmann 2005). To address the problem of misusing public funds for civil servants' subsidies, Article 78 of the Law of the Civil Servant outlawed the adjustment of civil servants' salary without central endorsement.

Wage reform makes careers in civil service attractive. In 2005, 365,000 candidates competed for 10,282 positions in central and provincial-level governments. The vacancy/candidate ratio of 1:36 was much higher than the median ratio of 1:10 at the turn of the last century. In December 2007, about 640,000 candidates participated in the national civil-service examinations; on average approximately 60 candidates competing for each post ('Ancient imperial exams' 2006). The keen competition may also be explained by the expansion of tertiary education and the resulting large number of unemployed university graduates. Without the corresponding increase in job opportunities, the estimated number of unemployed with higher education qualifications hit 4.95 million in mid-2007 (Shen 2007).

The pay rise, however, conflicted with some sound principles of spending control. As discussed in Chapter 4, public spending can be better controlled by slashing extra-budgetary funds. Table 5.9 shows that the amount of operating and administrative expenses (*xingzheng shiye fei zhichu* – a proxy of personnel cost) and its share in extra-budgetary expenditures was rising. The implications were such that the budgetary fund was stretched too much to finance wage payment. Local governments were pressured to rely more on extra-budgetary funds. In addition, wage arrears were common in some less-developed regions. In 2004, 624 departments and public-service units in the township-level governments of Shandong province failed to pay their employees at state-stipulated levels (Department of Finance, Shandong Province 2006: 21). To deal with the financial crisis, some local governments had to violate financial regulations and divert the funds earmarked for other purposes to pay civil servants.

Table 5.9 Operating and administrative expenses and its share in extra-budgetary expenditure

Year	Operating and administrative expenses (billion yuan)	Share in extra-budgetary expenditure (%)	Year	Operating and administrative expenses (billion yuan)	Share in extra-budgetary expenditure (%)
1997	268.56	47.58	2001	385.00	64.94
1998	291.83	54.45	2002	383.20	69.45
1999	313.91	57.96	2003	415.64	68.27
2000	352.90	63.17	2004	435.17	71.95

Source: National Bureau of Statistics (2006: 298).

The pay rise cannot help to hire and retain certain talents with the expertise of high market values. In response, Jilin province experimented to recruit 'contract employees' by the end of 2003. 'Contract employees' refers to the employees hired to offer technical services for a fixed period or on a project basis. The salary of contract employees may be 2–15 times higher than the civil servants hired by the conventional terms of employment. Wuxi city of Jiangsu province and Zhuhai city of Guangdong province followed suit (Ma 2004). This practice was later endorsed by the Law of the Civil Servant, stating in Article 95 that the contract system may be used for hiring talents in specialised professions. The hiring departments were allowed to decide the recruitment methods and compensation package on the condition that decisions were made according to establishment and budget plans, and the employees were not charged with duties involving state secrets. The employment period may last from one to five years, with a probation period from one to six months.

A mid-term evaluation on the achievement of the third objective of the wage – reduction of egalitarian fringe benefits as a proportion of the whole compensation package – suggested that fringe benefits (all items except foundation wages in combination) remained significant in the whole compensation package, ranging from 72.8 per cent (the State Council and Guangxi Autonomous Region) to 85.5 per cent (Shenzhen city) of a civil servant's total income (see Table 5.10). Equity consideration is still important in some wage-reform policies: the amount of subsidy may vary substantially within the same local government. Some departments with excellent revenue-generating ability may dispense a subsidy three to five times higher than others. In response, Beijing municipality decreed in 2003 to even out the salary of civil servants of the same rank working

Table 5.10 The composition of compensation cost on civil servants in selected governments, 1998*

	State Organs			
	State Council	Shanghai City Government	Guangxi Autonomous Region	Shenzhen City Government
Total compensation cost (%)	100	100	100	100
Gross Wage (%)	55.8	68.2	41.6	75.8
– Basic income	27.2	25.8	27.2	14.5
– Subsidy	15.0	25.4	14.4	39.1
– Bonus	13.6	17.0	–	19.2
Welfare (%)	9.2	14.1	48.6	–
Housing investment (%)	35.0	17.7	9.8	24.2

Source: Wen *et al.* (2001: 32, 153, 242, 271).

Note
* Fringe benefits here refer to 'subsidies', 'bonus', 'welfare' and 'housing investment'.

in different departments. As a result, 70 per cent of the civil servants enjoyed a pay rise; 20 per cent with zero growth; the other 10 per cent faced a subsidy cut. The biggest cut was up to one-third of the original level (Liu 2004: 26). There are no serious measures at local governments to reform the egalitarian tendency.

Conclusion

Civil-service reform in China is an important part of the reform of administrative capacity. Under this reform, the structures and processes of China's public personnel system were rationalised. A distinctive civil-service system was established. The principles of merit, openness and fairness were institutionalised in staffing, staff development and wage policies. In contrast with Western structural reforms that promote deregulation, flexibility and power devolution, China's civil-service reform follows a top-down approach, marked by a stress on regulation, hierarchy and control. Such a difference may be traced to the motives of reformers: the reforms in Western countries began in the context of a high level of institutionalisation and the consequential rigidity and red tape. Deregulation and reforming bureaucracy are believed to be effective in improving the vitality of the administration. China started its reform when the administration was far less institutionalised and therefore a Weberian approach in structuring the personnel system was deemed necessary (Burns 2001).

Civil-service reform may be construed as a continual conflict between the central agenda and local priorities. Central policy makers wanted to optimise economic rationality whereas local leaders placed more emphasis on coping with the conflicts arising out of the implementation of the reform: open recruitment was in conflict with the state's obligation to assign jobs to demobilised military officers. The conflict-aversion tendency of Chinese officials was not compatible with the possible discriminating effects of a performance-appraisal reform. The huge financial implication of wage reform is a thorny issue for impoverished governments as they can hardly finance substantial pay hikes. Reducing the proportion of fringe benefits in the whole compensation package ran counter to egalitarian work styles. The conflictual policy context motivated policy implementers to compromise the reform in order to lessen the conflict. These challenges rendered some institutional set-ups existent in form but not in substance.

6 Implementation of Administrative Licensing Law

Regulatory reforms have been undertaken in many Western countries to deal with a range of economic problems, such as the failure of public ownership and Keynesianism in sustaining economic growth, the pressure of globalisation for policy convergence and the demand on governments for improving the investment environment and economising public resources (Janow 1998: 216). One of these reforms is to overhaul the regime of business licences. It involves slashing the number of licences required in business activities, simplifying the procedures in obtaining licences and making the licensing regime more transparent. As these measures entail curtailing a government's licensing authority, reforming the system of business licences has the potential of improving administrative efficiency, economising the use of state resources and fighting corruption.

The reform merits scholarly attention, first, because of its implications for the private sector and economic development. Business activities are conducive to job creation. A study of 80 countries concluded that from 1984 to 1998, private firms created 4–80 times as many jobs as public-sector firms did. In China, almost all the 27 million new jobs created between 1996 and 2001 were in the private sector (Asian Development Bank 2003: 97). Huang and Di (2004) traced the economic development of Zhejiang and Jiangsu – the two eastern Chinese provinces almost identical in broad economic and social fundamentals – back to the late 1970s. They argued that Zhejiang's economy outperformed Jiangsu's in the end because of the former's thriving private sector promoted by a more business-friendly environment with fewer regulatory burdens. Measured by the World Bank's regulatory quality indicator (an indicator measuring the incidence of market-unfriendly policies and businesspeople's perceptions of regulatory burden), China's regulatory quality has deteriorated relative to other countries'. In 1996, the regulatory quality of approximately 47 per cent of the surveyed countries was rated lower than China's. In 2004, the percentage dropped to 35 per cent (World Bank 2004). The figure may not suffice to prove that the quality of China's regulatory framework has worsened, but it signifies that the Chinese government lags behind other countries in improving regulatory quality. A survey of the business managers of 138 domestic firms in six Chinese cities at the turn of this century revealed that a burdensome licensing process topped the

Table 6.1 Types of entry barriers reported by the managers of 138 Chinese firms

Licenses	Policy restriction	Local protection	Industry monopoly	Market size
34.8%	29.0%	11.6%	17.4%	7.2%

Source: Garnaut *et al.* (2001: 45).

list of the five most widely cited barriers of market entry (see Table 6.1). The other four challenges (policy restriction, local protection, industrial monopolies and limited market size) were to different extents caused by regulatory frameworks. Similar problems were reported by the American Chamber of Commerce in Shanghai. Since 1999, the top four challenges that American firms face in doing business in China (lack of transparency, inconsistent regulatory interpretation, unclear regulations, and bureaucracy) can also be traced to the cumbersome regulatory framework (AmCham Shanghai and AmCham-China (Beijing) 2007: 13).

Second, studying the reform can help to better evaluate the Chinese government's success in enforcing its World Trade Organisation (WTO) commitments, namely increasing its regulatory transparency, ensuring consistency among different levels of legislation and administering its trade regime uniformly across the country. During the reform era, the Chinese government has retreated from directing economic production and resource distribution and, at the same time, acquired new regulatory power based on secretive official documents known as *hongtou wenjian* (red-heading documents). These red-head documents carry the same (sometimes even heavier) weight as laws. Unlike laws, red-head documents are often unpublished. These documents once formed 80 per cent of all administrative licences. Until recently, local governments of all levels were able to arbitrarily issue these official documents which could have been inconsistent with national laws and administrative decrees. In 2001, 14 per cent of these documents reportedly conflicted with various laws and regulations (Lai 2003: 171–2; Yu and Tan 25 January 2006). The secrecy and inconsistency of the regulatory regime have made the investment environment unpredictable and conflicted with China's WTO commitments. An investigation into the reform is conducive to evaluating how far the Chinese government has implemented its WTO commitments.

Licensing reform in China: a background

Carlile and Tilton (1998) identified two models of regulatory reform. One is an Anglo-American tradition and an increasingly European trend of correcting market failure. Behind this model are mistrust of government and worship of the market: government should refrain from intervening in markets. It should focus on laying a level playing field and dealing with market failures. A desirable regulatory reform would reduce the regulatory costs on firms (the costs of adapting business processes to regulatory requirements, licensing fees, delays in obtaining regulatory approval, the time cost and the bribery used for dealing with officials) to a level not higher than necessary for tackling market failure. The advocacy of antitrust, transparency and competition may be traced back to this model. The second model is a developmental state model represented by Japan, Korea and Taiwan. The advocates of this model have a high trust in government and believe that bureaucrats should play an active role in economic development by fostering technological development and designating particular industries and businesses for support. This model is characteristic of government's extensive use of licences to influence economic development. Companies, both domestic and foreign, have to acquire appropriate licences for entering particular industries, altering their modes of production and importing particular products in order to protect domestic industries from excessive competition. With protection, domestic enterprises may have enough time to accumulate the technological foundation for quick modernisation so that late developers can eventually catch up with already industrialised countries.

Regulatory reforms are a desirable means to resolve economic problems because of the potential for promoting private investment and bolstering the GDP without incurring government expenditure and debt. Recent studies in OECD economies show that the level of private investment and the productivity of the investment are higher in countries with a lighter regulatory burden. Estimates for a group of developing countries suggest that reducing business registration costs to the United States' level (0.6 per cent of per-capita income) could increase private-sector investment by more than 20 per cent. A growing number of countries reducing administrative licences and simplifying licensing procedures have achieved significant results. For example, the World Bank reported that after the municipal government of La Paz, Bolivia, simplified the procedures of business registration, the number of registered businesses increased by 20 per cent. Similar measures in Vietnam increased new businesses from 6,000 in 1999 to more than 21,000 in 2002. In Uganda, the new businesses increased by four times (World Bank 2005: 99–104; International Finance Corporation 2000).

In comparison to other developing countries, China's system of business licences is not particularly burdensome (see Table 6.2). However, the licensing system is still arbitrary, cost inflating and inconsistent. An unidentified city was reported to have illegally revoked the business licences of approximately 100 joint ventures on a single day. Beijing city once revoked the permission granted to the fast-food chain giant McDonald's for establishing a restaurant in a prime location (Ambler and Witzel 2004: 84). In 2003, the public security bureau of Leqing city of Zhejiang province withdrew 150 business licences of man-powered tricycles auctioned in 1999, and penalised those who refused to return the licences (Liu, X. 2006). Without giving compensation or a grace period, another unidentified city withdrew the operation licences of schools that failed to meet an arbitrarily imposed qualifying benchmark (Zhao 2006). Setting up a local retail business may require up to 112 licences from different departments.

Table 6.2 Selected indicators of business regulation in eight developing countries, 2005

Indicators	Countries								
	China	India	Indonesia	Malaysia	Thailand	Philippines	Brazil	Argentina	World average (countries of low and middle income)
Number of start-up procedures	13	11	12	9	8	11	17	15	10
Time to start a business (days)	48	71	151	30	33	48	152	32	53
Rigidity of employment index*	30	62	57	10	18	45	56	48	43

Source: World Bank (2006: 274–6).

Note
* Rigidity of employment index ranges from 0 (less rigid) to 100 (very rigid).

Obtaining approval for importing certain types of foreign equipment may take at least six months (Meng 2004). Licensing barriers also precluded the private sector from entering the market sectors dominated but often badly served by state-owned enterprises. Many investors were forced to rely on personal relationships and bribery to get around the red tape. The resultant unpredictable business environment made it difficult for investors to calculate the risk involved in investment projects and delayed their investment decisions. The consequences were heavy business costs, rampant corruption and a lower level of private investment (Asian Development Bank 2003).

The burdensome framework of market regulation has not arisen in a vacuum. It was established when the market system was budding and the private sector was insignificant. Many rules target large state-owned companies and emphasise economic security rather than business promotion. Investors are required to put down significant registered capital and undergo strict examinations before starting businesses so that the risks of creditors – which were from the state sector – can be minimised. Thus the minimum capital requirement in China as a percentage of GNI per capita once was the second highest in the world, only after the 5,627 of Syria (see Table 6.3). There is a high level of intervention in market regulations. Investors have to prove their technical abilities measured against government-imposed standards before they can enter markets (AmCham Shanghai and AmCham-China (Beijing) 2007; Jiao 2005; All-China Federation of Industry and Commerce 2005: 20).

The decentralised public-finance system is another barrier to the formation of a business-friendly regulatory regime. The Chinese government has decentralised much of its economic authority to local governments to motivate them to achieve higher economic growth, and turn the Chinese economy into 'market-preserving federalism' (Qian and Weingast 1995). Local governments are required to cover their expenditures and meet the revenue quota assigned by upper-level governments (see Chapter 3). However, local governments are not authorised to adjust the rate of local taxes or to create new taxes. Without adequate tax revenue, local governments have to rely on extra-budgetary revenue such as various fines and licence fees (Lü 2000: 218; Wong 1997: 60; Breslin 1996: 129). The amount of licence fees is huge. The 'administrative and institutional fees' (*xingzheng shiyexing shoufei*) – a proxy of the revenues of licence fees – accounts for 64–85 per cent of the gross extra-budgetary revenue (see Table 6.4). The licence fees on 78 economic and social activities that Zhejiang province sought to abolish amounted to 120 million *yuan* a year (Luo and Yu 2005: 21). The licence fees on the 152 items that Heilongjiang province was going to cancel was worth 300 million *yuan* in 2006. Between May and September 2003, Yanggang city, a medium-sized city in western Guangdong province had to give up 22.97 million *yuan* due to licensing reform (Xiao 2006). Owing to the significance of licensing fees to local public coffers, local governments have great incentive to create a cumbersome licensing system.

The decentralised public-finance system provides much discretion for local governments on wage policies. To generate higher revenue, local governments

Table 6.3 A comparison of the minimum capital requirement in eight developing countries in 2003

	Countries								
	China	India	Indonesia	Malaysia	Thailand	Philippines	Brazil	Argentina	World average (countries of low and middle income)
Minimum capital requirement (% of GNI per capita)	3,856	430	303	0	0	10	0	0	118

Source: World Bank (2004: 262–4).

Table 6.4 Administrative and institutional fees

Year	Revenue of administrative and institutional units (billion yuan)	Share in extra-budgetary expenditure (%)	Year	Revenue of administrative and institutional units (billion yuan)	Share in extra-budgetary expenditure (%)
1997	241.43	85.16	2001	309.00	71.86
1998	198.19	64.29	2002	323.80	72.32
1999	235.43	69.32	2003	333.57	73.09
2000	265.45	69.19	2004	320.84	68.30

Source: National Bureau of Statistics (2006: 298).

often link the level of licence fee and extra-budgetary revenue with officials' bonus and penalty. Despite the prohibition from the central government, Yulin city in the Guangxi Autonomous Region imposed a fee-collection target of 12 million *yuan* on the city's round-city highway management office in 1995. If they failed to meet the target, the subsidies of relevant officials would be cut back; they could retain 80 per cent of the surplus portion for subsidies if they generated more than the target (Qin 1996). In China, subsidies accounted for 70–85 per cent of the total income of individual officials in the late 1990s (Chou 2004: 230). In view of the impact of extra-budgetary revenue on their well-being, local leaders are highly motivated to create and defend licence revenue, and assign a quota of extra-budgetary revenue that individual departments must generate. Quite often, licensing items were created purely for generating revenue, but not for regulating markets. An entrepreneur of Yanggang city complained that the city labour bureau required him to apply for 'appointment cards' (*shang gang zhen*) on behalf of all his employees. Each appointment card cost him over 100 *yuan*. The fee collected was purported to finance government-sponsored training courses for new employees. No training was provided in the end, however. Another agricultural entrepreneur complained that the traffic bureau of the city charged him 1,000 *yuan* for vehicle-maintenance fee every year without providing any meaningful maintenance service in return (Xiao 2006).

The implication of licences is furthered complicated by the local leaders' opportunism shaped by a job-rotation system and the narrow focus of the local leaders' performance appraisal based on local economic development. The job-rotation and performance-appraisal systems encouraged local leaders to promote local economic development with little consideration of the policies' impact on neighbouring regions and the country as a whole. Because of their short office terms, they are likely to work for immediate work achievement at the expense of long-term benefits, such as the improvement of the business environment and product quality. Thus many local leaders pursue regional protectionist measures: through licensing systems, they can raise the barriers of market entry to fend off outside competition against local entrepreneurs, or impose a ban on the import of certain types of products to protect local products. A bus company in an unnamed city of Anhui province, for example, received an approval from city government to purchase new buses. On discovering that the new buses were not manufactured in Anhui province, the city government prohibited the buses from being used (Zhao 19 January 2006). The municipalities of Shanghai and Beijing supported their own car industry by instructing the taxi companies to use locally produced sedan cars. Shanghai even charged the non-Shanghai-made sedan cars higher licence fees to undermine their competitiveness (Lardy 2002: 29–62). Shanxi Transportation and Sales Corporation once took over a large market share of Shanxi province's coal business. To compete with the Corporation's business on behalf of their affiliated enterprises, the Shanxi Provincial Department of Coal Industry issued new regulations in 1995 requiring all small coal mines to obtain a permit of coal sales from the department before they could sell the products. The corporation was denied permits and lost much of the coal business (Su 2004: 241).

Regulatory barriers have not stopped the Chinese economy from booming. Private-sector development remains robust. Foreign direct investment is huge. Economic logic is not as significant as WTO accession behind licensing reform. In fact, China's system of business licences fails to live up to China's three major commitments to the WTO:

1   Transparency: Local governments' use of secretive *hongtou wenjian* to create new regulations is incompatible with the paragraph 332 of the Report of the Working Party of the Accession of China (hereafter 'the Report of the Working Party'). The paragraph stated that China would:

> publish in the official journal, by appropriate classification and by service where relevant, a list of all organizations, including those organizations delegated such authority from the national authorities, that were responsible for authorizing, approving or regulating services activities whether through grant of licence or other approval. Procedures and the conditions for obtaining such licences or approval would also be published.

2   Uniform administration of trade regime: Inconsistency of regulations among different levels of government contradicts paragraphs 73, 75 and 68. Paragraph 73 reads:

> the provisions of the WTO Agreement … would be applied uniformly throughout its customs territory, including in SEZs [Special Economic Zones] and other areas where special regimes for tariffs, taxes and regulations were established and at all levels of government.

Paragraph 75 reads:

> All individuals and entities could bring to the attention of central government authorities cases of non-uniform application of China's trade

regime ... Such cases would be referred promptly to the responsible government agency, and when non-uniform application was established, the authorities would act promptly to address the situation utilizing the remedies available under China's laws, taking into consideration China's international obligations and the need to provide a meaningful remedy.

Paragraph 68 reads: 'the central government would undertake in a timely manner to revise or annul administrative regulations or departmental rules if they were inconsistent with China's obligations under the WTO Agreement and Draft Protocol.'

3   Licensing issues: Blocking market access through licences and charging exorbitant licence fees conflict with paragraphs 308 and 308(d) respectively. Paragraph 308 reads: 'China would ensure that China's licensing procedures and conditions would not act as barriers to market access and would not be more trade restrictive than necessary.' Paragraph 308(d) states: 'Any fees charged ... would be commensurate with the administrative cost of processing an application' (World Trade Organisation 2004).

The impacts of these commitments are as follows:

1   the Chinese government is obliged to reform its market regulatory framework as soon as possible;
2   local governments can no longer use secretive documents to create licensing authority. Their licensing authority refers to national legislations which, in turn, have to be consistent with the WTO requirements;
3   licence fees should not cost more than administrative costs; and
4   creation of regional trade blocs through licensing is prohibited.

If successfully implemented, these measures have the potential of promoting private-sector development.

Reform strategies

Curtailing local governments' licensing authority and their opportunities of extracting rent are major strategies in the reform of the licensing system. The reform may be construed as the second stage of structural reform since the early 1980s. The first stage of reforms was characterised by de-bureaucratisation, de-nationalisation and greater use of market principle. The reform measures include the strategies of bureaucracy downsizing, departments merging, reform of state-owned enterprises, transformation of government departments into quasi-governmental organisations and civil-service reform. The control of business opportunities was relaxed. Monopolies over foreign trade were broken up. Industrial ministries were either absorbed into other ministries or transformed into economic entities and industrial associations. Many forms of administrative licences disappeared together with these industrial ministries. Market forces were phased in to replace bureaucracy to direct economic production and resource distribution. Bureaucracy was trimmed. Those remaining in bureaucracy were better educated, younger and better prepared to embrace market principles. State-owned enterprises were incorporated and exposed to greater competition. While the state retreated from enterprise ownership and economic planning, it set up new ministries and departments charged with regulatory functions over environment, food safety, work safety, financial services, telecommunications and intellectual property rights. Meanwhile, it restricted administrative discretion and bureaucratic interference in private businesses through institutionalising legal frameworks, represented by the 1990 Administrative Litigation Law, the 1994 Compensation Law and the 1999 Administrative Punishment Laws.

The second round of structural reform – the reform of the licensing regime – started at the turn of this century. In September 2001, the State Council set up the Leadership Small Group on the Reform of the System of Administrative Licensing (*Guowuyuan xingzheng shenpi zhidu gaige gongzuo lingdao xiaozu*) for better coordination of the reform. After several rounds of licence downsizing, the State Council gave up its authority over 1,795 licensing items. Some of these abandoned licensing items were annulled altogether, whereas others were handed over to industrial associations and other intermediary agencies (Meng 2004). The reform soon penetrated many local governments (see Table 6.5). The process of issuing licences has been made more transparent. Jinan city placed official documents concerning licences in public libraries and published them on government websites for public access. Guangzhou city of Guangdong province published *hongtou wenjian* in the Guangzhou Administrative Report and accepted subscriptions from the public. Wuhan city of Hubei province published its new *hongtou wenjian* in the Public Bulletin of Wuhan People's Government every two weeks, and distributed the bulletin to the public free of charge. Since 2002, Chongqing municipality published most of its *hongtou wenjian* in the Administrative Affairs Bulletin. The cities of Wuxi in Jiangsu province and Shenzhen in Guangdong province overhauled their systems of *hongtou wenjian*.

Table 6.5 The number of licensing items in selected governments

Year	Governments	Original items	Items relinquished	Percentage of items relinquished (%)
1999	Heilongjian province	2,325	1,283	55.18
1999	Henan province	2,706	1,764	65.19
2000	Zhejiang province	1,372	751	54.7
2000	Tianjin municipality	935	N/A	More than 40
2000	Shenzhen city	1,091	463	42.44
2001	Shenzhen city	652	277	42.48
2001	Shanghai city	N/A	N/A	40

Sources: L. Wang (1998); G. Li (2000: 15); 'Shizhengfu tisu xiaoguo xianzhu' (City government made progress in improving administrative efficiency) (2001: A1); A. Hu and Y. Guo (2002: 245).

By June 2002, Shenzhen city had reviewed 2,500 internal documents, annulled 878 of them and revised 1,700 (Lai 2003: 171–2). The amount of licence fees was made open. Licence applicants deposited the fees in the bank accounts under the scrutiny of the Treasury so that government departments could not embezzle the fees. One-stop centres were opened to speed up the processing of licence applications. Complaint centres and telephone hotlines were set up to keep rent-seeking acts in check (Yang 2004: 154–75).

The reform efforts, however, were watered down by the re-establishment of many annulled licensing items. The number of licensing items in Shenzhen city rose to 652 in 2001 after having been slashed from 1,091 to 463 in 2000 ('Shizhengfu' 2001). Guangdong province slashed the number of licensing items to 1,205 in June 2000. Soon afterwards, it rose to 1,519 items ('Guanche shishi' 2006). To prevent the annulled licensing items from being re-established, the National People's Congress (NPC) enacted the Administrative Licensing Law (hereafter 'the Law') to restrict administrative power in licence creation and make licensing procedures more transparent. The drafting of the Law began in the mid-1990s and consultation with various stakeholders took almost five years. In 2000, the State Council started drafting the Law. The NPC Standing Committee reviewed the draft law in 2002 and endorsed it on 27 August 2003. The effective date of the Law was postponed to 1 July 2004 so that local governments could have adequate time to update and coordinate their licence regulations with the Law ('Xingzheng xukefa' 2006).

In 2004, the Legal Office of the State Council provided two Explanations on the scope of administrative licensing. In the First Explanation, the Office pointed out that administrative licensing involves the regulatory activities of a government department in relation to economic or social activities. Approval of land use is one example of these activities. Since administrative licensing does not include the recognition of civil rights or civil relations, such activities as marriage, household and vehicle registration do not constitute administrative licensing. In addition, administrative licensing is a decision of a government department in relation to approval, after examination, of an application by a citizen, legal person or other organisation to engage in a relevant activity. Thus, government departments' testing and measurement of market products does not constitute administrative licensing. The Second Explanation responds to 16 specific questions on the nature of an administrative licence in order to clarify the difference between administrative licensing and non-administrative licensing (Bath 2008).

The Law is aimed at improving the business environment and harmonising the market regulatory framework to China's commitments to the WTO. Article 12 of the Law specifies six market sectors that require licences for entrance.[1] Local governments are prohibited from using licences to restrict market entry and the import of products, services and labour. Article 13 signifies the retreat of governments from licensing, stating that government departments should not create licensing items when business activities can be effectively regulated by: (1) citizens, legal entities and 'other organs'; (2) market competition; (3) industrial associations; (4) post-verification. Article 25 removes the authority of sub-provincial governments to create licences. Their licensing authority must be either based on national laws or delegated from provincial-level governments. Provincial-level governments, in turn, are restricted by Article 15: The licensing items created by provincial-level governments may stand valid for up to one year. Afterwards, an enactment from the provincial people's congresses is required to keep the licensing items valid. The centralisation of the licensing authority was consistent with the recent trend of the recentralisation of authority in China's administration with the purpose of reducing stress on the provincial governments and aligning local practices with central priorities. Functional departments used to be answerable to local governments, but since the late 1990s, industry and commerce bureaux, quality technology supervision bureaux, pharmaceutical supervision bureaux and securities supervision commissions have answered to the functional departments at upper levels.[2]

Several provisions take on rent seeking. Article 27 prohibits licence-issuing departments from compelling licence applicants to purchase products supplied by their subsidiary enterprises. Article 58 specifies the two conditions under which licence fees are permissible: (1) the fees are stipulated in law or administrative decrees; and (2) the public has prior knowledge of the fees. This provision reflects the Law's convergence with paragraph 308(a) of the Report of the Working Party, reading: 'China's licensing procedures and conditions were published prior to becoming effective.' Article 58 requires licensing departments to cover the administrative costs of issuing licences by their budgets. This requirement is divergent from the user-charge principle widely practised in industrialised countries, and is even stricter than the commitment in the Report of the Working Party paragraph 308(d) discussed above, which permits charging licence fees to cover operating costs.

Transparency issues are addressed in the following provisions: Article 5 states that secretive *hongtou wenjian* cannot be used as legal bases of licensing authority unless state secrets, business secrets or privacy are involved. Article 19 states that before introducing new licensing items, provincial-level governments should consult the public through public hearings. Under Article 42, government departments have to inform the applicants of their licence application results in 60 days. Article 50 embraces the rule of 'silent consent' – if departments fail to respond to licence holders' application for renewing their licences in 30 days, the licences will be automatically renewed. These articles are convergent with the requirement in the paragraph 308(f) of the Report of the Working Party about timely decisions on licence applications.

Despite an absence of provisions on a redress system from the Law, there are still channels for seeking redress on licensing issues: Administrative Review Law confers the right of seeking redress on licensing issues. Under the Administrative Litigation Law, citizens may sue departments abusing their licensing authority. Citizens' challenges of licensing decisions were widely reported. In Sichuan province, the number of court cases involving administrative licences rose from 91 between January and December 2003 to 638 during the period between 1 July 2004 (the day on which the Law came into effect) and 30 May

2005 (Gao 2006). Within one year after the Law became effective, Guangzhou city received nine cases of administrative review and 20 cases of administrative litigation (Luo *et al.* 2006).

In response to paragraph 308(a) of the Report of the Working Party about publishing China's licensing procedures and conditions prior to their effective day, the State Council issued Directive No. 412 to publish a list of 386 licensing items two days before the Law came into effect. No departments can issue licences on matters beyond these 386 items, down from 4,000 items in 2002 (Meng 2004). Most of the licensing items fall under the jurisdiction of the ministries charged with market regulation, such as the General Administration of Civil Aviation, the Ministry of Information Industry, the China Insurance Regulatory Commission, the China Securities Regulatory Commission, the National Development and Reform Commission, and the Ministry of Commerce (see Table 6.6).

Table 6.6 Distribution of licensing items among central bureaucracies

Ministries and Commissions under the State Council	No. of items	Organisations directly under the State Council	No. of items
Ministry of Information Industry	21	General Administration of Civil Aviation	44
Ministry of Railways	21	General Administration of Press and Publication	14
National Development and Reform Commission	17	General Administration of Customs	12
Ministry of Commerce	18	State Administration of Radio, Film and Television	11
People's Bank of China	15	State Environmental Protection Administration	8
Ministry of Public Security	9	State Food and Drug Administration	8
Ministry of Finance	7	State Administration for Religious Affairs	7
Ministry of Water Resources	7	General Administration of Quality Supervision, Inspection and Quarantine	7
State Commission of Science, Technology and Industry for National Defence	7	State Forestry Administration	5
Ministry of Health	6	State Administration for Industry and Commerce	4
Ministry of Communications	6	National Tourism Administration	3
Ministry of Education	6	State Administration of Taxation	2
Ministry of Justice	5	State Administration of Work Safety	1
Ministry of Labour and Social Security	5	General Administration of Sport	1
Ministry of Culture	4		

continued

Table 6.6 Continued

Ministries and Commissions under the State Council	No. of items	Organisations directly under the State Council	No. of items
Ministry of Construction	3	*Administrative Offices under the State Council*	*No. of Items*
Ministry of Personnel	2	Information Office	2
Ministry of Agriculture	2	Overseas Chinese Affairs Office	1
Ministry of Land and Resources	2	Hong Kong and Macao Affairs Office	1
Ministry of State Security	1		
Ministry of Civil Affairs	1	*Administrations and bureaux under the Ministries and Commissions*	*No. of items*
Ministry of Science and Technology	1	State Administration of Foreign Exchange	31
		State Oceanic Administration	6
Institutions directly under the State Council	*No. of items*	State Administration of Foreign Experts Affairs	5
China Insurance Regulatory Commission	38	State Bureau of Cultural Relics	6
China Securities Regulatory Commission	23	State Tobacco Monopoly Administration	2
China Banking Regulatory Commission	5	State Bureau of Surveying and Mapping	1
Xinhua News Agency	2	State Post Bureau	1
China Earthquake Administration	1		
China Meteorological Administration	1		

Total number of licensing items: 419*

Source: *Zhonghua renmin gongheguo guowuyuan ling di xiyier hao* (Directive No. 412 of The State Council of the People's Republic of China).

Note

* The figure is higher than the 386 licensing items stipulated in Directive No. 412. The discrepancy in figure is due to the involvement of more than one department in certain licensing items and the consequent double counting.

The State Council has centralised most of the licensing authorities. Central bureaucracies are responsible for almost 70 per cent of the licensing items (see Figure 6.1). Centralisation may go to the extent that the provincial and sub-provincial branches of some central organs like the Securities Regulatory Commission, the Insurance Regulatory Commission, the Banking Regulatory Commission, the Ministry of Railways and the State Environmental Protection Administration have been turned into central organs' executive agents without any licensing authority at all. The provincial branches of the Ministry of Information Industry and Bank of China are allowed to keep only two licensing items. Less than 16 per cent of the licensing items have been assigned to sub-

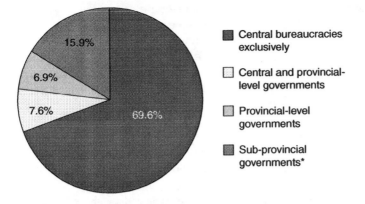

Figure 6.1 Distribution of licensing items (source: *Zhonghua renmin gongheguo guowuyuan ling di xiyier hao* (Directive No. 412 of The State Council of the People's Republic of China)).

Note
* The category of 'Sub-Provincial Governments' refers to the licensing items either under the exclusive jurisdiction of sub-provincial governments, or jointly with provincial-level governments and/or central bureaucracies.

provincial governments. This centralisation policy is conducive to standardising commercial practices, implementing trade-related policies uniformly across the country and tackling the problems of inconsistent regulations.

To reinforce the reform measures, the State Council promulgated 'Several Opinions on Supporting and Directing the Development of the Non-State Sector Like the Private Sector' in February 2005. This decree covers a wide range of policies, such as bank credit, market access, corporate governance and licence charges. It aims to restrict local governments' authority in entrenching regional protectionism and collecting exorbitant fees through licensing systems. Article 1 rules out restrictions on the non-state sector to all market sectors except those stipulated by law. Article 33 prohibited local governments from charging private enterprises fees unless the fees were stipulated by law.[3]

Evaluation and analysis

Successful cases of implementing the Administrative Licensing Law have been reported. Central government and Guangdong province declared the previous regulations on chemical industries void and revoked the subordinate departments' licensing authority on chemical industries (Yu and Tan 2006). Wuhan city of Hubei province declared 48 government documents on licensing ineffective. Ningxia province annulled 170 items of administrative licensing. Liaoning province annulled almost half of its licensing items ('Xingzheng xukefa' 2006). Gulou district of Nanjing city reduced its licensing items from 278 to 53 (Mao and Ming 2006). Chongqing municipality planned to reduce the processing time of licence applications for construction projects involving land acquisition from 350 days to 110–50 days. The municipal government estimated that the saving of licence fees from the reform amounted to hundreds of thousands of *yuan* (Lan 2006). Guangdong province annulled the Regulations on Pesticide Management and cancelled the licences for trading pesticides. Foreign investors were permitted to trade pesticides by the end of 2004 and fertilisers by the end of 2006. Domestic private entrepreneurs were permitted to enter all the markets open to foreign investors (Yu 2006). Significant numbers of American firms agreed that the top four challenges in doing business in China that can be traced to the regulatory and licensing regime – lack of transparency, inconsistent regulatory interpretation, unclear regulations and bureaucracy – have been alleviated (see Figure 6.2).

Caution is necessary for interpreting the success. The data about annulling licensing items and the government activities in implementing the Law were supplied by local governments. The validity of the data requires further investigation. Attribution problems should also be considered. The licensing reform is aimed at improving the business environment, increasing government efficiency and resolving regional protectionism. Most business managers interviewed in a survey felt that government efficiency had been improved and regional protectionism had been alleviated after the Law came into effect. However, the change in the managers' perception was reported before the Law came into effect, as suggested by an earlier longitudinal survey (see Table 6.7). There is no way of knowing whether the improvement is due to the reform or other measures. The most chosen option – 'unchanged' – reflects that small improvements have been made.

Besides that, a survey conducted by the Social Survey Institute of China at the end of 2004 revealed that 73 per cent of the 1,500 respondents in seven cities

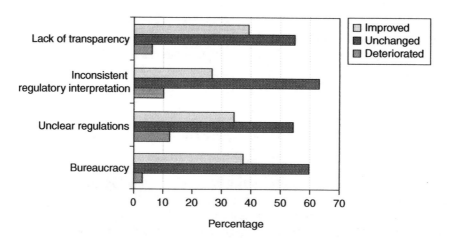

Figure 6.2 Perceived changes in top four business challenges over the last two years, 2007 (source: AmCham Shanghai and AmCham-China (Beijing) (2007: 64)).

Table 6.7 Surveys of managers on business environments

Questions	2003			2005		
	Improved (%)	Unchanged (%)	Deteriorated (%)	Improved (%)	Unchanged (%)	Deteriorated (%)
Do you think government efficiency has improved?	41.6	47.2	11.2	40.2	46.3	13.5
Do you think the problem of regional protectionism has improved?	25.4	59.7	14.9	31.8	60.0	8.2

Sources: Centre of Human Resources Research and Training, Development and Research Centre, the State Council, *Qiye jingyingzhe dui hongguan jingji xingxi ji gaige redian he panduan* (The opinions and suggestions of entrepreneurs towards the economy); Centre of Human Resources Research and Training, Development and Research Centre, the State Council, *Qiye jingyingzhe dui jingji huanjing he gaige redian de panduan – 2005 zhongguo qiye jingyingzhe wenquan diaocha baogao* (The opinions of entrepreneurs towards the context and hot issues of economy).

did not feel the Law had improved administrative efficiency; 76 per cent of the respondents thought that local governance had watered down the Law; 49 per cent believed that individual bureaucrats had to circumvent the Law (Jin, L. 2006). A survey of business managers in 2005 revealed that 34 per cent, 58.1 per cent and 7.9 per cent of the respondents thought the problems associated with barriers to market entry have been alleviated, unchanged and worsened, respectively. Discriminatory administrative licensing procedures remained the most cited factor impeding business expansion, according to 42.9 per cent of the respondents, followed by a discriminatory quality-inspection standard (38.2 per cent), exorbitant fees and unpredictable taxation policies (27.8 per cent), restrictions on import and sale (23.5 per cent) and discriminatory price restriction (17.3 per cent) (Centre of Human Resources Research and Training, Development and Research Centre, the State Council 2006). It has to be noted that about 17 per cent of the respondents in the survey are affiliated with state-owned enterprises. State-owned enterprises are better protected by governments at various levels and more easily bypass administrative barriers. If respondents from state-owned enterprises had been excluded and only private entrepreneurs had been counted, the percentage of respondents expressing negative opinions about licensing issues would have been even higher.

It may take several more years before the real impact of the reform becomes obvious. At this stage, it can be cautiously concluded that the success is mixed. Lü characterised distortion of national policies by policy implementers in communist countries as communist neo-traditionalism, a concept first used by Walder in analysing bureaucratic behaviour in China (Walder 1986). Lü argued that bureaucrats in communist regimes were reluctant to adapt themselves to the 'modern' (rational, empirical and impersonal) bureaucratic structures imposed by political elites. Instead, they reshaped the processes behind the structures to reinforce and elaborate traditional (or patrimonial) modes of operation (Lü 1999). The reform may illustrate this notion. Many local governments have adapted the Administrative Licensing Law to old licensing practices. According to the State Council Directive No. 412, provincial governments are permitted to keep 144 licensing items (*Zhonghua renmin gongheguo guowuyuan ling* 8 February 2006). However, Sichuan province kept 383 items in the end (Gao 2006). Fujian province kept 445 items ('Fujian' 4 April 2006). Selective implementation may appear in the form of substantial delay. Private businesspeople are allowed to trade in agriculture-related inputs such as seeds, fertilisers and pesticides, according to Article 12 of the Law. By the end of 2005, Guangdong provincial bureau of industry and commerce had not put an end to the state monopoly of the trade. Private businesspeople were blocked from entering the market (Yu and Tan 2006; Yu 2006). In Guangzhou city of Guangdong province, the government was accused of using a licensing regime to deny private entrepreneurs' entry into the trade of agriculture-related inputs. It was believed that this means enabled the firm run by the city's agriculture bureau to maintain its monopolistic position in the market (Yang 2006). Certain localities violated Article 58 of the Law concerning prohibition of licences fees. A licence to sell chemical products in Guangzhou city of Guangdong province was worth more than 20,000 *yuan* in early 2006, one-and-a-half years after the Law came into effect (Yu and Tan 2006). Foreign-invested enterprises in Lianyungan city of Jiangsu province with a registered capitalisation of US\$3 million or above have to obtain at least 11 licences and pay a licence fee of 15,000 *yuan* before starting any businesses. The city also violated Article 26 and failed to designate a single department to handle licence applications involving more than one department. Among its 50 departments with licensing authority, only the urban management department followed this Article. Also the city government did not annul the licensing items according to law: 109 out of its 428 licensing items remained in force illegally (Yan 2005: 44; Chen 2005: 75). The efforts of alleviating legislative inconsistency and creating a uniform trade regime have been compromised. Some departments of Guangzhou city of Guangdong province have broken Article 5 of the Law and referred to internal documents or even the personal opinions of the department director when considering licensing issues. The city's industry and commerce bureau justified some of its licensing authority by quoting the internal *hongtou wenjian* 'State Council Directive No. 68' issued in 1988 (Yu and Tan 2006).

Owing to the selective implementation of the Law at the local level, local governments were perceived to be uncommitted to the market opening. In a survey by the American Chamber of Commerce published in 2007, 38 per cent of respondents to the survey believed that central government was 'willing, able and prepared to implement changes in the spirit of the WTO'. Only 6 per cent thought that the central government was 'actively seeking loopholes' in the WTO agreement, and 4 per cent 'unwilling to implement the required changes'. When it came to local governments' attitude towards market opening, the figure in these three areas was 12 per cent, 25 per cent and 11 per cent, respectively (see Figure 6.3).

Licensing reform may be considered deep economic integration – a country's convergence of its economic policies with international rules. Haggard argued that while the agenda of trade liberalisation in deep integration has the potential of augmenting the overall welfare benefits, it remains unclear whether deep integration can augment welfare benefits to particular countries, regions of a country, and/or industries. Infant industries in developing countries may lose out if developing countries harmonise their regulatory policies around the norms of developed countries (Haggard 1995: 2–4). In view of the damage to the losers, the WTO permits developing and the least-developed member countries to maintain certain protectionist measures for safeguarding their infant industries. China's regional development varies greatly and different regions require a different extent of trade liberalisation in order to fully benefit from WTO accession. Not committing to a uniform administration of a trade regime may be a more sensible option for China and other countries which have no effective mechanism to redistribute the gains of free trade from beneficiaries to losers.

The selective implementation of the Law can be explained by an analysis of the local political landscape. Various levels of government and their

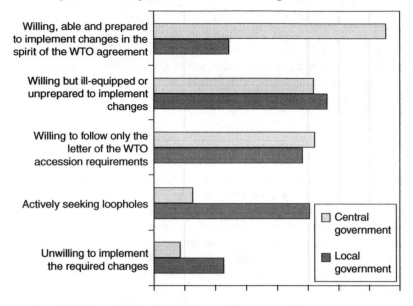

Figure 6.3 Perceived attitude of central and local governments towards market opening, 2007 (source: AmCham Shanghai and AmCham-China (Beijing) (2007: 63)).

departments have some sort of licensing authority and are involved in licence downsizing. The implementation of downsizing is contingent on the concerted actions of numerous local actors with diverse interests. Consensus with the action plans and the schedule of downsizing is rarely agreed upon. To address the problem of authority fragmentation and the difficulty in coordination and supervision, the central government has centralised certain regulatory authority from sub-provincial to provincial-level governments since the late 1990s. The 31 provincial-level governments have been given more authority in monitoring sub-provincial governments and aligning local practices with national and provincial legislation. In his study of China's financial industry, Heilmann (2005) pointed out that the partial centralisation cannot help to tap much more information. The Shanghai securities regulators who were previously directed by Shanghai Municipality were incorporated into a central government regulatory commission, but consultations and coordination remained inadequate. Vast geographical distance was the main reason; communications between central and Shanghai regulators were not based on regular exchanges but on ad hoc meetings and unsystematic data transfers. Moreover, many local bureaucrats were resistant to the partial centralisation policy. They believed that if their departments remained accountable to local government at a corresponding level but not the departments at the next higher level, they had a greater chance of being appointed to people's congresses or people's political consultative conferences. By this means, they can retain political influence after their retirement (Yang 2004).

O'Toole argued that a bottom-up model is more effective in soliciting policy implementers' compliance. Policy makers should either modify the incentive systems in the administration or adjust policy content by involving policy implementers in the policy-making process. By this means, policy implementers' interests can be aligned with broader collective benefits, and appropriate behaviour can be induced on the part of the policy implementers (O'Toole 1989). Nevertheless, licensing reform remains a top-down exercise. Input from local actors in the policy-making processes is not actively solicited. The incentive systems marked by a linkage of extra-budgetary revenue with the level of subsidy and bonus remain unreformed. In 2004, Beijing municipality severed the link to reduce the incentive of individual departments and bureaucrats in defending their licensing authority by levelling out the subsidies of the officials. Officials of the same rank were entitled to the same amount of subsidies, regardless of the level of extra-budgetary revenue their individual departments generated (Chou 2008: 65). Nevertheless, not many local governments can follow the Beijing model as their tax bases are much narrower. A licensing authority can help to create a source of revenue. They may annul only the items with limited potential of revenue generation and keep others illegally (Yan 2005: 44; Chen 2005: 75).

Furthermore, licensing reform is contradictory with the industrial growth of the regions where the industries are not competitive enough to survive without protectionist measures. A licensing authority contributes to the creation of locally owned conglomerates with certain monopolised power and forms a stable source of tax revenue to local governments. Without adequate compensation, it is difficult for local governments to relinquish their licensing authority. As discussed in Chapter 5, local leaders are evaluated on their ability to develop the local economy. They tend to focus on local economic growth and ignore collective interests of the wider regions. Undoubtedly licensing reform can improve the local business environment, attract more investment, enlarge tax bases and fuel economic growth in the long run. But regular job rotation discourages local leaders from committing to policies that cannot achieve immediate results.

Several institutional features entrench local leaders' incentive to weaken licensing reform. The first is a lack of pro-reform interest groups or a strong functional bureaucracy representing the societal actors who benefit from licensing reform. After investigating 50 countries' regulatory reforms in the telecommunications industry, Li *et al.* (2005) argued that successful regulatory reforms are more likely in countries with strong pro-reform interest groups such as the financial sector and urban consumers who are frequent users of telecommunications services and beneficiaries of a reformed telecommunications industry. The major opponents are the incumbent telecommunications operators who benefit from their monopolistic power buttressed by old regulatory systems. The countries whose regulatory reforms are less successful are those without institutionally significant beneficiaries of the reforms. With regard to licensing reform, the major beneficiaries are private entrepreneurs while the licence-issuing bureaucracies have vested interests in the old licensing regime. The institutional position of Chinese private entrepreneurs is very weak. The strict control on the formation of civic associations makes it difficult for private entrepreneurs to organise collective action for promoting licensing reform. All-China Federation of Industry and Commerce, the state-sanctioned national association representing private enterprises, is more like a government's executive arm than their Anglo-American counterparts, which proactively advocate the interests of their members, joining alliances with legislators and the functional bureaucracy and lobbying on behalf of their members. Without politically powerful beneficiaries having strong institutionalised positions, licensing reform easily loses momentum in the face of bureaucratic resistance.[4]

The second feature is the ineffectiveness of the legislation review mechanism. To ensure consistency among different levels of laws and regulations, several OECD countries have established central regulatory registers and enforced only the rules in the registers (OECD 2002: 373). China has its own legislation review system. The Law of Legislation promulgated in 2000 identifies a hierarchy of Chinese laws with the Constitution as supreme, followed by the laws enacted by the NPC and its Standing Committee, local laws and local administrative decrees (Articles 78–80). The Standing Committee of the NPC is responsible for reviewing and striking down lower-level legislation contradictory with the Constitution and laws (Article 88).[5] The Standing Committee of the NPC set up the Judicial Review Office (*Fagui shencha beian bangongshi*) under its Law Committee to provide the Law Committee with expert advice on the conflict of national laws with central regulations. Review of the consistency between central and local regulations and among local regulations themselves was left to the State Council, its Ministries, or local-level administrative agencies (Article 86). Since the promulgation of the Law of Legislation, the Standing Committee of the NPC has received some 20 requests for legislation review. But the Standing Committee of the NPC could not take any concrete action in response because of the lack of an operationalised procedure. The Judicial Review Office had only a staff of fewer than 30 officers, far from enough for reviewing all legislation and decrees (Wen and Chang 2004: 31).[6]

The third institutional feature is the ambiguity in relevant laws. Administrative Punishment Law obliges local governments to hold a public hearing before they impose a 'relatively large amount of penalty' or introduce provisions about 'revoking' (*diaoshao*) licences. To evade the constraints, some departments do not impose penalties but collect 'guarantee money'. They do not revoke but 'recall' licences (Ma, H. 2006). The Regulations of Management of Dangerous Chemical Products states that manufacturers of dangerous chemical products, including 'mildly poisonous agricultural-use pesticides' have to obtain licences first before they can start their businesses. But the definition of 'mildly poisonous pesticides' is unclear. Some agricultural bureaux classified fertilisers and pesticides as dangerous chemical products to justify their licensing authority over the trade of fertilisers and pesticides. By these means, the bureaux can keep their authority over denying private entrepreneurs necessary licences to run businesses involving fertilisers and pesticides, and fend off competition against similar businesses affiliated with the bureaux (Yang 2004). Some local governments circumvent the Administrative Licensing Law by transferring their licensing authority to subordinate industrial associations or public-service units. Since the licensing items that industrial associations and public-service units oversee are not construed as administrative licenses, these licensing items and related licensing authorities are not bound by the Law (Han and Yang 2006).

Courts have the potential to curb power abuse. Unfortunately, the fact that China's courts lack the power to rein in the administration is the fourth institutional feature that entrenches local leaders' incentive to safeguard their licensing authority. The power of interpreting laws and administrative decrees does not rest with the courts but the people's congresses at various levels. Most of the deputies of people's congresses, however, work for congresses on a part-time basis and have no legal training. No subsidies are given to them to hire legal consultants or support staff. It is difficult for them to accumulate expertise and spend their spare time on legal interpretation. Unlike Western democratic countries which guarantee judicial stability and impartiality through life employment, Chinese judges' terms of office are decided by Party branches. Courts are dependent on Party branches and local governments and vulnerable to intimidation from the Party and government officials. Thus Chinese judges are reluctant to challenge government decisions. More importantly, Chinese political leaders reject the liberal notion of a neutral state. Courts have to decide cases according to a normative agenda determined by the regime (Peerenboom 2001). Horsley (2007: 7) emphasised successful lawsuits relating to administrative licences in China, but the lawsuits cannot deny the fact that local governments are able to foul the enforcement of court judgments. In 2006, the court of Tolufan city in Xinjiang Autonomous Region ruled that a township government violated an entrepreneur's property right and had to compensate him. The township government ignored the court decision, and the decision was unable to be implemented (Lu 2006). Xingguo county of Jiangxi province once instructed the court not to hear the charges filed by an enterprise against the county government's refusal to repay debts (Song *et al.* 2004: 59). The limitation of existing laws and the judiciary makes it difficult for businesspeople to challenge administrative decisions and safeguard their rights. Without effective constraints, many local leaders have motives to ignore the laws and policies that go against their own interests, Administrative Licensing Law and other measures of licensing reform included.

Conclusion

Ideological suspicion against private-sector development has been gradually dissipating in China. Ideological change has prompted the CCP to revise its constitution and allow private entrepreneurs Party membership. The state constitution was also amended to enshrine the private economy as an important pillar of the national economy. Creating jobs for first-time job seekers and laid-off workers through a developing private sector is high on the CCP's agenda. Private enterprises are now permitted to enter many sectors once monopolised by state sectors and to create new market sectors. Both foreign-invested and domestic companies face less restriction in acquiring state assets. Further private-sector development requires a reform of the regulatory regime to make it more business friendly and encourage investment. Reforms of the regulatory regime include two parts: downsizing licensing systems and enhancing the government's regulatory capacity to police markets and to cope with various forms of market failure.

On top of improving the business environment, licensing reform has the potential to change bureaucrats' behaviour in favour of private-sector development through institutionalising the operation mode of the administration in terms of China's WTO commitments. The reform centres on removing the licensing authority of local bureaucrats and changing the practice of creating market barriers and rent seeking by the use of an overly complicated licensing system. The Chinese government has slashed most licensing items, and issued laws and regulations to prevent annulled licensing items from being re-established. Sub-provincial governments have to refer to national laws and regulations before making decisions on licensing issues. Provincial-level governments are authorised to scrutinise lower-level government in the establishment of new licences. Provincial people's congresses have taken some of the licensing authority from provincial-level governments and weakened the latter's ability in licensing issues.

As Clarke (2007: 576) argued, the Administrative Licensing Law established the important principle that the licensing of business activities should be justified only by public necessity – in other words, the mere existence of a business is no longer sufficient justification for requiring it to be licensed; some public benefit from a licensing scheme must be shown. The question is such that there is no institutional method of realistically challenging local-government decisions that a particular licensing scheme has public benefits. While the law may change the general culture of administrative licensing, its immediate effects are limited. The selective implementation of the reform illustrates that the masterminds behind the policy have inadequately considered the structural features of local institutions through which the reform is carried out. The policy entails numerous implementers whose interests are diverse and activities are badly coordinated. A command-and-control approach in implementing the policy neither solicits voluntary compliance from implementers, nor generates adequate information for policy makers to monitor policy implementation and exercise sanctions. The incentive systems at local governance go against the policy in the implementation process: The performance-appraisal systems of local leaders and job-rotation system encourage local leaders to focus narrowly on the short-term economic growth of small localities, but ignore the welfare of wider regions and the long-term improvement in the investment environment. Licensing authority is conducive to achieving the immediate result of economic growth by fending off competition against local enterprises and products. Since local governments are required to be financially self-sufficient, the potential of the licensing authority to form a major source of revenue provides a strong incentive for the local governments without a broad tax base to thwart licensing reform. Other institutional features such as the weak institutional position of private businesses, ineffective legislation review mechanism and deficient legal system make it possible for local leaders to bypass the formal rules.

7 Conclusion

The government and policy-making reforms in China are institutional reforms in response to the domestic socioeconomic transformation, challenges to the legitimacy and capacity of the CCP and the desire of Chinese leaders to closely integrate with the world economy; with the state relaxing its social control, NGOs have emerged as advocates of the causes supported by their leaders and to deliver social goods that the state is reluctant and/or unable to provide. The public grievances and social unrest triggered by market-oriented reforms have prompted the government to reform state-sanctioned mass organisations and enhance their capacity in aggregating, representing and articulating sectoral interests. Due to a more relaxed political atmosphere and a higher stake in many public policies, the public has more incentive to participate in public policies and mount pressure on the government to provide new channels for collecting public opinions. The declining capacity of the central government in resource extraction caused by the post-Mao decentralisation has engendered the recentralisation of fiscal authority and expenditure assignments. The need to enhance the CCP's ruling legitimacy is threatened by corruption, and the abuse of public monies has resulted in spending-control reforms. Civil-service reform is a remedy to the weaknesses of an administration in realising state objectives and the failure to deliver performance legitimacy. The opening up of the economy to foreign investment has convinced political elites of the benefits of trade liberalisation. Further trade liberalisation requires accession to the WTO and implementing the WTO's demand for a business-friendly regulatory framework and the uniform implementation of the framework across the country. The common ground of these reform measures is such that their design is based on technical rationality. None of them have the potential to redistribute political power or pose challenges to the CCP's supremacy. This characteristic reflects the determination of the central leaders not to share political power with independent societal forces.

The study of the institutional reforms underlines two significant notions useful for answering the central question of this book: Why are the institutional reforms in China limited in their success? First, government and policy-making reforms in China are path dependent, following the trajectory of centralising the decision-making authority when faced with the problems of decentralisation.

The CCP has historically used centralisation to deal with the problems of decentralisation. Past institutions locked decision makers into a certain path and constrained their choices of policy instruments.

Two forms of centralisation can be identified: transfer of authority from lower-level to upper-level governments, and from spending departments to departments charged with supervising the spending departments. The 1994 tax-sharing reform worked to centralise tax bases and enhance central governments' resource-extractive capacity at the expense of local governments'. The reform of spending control unifies the authority of budget preparation and execution under the management of finance bureaux and the scrutiny of audit offices. Certain budgeting authority is transferred upwards from township to county-level governments, and from prefectural to provincial-level governments, respectively. The strengthening of establishment control in civil-service reform transferred the authority of position creation from lower to upper-level governments. Under the policy of institutionalising wage payments and equalising civil servants' bonuses, individual departments were required to give up much of their authority over pay determination and bonus distribution to corresponding finance bureaux. Performance contracts of local leaders have the potential of asserting central control over local leaders by aligning local leaders' interests with a central agenda characterised by a high emphasis on economic development, public order and family planning. Administrative licensing reform prohibits sub-provincial governments from arbitrarily creating new licences. Their licensing authority must be derived from the delegation of central and provincial governments which, in turn, are constrained by a legal framework. The policy of centralisation contrasted with the decentralisation in the 1980s which successfully motivated local leaders to pursue the central policies of economic development. The policy is also divergent from the paradigm of new public management, advocating empowerment of department managers and moving the decision-making authority closer to the target population. Centralisation is a result of the political elites' awareness that decentralisation has led to an increasing information gap, difficulty in scrutinising local actors and, above all, has strained the ability of central government to steer national development. These problems have fuelled corruption and weakened the central government's capacity in resource extraction.

The impact of centralisation on the central government's capacity is evident. Central tax revenue has increased substantially, as has the proportion of central tax in the gross tax revenue. The authority of lower-level governments in creating public offices, using public monies and issuing licences has been undercut. This brings lower-level governments and spending departments under closer scrutiny, narrows the information gap and rectifies agency problems: Agents represented by the leaders of local governments and directors of functional departments have incentives to ignore the responsibilities delegated by their principals in case they are required to undertake duties that conflict with their priorities. A narrower information gap makes agents more difficult to avoid.

The second notion is that the reform follows a top-down approach. The CCP's high priority of political survival and central control has led to the use of

the top-down approach. Illustrative of this is the higher degree of citizen participation in the policy process. Central government maintains control over which
spectrum of issues welcome citizen participation and which do not, which types
of participation are allowed, and who may participate and air their opinions. The
participants are aware that their participation is not taken for granted but is at the
discretion of the authorities. Jet Li, a famous film actor and the founder of One
Foundation (an NGO specialising in disaster relief and charity promotion) said
in the aftermath of the 2008 Sichuan earthquake that he hesitated to act immedi-
ately after the earthquake happened. The reason was that he might have encountered trouble with the authorities and be accused of releasing state secrets if the
government had wanted to conceal news of the earthquake (Lei 2008).[1] Furthermore, their advisory nature makes it difficult for participatory activities to have a
real impact on the substance of public policies, as well as on agenda setting. The
impact of citizen participation is confined to the programme design and opera-
tional details of public policies, the mode of public-service delivery and the
enforcement of public policies.

A major shortcoming of the top-down approach is that the reform measures
are introduced to satisfy the needs of central elites who are not held responsible
and who need not be responsive to local constituencies. Therefore local agendas
and uniqueness are not taken into consideration during the policy-making stage.
Tax-sharing reform is entirely oriented to the interests of the central government,
seeking to enhance the resource-extracting capacity of the central government at
the expense of a local government's fiscal adequacy. In the wake of the reform,
the proportion of central tax within the total tax revenue has increased substantially; the percentage of total tax revenue in the GDP has risen slightly. The
reform, however, comes at a heavy price for local governments. Deprived of
important tax sources, local governments have to rely on imposing exorbitant
fees to raise capital and invest less in public service to save costs. The policy of
the uniform pay increment for civil servants reflects the central elites' inadequate
consideration of the different levels of economic development among different
regions, and the negative impact of pay rises on the fiscal health of governments.
From a local perspective, establishment control and downsizing are not sensible;
the reforms fail to take account of the role of lower-level governments as major
employers. Curtailing the authority of lower-level governments in job creation
may cause widespread unemployment and affect social stability. The reform of
the licensing regime aims to undertake the central government's WTO commitments on uniform implementation of business-friendly policies and the abolition
of trade barriers. As argued in Chapter 6, less-developed regions require more
protectionist measures so that domestic firms can have more opportunities to
grow before they are able to compete on an equal footing with more efficient
foreign-invested companies. Full implementation of the WTO commitments
would have seriously hurt local economies. Furthermore, simplifying the licensing regime entails taking away local governments' licensing authority which is a
significant source of revenue. Without financial compensation, the cash-strapped
local governments defend their licensing authority and blunt the efforts of central

government to improve the business environment so as to be in line with their WTO commitments.

Spending control is also illustrative of the limits of the top-down approach. The reform of public-spending control reflects the central leaders' distrust of their agents in using public monies. Under the reform, the leaders of local governments and the directors of spending departments are obliged to give up certain authority of financial management, such as the use of extra-budgetary revenue and procurement funds. Unlike the reform in many OECD countries, theoretically, local leaders and department directors in China have no discretionary power over spending the saved funds or using the capital for unbudgeted items as long as the total expenditure does not exceed the budget. Therefore spending control has reduced the amount of funds that local leaders and department directors can allocate, increased the conflict level of the policy context, and above all, provided incentive for local leaders and department directors to circumvent the spending-control regulations.

As a result of the little input from local government in the policy making of the reform measures, local governments have to reshape or even kill off some of the measures in order to adapt them to the local context or to alleviate the conflicts between the measures and local agendas. It is true that China is a monolith unitary regime and that local governments are expected to be absolutely subservient to the Party centre, but the unavoidability of the information gap occasionally gives local governments a free hand to act and avoid the scrutiny of the central government. The problem of avoidance cannot be resolved unless an incentive-compatible mechanism is institutionalised to align the interests of local actors with the agendas of the Party centre. Even if the Party centre has knowledge of a policy's failure, taking corrective action is not necessarily desirable: If the Party centre had intervened and sanctioned the local governments whenever policy non-implementation was found and policy adjustments were required, local governments would have become demoralised and passive. To avoid sanctions, local governments might have simply waited for central instructions on every single issue. Then the Party centre would have been overloaded and unable to concentrate on agenda setting, consensus reaching and policy evaluation.

What merits further evaluation is how effective are the remedial actions that the Chinese government undertakes to address the problems caused by the reform measures. To compensate local governments' loss of revenue, central government has increased the fiscal transfer and partially centralised the expenditure responsibilities on education, health care and social welfare. This measure led to a dilemma on the issues of equity and sustainability: To qualify for a certain fiscal transfer, the recipients are required to set aside a certain amount of matching funds in order to improve the incentive of local governments in capital generation and cost saving, prevent the abuse of a fiscal transfer and force local governments to utilise their secretive extra-budgetary funds for the causes that central government supports. The intention is good, but the outcome may not be equitable. Affluent localities are more able to generate matching funds, and therefore it is easier for them to get a fiscal transfer than it is for their cash-strapped, less-developed counterparts. Besides that, much of the fiscal transfer is in the form of earmarked funds for capital investment. Therefore the fiscal transfer cannot help to alleviate the local fiscal stress caused by burdensome payroll expenditure. The unresolved fiscal problems force some local governments to divert the central appropriation on local education, health care and social welfare to other uses. Furthermore, the fiscal transfer is not well-institutionalised. Local governments have no knowledge of whether the fiscal transfer will be suspended one day. Many local governments therefore hold back the use of fiscal transfer for future use, and thus dilute the impact of fiscal transfer. A systematic analysis dealing with these issues is useful for understanding the organisational and managerial abilities of political elites in policy learning, an essential part of policy capacity.

The role of the people's congresses at various levels on reviewing budgets is enhanced by spending control. They are provided with more full-time staff to give policy and legal advice to the deputies. Local governments are required to table more detailed budgets so that deputies have more information on budget issues. However, some of the weaknesses of the people's congresses and the budgeting process remain unaddressed. For example, many of the deputies are government officials and can hardly serve as vigilant watchmen over government acts. Deputies work in the people's congresses on a part-time basis. Some of them are appointed not because of their expertise, but because they are model workers; they may not be prepared intellectually for sophisticated analysis. How well they can accumulate adequate expertise for the role of budget scrutiny deserves scholarly attention. In addition, the budget cycles of various levels of government start before budgets are tabled and the amount of fiscal transfer from upper-level governments is decided after budgets are approved by the people's congresses. The ways of addressing these problems and the effectiveness of other remedial actions, such the inducement of lower-level governments to downsize and the stepping up of anti-corruption measures in various aspects of administration, are of interest to policy and academic communities.

Notes

1 Introduction

1 The 205 countries and regions include 86 for which relevant data is missing.

2 Citizen participation in the policy process

1 For example, Shi (1997) has undertaken a survey of political participation in the capital, Beijing. Walder (1986) has examined the attempts of urban citizens to influence the implementation of public policies through work units.

2 Electoral participation aims to elect representatives and vote on pertinent issues. This category involves such activities as voting and working for a political candidate or in support or opposition to an issue. Obligatory participation involves the mandatory responsibilities that are the legal obligations of citizenship. This category includes such activities as paying taxes, jury duty and military service. Citizen action is initiated and controlled by citizens for purposes that they determine. This category involves such activities as lobbying and public advocacy. Citizen involvement seeks to improve and/ or to gain support for decisions, programmes or services. This category involves such activities as public hearings, consultation with advisory committees and attitudinal surveys.

3 It was found in a survey that 'contacting the leading cadres of work units' was the most popular among the eight most common forms of citizen participation (Chang 1994: 89). Shi's (1997) study also reported similar results. 'Contacting the leaders of work unit' was the second most popular act of political participation and was ranked after 'voting for deputies to local people's congress'.

4 Y. Kong, a trade union official in Liaoyang, antagonised local officials by fighting doggedly for the rights of recently laid-off workers. Afterwards, he was sentenced to 15 years in prison on false charges (Pocha 2007).

5 Interview with a Beijing resident in June 2004.

6 According to the framework, access to information is the lowest level of participation. Consultation, a two-way relationship in which citizens provide feedback to government, is of a higher level. The highest level of participation is active participation – a relation based on partnership with the government in which citizens actively engage in defining the process and content of policy making. It acknowledges equal standing for citizens in setting the agenda, proposing policy options and shaping the policy dialogue (OECD 2001: 23).

3 Taxation reform

1 For detail of the division system, see Wang and Hu (1999: 216–19).

2 The composition of local taxes and shared taxes has changed since 1994. Basically

more and more local taxes have been classified into shared taxes. From 1994, central taxes comprise: customs duties; the consumption tax; value-added tax revenues collected by customs; income taxes from central enterprises and from banks and non-bank financial intermediaries; the remitted profits, income taxes, business taxes and urban construction and maintenance taxes of the railroad, bank headquarters and insurance companies; and resource taxes on offshore oil extraction. Local taxes consist of business taxes; income taxes and profit remittances of local enterprises; urban land-use taxes; personal income taxes; the fixed-asset investment-orientation tax; the urban construction and maintenance tax; real-estate taxes; the vehicle-utilisation tax; the stamp tax; the animal slaughter tax; agricultural taxes; the title tax; inheritance and gift taxes; the capital-gains tax on land; state land-sales revenues; and resource taxes on land-based resources. Shared taxes are securities-trading tax and value-added tax, with the former shared 50:50 and the latter shared at a fixed rate of 75 per cent to central government and 25 per cent to provincial-level governments.

3 In the coastal regions, it was the central, provincial, city and township-level governments contributing to the fund.

4 Reform of spending control

1 A copy of the Regulations can be found in *Zhongguo fayuan wang* (China Court Web). Available online: www.chinacourt.org/flwk/show1.php?file_id=117863 (accessed 13 May 2007).

2 Official figures indicate the value of government procurement in 2005 totalling 292.75 billion *yuan*. However, the figure did not include procurement conducted by public-sector organisations which are not covered by the Law of Government Procurement, such as procurement by state-owned enterprises and for the 2008 Beijing Olympic Games. If procurement by these organisations had been included, the estimated value of government procurement might have been as high as 1.8 trillion *yuan* (AmCham Shanghai and AmCham-China (Beijing) 2007).

5 Civil service reform

1 Administrative functions include four parts: national construction; economic management; welfare development; and environment protection (Huang and Wang 1993: 33).

2 A copy of the Law can be found in 'Zhonghua renmin gongheguo gongwuyuan fa' (The Law of Civil Servant, the People's Republic of China), *Zhonghua renmin gongheguo renshibu wangzhan* (Ministry of Personnel website). Available online: www.mop. gov.cn/gjgwy/content.asp?id=48 (accessed 14 May 2005).

3 A copy of the Regulation can be found in *Renshi zhengce fagui zhuankan* (A Collection of Personnel Policies and Regulations), 68, 1994, 17–20.

4 A detailed account of an instance of appointment of leading civil servants through open competition can be found in: Leading Cadre's Office of Open Recruitment in Guangdong Province (2001).

5 An OECD study reviewed the merit pay in the civil service of five member countries. The study concluded that the pay amount (ranging from 1.8 per cent to 12.3 per cent of their salary and the median was around 3.3 per cent) was too small to motivate employees (OECD 1997: 44, 59).

6 The argument was based on a review of a sample of one provincial-level city (Beijing city), three provinces (Hubei, Hunan and Sichuan), and one prefecture-level city (Urumqi of Xinjiang autonomous region) (Chou 2003c).

7 Interview with a former civil servant of a district government in Shanghai in 2006.

6 Implementation of Administrative Licensing Law

1 These six sectors are: (1) industries involving 'national security, public safety, macro-economic management, environmental protection, public health, personal safety and property protection'; (2) industries involving scarce natural resources exploitation and public resources allocation; (3) professions involving public interest and public service (such as legal and accounting professions); (4) sale of equipment, facilities, products involving public safety, public health and personal safety and property; (5) restricted industries; (6) other industries covered by other laws promulgated by the National People's Congress and its Standing Committee and administrative decrees by State Council.

2 Since the late 1990s, the Chinese government has partially centralised some regulatory authority from sub-provincial to provincial governments. Certain regulatory bureaux are no longer responsible to the local governments at corresponding levels, but answerable to superior functional bureaucracies which, in turn, report to provincial-level governments (Mertha 2005; Heilmann 2005).

3 In the 2003 administrative reform and merging of central ministries, the price-control bureau was put under the National Development and Reform Commission ('Guowuyuan guanyu guli zhichi' 13 April 2006).

4 For details of how private entrepreneurs influenced local governments and their institutional positions in the policy process, see Sato (2003) and Dickson (2003).

5 In reality, this provision can be applied in different ways. In 2005, the Standing Committee of NPC received a petition from a peasant in Hebei province protesting that the provincial regulations on land management violated the national Law of Land Management. Before the State Committee of NPC took action, Hebei provincial people's congresses amended the provincial regulations to keep them consistent with the Law. For details, see Yang (2004).

6 A more comprehensive evaluation of the Law of Legislation can be found in Zou (2004).

7 Conclusion

1 X. Lei, 'Yi jijin zhen hou de erbai sishi xiaoshi' (One Foundation and 240 hours after the Earthquake), *Sina.Com.* Available online: http://finance.sina.com.cn/g/20080529/09484923805.shtml (accessed 23 July 2008).

Bibliography

'3.6b of state funds misused', *China Daily*, 20 September 2007.

'Activists held over Xiamen rallies', *South China Morning Post*, 19 July 2007.

Ahmad, E. (1995) 'A comparative perspective on expenditure assignments', in E. Ahmad, Q. Gao and V. Tanzi (eds), *Reforming China's Public Finances*, Washington, DC: International Monetary Fund, pp. 77–96.

All-China Federation of Industry and Commerce (2005) *Zhongguo minying jingji fazhan baogao no. 2* (The Development Report of Non-State-Owned Economy in China, No. 2), Beijing: Social Sciences Academic Press.

Almond, G.A. and Powell, G.B. (1966) *Comparative Politics: A Developmental Approach*, Boston: Little, Brown and Company.

Ambler, T. and Witzel, M. (2004) *Doing Business in China*, London; New York: RoutledgeCurzon.

AmCham Shanghai and AmCham-China (Beijing) (2007) *2007 White Paper: American Business in China*, Beijing. Available online: www.amcham-shanghai.org/AmCham-Portal/MCMS/Presentation/Publication/WhitePaper/WhitePaperDetail.aspx?Guid={F121DEE5–8B38–49E2-B9B3-FDFA7D1D94CC} (accessed 20 August 2007).

'Ancient imperial exams with modern relevance', *China Daily*, 23 February 2006. Available online: www.chinadaily.com.cn/english/doc/2006-02/23/content_523094.htm (accessed 2 March 2006).

Anderson, J.E. (2000) *Public Policymaking: An Introduction*, Boston; New York: Houghton Mifflin.

Asian Development Bank (2003) *Private Sector Assessment: People's Republic of China*, Manila: Asian Development Bank.

Bath, V. (2008) 'Reducing the role of government – The Chinese experiment', *Asian Journal of Comparative Law*, 3 (1), 1–37.

Beijing Local History Editorial Committee (ed.) (2000) *Beijing nianjian 2000* (Beijing Yearbook 2000), Beijing: Beijing Yearbook Press.

Benewick, R., Tong, I. and Howell, J. (2004) 'Self-governance and community: A preliminary comparison between villagers' committees and urban community councils', *China Information*, 18 (1), 11–28.

Bernstein, T.P. and Lü, X. (2003) *Taxation without Representation in Contemporary Rural China*, Cambridge: Cambridge University Press.

Bing, Z. (2005) 'Sheng yi xia caizheng guanli tizhi gaige gouxiang' (Blueprints of reforming the financial management of sub-provincial governments), *Zhongguo caizheng* (China State Finance), 12, 12–14.

Bo, Z. (2004) 'The institutionalization of elite management in China', in B.J. Naughton and D.L. Yang (eds), *Holding China Together: Diversity and National Integration in the Post-Deng Era*, Cambridge: Cambridge University Press, pp. 70–100.

Breslin, S.G. (1996) *China in the 1980s: Centre-Province Relations in a Reforming Socialist State*, London: Macmillan Press.

Brosio, G. (1995) 'Local taxation in an international perspective', in E. Ahmad, Q. Gao and V. Tanzi (eds), *Reforming China's Public Finances*, Washington, DC: International Monetary Fund, pp. 178–93.

Budget Bureau, Ministry of Finance (2006) 'Shishi "sanjiang yibu" jili yueshu jizhi. Huanjie xian xiang caizheng kunnan' (Implementing 'three-award-and-one-subsidy' policy to alleviate the fiscal constraints of counties and townships), *Zhongguo caizheng* (China Finance), 9, 17–20.

'Bullet Time', *The Economist* (19–25 May 2007), 68.

Burns, J.P. (2004) 'Governance and civil service reform', in J. Howell (ed.), *Governance in China*, New York; Oxford: Rowman & Littlefield Publishers, Inc., pp. 37–57.

—— (2001) 'Public sector reform and the state: The case of China', *Public Administration Quarterly*, 24 (4), 419–36.

—— (1994a) 'Civil service reform in China', *Asian Journal of Political Science*, 2, 44–72.

—— (1994b) 'Strengthening Central CCP control of leadership selection: The 1990 nomenklatura', *The China Quarterly*, 138, 458–91.

—— (1993) 'China's administrative reforms for a market economy', *Public Administration and Development*, 13 (4), 345–60.

—— (1989a) 'Chinese civil service reform: The 13th Party Congress proposal', *The China Quarterly*, 120: 739–70.

—— (1989b), *The Chinese Communist Party's Nomenklatura System: A Documentary Study of Party Control of Leadership Selection, 1979–1984*, New York: M.E. Sharpe.

—— (1988) *Political Participation in Rural China*, Berkeley, CA: University of California Press.

—— (1987) 'Civil service reform in contemporary China', *The Australian Journal of Chinese Affairs*, 18, 47–84.

Cai, C. (2007) 'Why can't regulations safeguarding labour rights be implemented?', *China Labour Bulletin*. Available online: www.china-labour.org.hk/public/contents/arti cle?revision%5fid=46543&item%5fid=44889 (accessed 28 July 2007).

Cai, H. (2005) 'Nongcun yiwu jiaoyu jingfei zhengfu fendan jizhi yanjiu' (A research on government expenditure on rural voluntary education), *Caizheng yanjiu* (Public Finance Research), 3, 15–17.

Cai, Y. (2006) *State and Laid-Off Workers in Reform China: The Silence and Collective Action of the Retrenched*, London; New York: Routledge.

—— (2004) 'Managed participation in China', *Political Science Quarterly*, 119 (3), 425–51.

Cao, Z., Liu, J. and Dai, G. (1994) 'Jianli you zhongguo tese de guojia gongwuyuan zhidu' (Establishment of civil service system with Chinese characteristics), in Ministry of Personnel (ed.), *Guojia gongwuyuan zhidu quanshu* (A Collection of Articles on State Civil Service System), Changchun: Jilin Literature and History Press, pp. 209–14.

Carlile, L. and Tilton, M.C. (1998) 'Regulatory reform and developmental states', in L. Carlile and M.C. Tilton (eds), *Is Japan Really Changing Its Ways?: Regulatory Reform and the Japanese Economy*, Washington, DC: Brookings Institution Press, pp. 1–15.

Centre of Human Resources Research and Training, Development and Research Centre, the State Council (2005) *Qiye jingyingzhe dui jingji huanjing he gaige redian de panduan – 2005 zhongguo qiye jingyingzhe wenjuan diaocha baogao* (The Opinions of Entrepreneurs towards the Context and Hot Issues of Economy). Available online: www.drc.gov.cn/view.asp?doc_ID=032802 (accessed 28 February 2006).

Centre of Human Resources Research and Training, Development and Research Centre, the State Council, *Qiye jingyingzhe dui hongguan jingji xingxi ji gaige redian he panduan* (The Opinions and Suggestions of Entrepreneurs towards the Economy). Available online: www.drc.gov.cn/view.asp?doc_ID=030466 (accessed 28 February 2006).

Chan, A. (1993) 'Revolution or corporatism? Workers and trade unions in post-Mao China', *The Australian Journal of Chinese Affairs*, 29, 31–61.

Chan, C.P. and Drewry, G. (2001) 'The 1998 State Council organizational streamlining: Personnel reduction and change of government function', *Journal of Contemporary China*, 10 (29), 553–72.

Chan, H.S. and Lam, T.C. (1996) 'China's new civil service: What the emperor is wearing and why', *Public Administration Review*, 56 (5), 479–84.

—— (1995a) 'The civil service system: Policy formulation and implementation', in C.K. Lo, S. Pepper and K.Y. Tsui (eds), *China Review 1995*, Hong Kong: The Chinese University Press, pp. 2.2–2.35.

—— (1995b) 'Designing China's civil service system: General principles and realities', *International Journal of Public Administration*, 18 (8), 1301–21.

Chan, M. (2007) 'Cadres face the sack if they miss green goals', *South China Morning Post*, 25 November 2007.

Chang, S. (1994) *Zhongguo 'zhengzhiren': Zhongguo gongmin zhengzhi zhisu diaocha baogao* (Chinese 'Political Men': A Report of the Political Efficacy of Chinese Citizens), Beijing: China Social Sciences Press.

Chen, C. (2003) 'Dang yu shehui, dang de zuzhi yu shequ zhili' (The CCP and the society: Party organizations and community governance), in S. Lin (ed.), *Shequ minzhu yu zhili: anli yanjiu* (Research on Cases of Community Democratic Governance), Beijing: Social Sciences Documentation Press, pp. 40–68.

Chen, F. (2004) 'Legal mobilization by trade unions: The case of Shanghai', *The China Journal*, 52, 27–44.

—— (2003) 'Between the state and labour: The conflict of Chinese trade unions' double identity in market reform', *China Quarterly*, 176, 1004–28.

Chen, W. (2003) 'Zhongguo chengshi shequ zizhi de fazhan daolu' (The way of developing the autonomy of city communities in China), in Li Fan (ed.), *Zhongguo jiceng minzhu fazhan baogao* (A Report on the Development of China's Grassroots Democracy, 2002), Xian: Xibei University Press, pp. 189–221.

Chen, W., Zhai, S. and Deng, X. (2006) 'Hunan Huaihua nongcun caiwu kuaiji gongzuo diaocha' (A survey in the village accounting of Huaihua city of Hunan province), *Zhongguo caijing bao* (China Financial and Economic Times), 1 September 2006.

Chen, X. (1997) 'Jingji qian fada diqu keji duiwu cunzai de wenti yu duice' (Problems in the science and technology development in economically backward regions), *Jiangxi renshi* (Jiangxi Personnel), 35, 6–8.

Chen, Z. (2005) 'Qian xi xingzheng xukefa shishi zhong chuxian de jige wenti' (Several problems in implementing Administrative Licensing Law), *Heihe xuekan* (Journal of Heihe), 116, 74–6.

Cheung, A.B.L. and Poon, K.K. (2001) 'The paradox of China's wage system reforms:

balancing stakeholders' rationalities', *Public Administration Quarterly*, 24 (4), 491–521.

Cheung, K.C. (2003) 'Not so much a model, more a way of life: China's fragmented authoritarianism in budgetary management', in J. Wann, L. Jensen and J. Vries (eds), *Controlling Public Expenditure: The Changing Roles of Central Budget Agencies – Better Guardians?* Cheltenham: Edward Elgar, pp. 211–30.

China Directory 2007, Tokyo: Radio Press, Inc.

China Directory 2004, Tokyo: Radio Press, Inc

China Directory 1999, Tokyo: Radio Press, Inc.

China Directory 1994, Tokyo: Radio Press, Inc.

China Labour Bulletin (2007) 'Zhongguo gongren yundong guancha baogao, 2005–2006' (A report of labour movement in China, 2005–2006). Available online: http://gb.china-labour.org.hk/gate/gb/big5.clb.org.hk/fs/view/downloadables/No9_labourmove-ment2006_TC.pdf (accessed 29 July 2007).

China Local Administration Editorial Committee (1995) *Zhongguo difang zhengfu jigou gaige* (Administrative Reform of Chinese Local Government), Beijing: New China Press.

China Personnel Yearbook Editorial Board (1991) *Zhongguo renshi nianjian 1988–89* (Chinese Personnel Yearbook 1988–89), Beijing: China Personnel Press.

'China punishes four Olympic licensees over labour abuses', *Earth Times*. Available online: www.earthtimes.org/articles/show/88494.html (accessed 1 August 2007).

'China's civil servants to get another 15% pay rise plus bonus', *China Daily*, 12 October 2001.

'China to release action plan on environment', the *Straits Times*, 2 June 2007.

China Youth Development Foundation (2006) *Xiwanggongcheng juankuan juanwu shouzhibiao* (A Balance Sheet of Donated Money and Goods to Project Hope). Available online: www.cydf.org.cn/shenjibaogao/0622–4.htm (accessed 29 September 2007).

Chou, Bill K.P. (2008) 'Does governance matter? Civil service reform in China', *International Journal of Public Administration*, 31 (1), 54–75.

—— (2007) 'Downsizing administrative licensing system and private sector development in China: A preliminary assessment', *Asian Development Bank Institute Occasional Paper*. Available online: www.adbi.org/discussion-paper/2006/08/23/1958.admin.licensing.prc (accessed 2 June 2007).

—— (2006) 'Challenges for China's reform of government procurement', *Journal of Contemporary China*, 48, 533–49.

—— (2005) 'Implementing the reform of performance appraisal in the civil service of China', *China Information*, 19 (1), 39–66.

—— (2004) 'Civil service reform in China, 1993–2001: A case of implementation Failure', *China: An International Journal*, 2 (2), 210–34.

—— (2003a) *Conflict and Ambiguity in the Implementation of Civil Service Reform in China, 1993–2000*, PhD dissertation, University of Hong Kong. Available online: http://sunzi1.lib.hku.hk/hkuto/record/B29822294 (accessed 8 May 2006).

—— (2003b) 'The conflicts and ambiguities in implementing compensation reform in the civil service of China, 1993–2000', paper presented at the Third International Convention of Asian Scholars, Raffles City Convention Centre, Singapore, 19–22 August 2003.

—— (2003c) 'Implementing recruitment and selection reform in the civil service of China in the 1990s: An application of ambiguity-conflict model of policy implementation', *Public Administration and Policy*, 12 (2), 97–100.

Chow, C.Y. (2007) 'Huawei halts lay-off plan after criticism ahead of contract law', *South China Morning Post*, 11 November 2007.

Chua, C.H. (2007) 'Red China's green revolution', *Sunday Times*, 17 June 2007.

'Citizen power halts chemical plant project', the *Straits Times*, 31 May 2007, 13.

'Civil service exams to be held in July' (text), Beijing *Xinhua Domestic Service* (in Chinese) (17 May 1995), transl. Foreign Broadcast Information Service. FBIS Daily Report – China, 14 November 1995 (PrEx.7.10: FBIS-CHI-95-103).

'Civil service recruitment opens up', *South China Morning Post*, 13 August 2003.

Civil Society Management Bureau, Ministry of Civil Affairs (ed.) (2005) *Minjian zuzhi nengli jianshe tansuo* (A Study of Capacity Building of Civil Society), Beijing: Chinese Social Sciences Press.

Clarke, D.C. (2007) 'Legislating for a market economy in China', *China Quarterly*, 191, 567–85.

Cline, K.D. (2000) 'Defining the implementation problem: Organizational management versus cooperation', *Journal of Public Administration Research and Theory*, 10 (3), 551–71.

Commission on Global Governance (1995) *Our Global Neighbourhood*, New York: Oxford University Press.

Contemporary China Editorial Committee (1994), *Dangdai zhongguo renshi guanli (shang)* (Contemporary Chinese Personnel Management, Vol. 1), Beijing: Contemporary China Press.

Cui, S., Li, S. and Zhou, Y. (2006) 'Shenshi Zhongguo guanyuan chuguo peixunre' (An investigation into the overseas training of Chinese civil servants), *Minzhu fazhi shibao* (Democracy and Law Post), 31 July 2006. Available online: www.mzyfz-news.com.cn/news/0606133702.html (accessed 30 November 2007).

de Leon, P. (1999) 'The stages approach to the policy process: What has it done? Where is it going?' in P.A. Sabatier (ed.), *Theories of the Policy Process*, Boulder, CO: Westview Press, pp. 19–34.

Deng, H. (2007) 'Lushi Zheng Enchong shi ruhe xielu guojia mimi de?' (How did lawyer Zheng Enhong leak state secret?) *Renmin wang* (PeopleNet). Available online: http://unn.people.com.cn/GB/14748/2172850.html (accessed 22 July 2007).

Department of Finance, Anhui Province (2006) 'Quanmian tuijin xiangcai xianguan gaige' (Implementing the reform of centralising the financial management of township governments to county governments), *Zhongguo caizheng* (China Finance), 9, 23–5.

Department of Finance, Shandong Province (2006) 'Fenlei zhidao, zonghe fuchi, jiaqiang xianxiang caizheng jianshe' (Instructing based on budget classification, comprehensively supporting and stepping up the establishment of county financial system), *Zhongguo caizheng* (China State Finance), 9, 21–2.

Department of Finance, Zhejiang Province (2006) 'Zhejiang: "Sixiang gongcheng" cujin chengxiang jiaoyu junheng fazhan' (Zhejiang promotes even development of education between cities and villages through 'four projects'), *Zhongguo caizheng* (China State Finance), 3, 17.

Derleth, J. and Koldyk, D.R. (2004) 'The *shequ* experiment: Grassroots political reform in urban China', *Journal of Contemporary China*, 41, 747–78.

Diamond, J. (2006) *Budget System Reform in Emerging Economies: The Challenges and the Reform Agenda*, Washington, DC: International Monetary Fund.

Dickson, Bruce J. (2003) *Red Capitalists in China: The Party, Private Entrepreneurs, and Prospects for Political Change*, New York; Cambridge: Cambridge University Press.

Ding, X. (2006) 'Zhongyang difang gongdan jianli nongcun yiwu jiaoyu jingfei baozhang jizhi' (Central government joined local governments to establish rural voluntary education funds), *Zhongguo caizheng* (China State Finance), 3, 9–11.

Dittmer, L. and Lü, X. (1996) 'Personal politics in the Chinese *danwei* under reform', *Asian Survey*, 36, 246–67.

Domberger, S., Hall, C. and Lee, E.A.L. (1995) 'The determinants of price and quality in competitively tender contracts', *Economic Journal*, 105, 1454–70.

Dresang, D.L. (1999), *Public Personnel Management and Public Policy*, New York: Longman.

Du, Z. (2006) '"Touzhi" zhongguo' ('Over-drafting' China), *Cheng Ming Yuekan* (Voice out Monthly), 6: 26–7.

Dye, T.R. (2004) *Understanding Public Policy*, Upper Saddle River, NJ: Pearson Prentice Hall.

Ebdon, C. and Franklin, A.L. (2006) 'Citizen participation in budgeting theory', *Public Administration Review*, May/June 2006, 437–47.

Edin, M. (2003) 'State capacity and local agent control in China: CCP cadre management from a township perspective', *China Quarterly*, 173, 35–52.

Elmore, R.F. (1985) 'Forward and backward mapping', in K. Hanf and T.A.J. Toonen (eds), *Policy Implementation in Federal and Unitary Systems*, Dordrecht: Martinus Nijhoff.

Fang, Y. (2006) 'Minzhu lifa fengqi yunyong – er ling ling wu Chongqing renda lifa jujiao' (Democratic legislation has caused a storm: A report of legislation by Chongqing People's Congress in 2005), *Gongmin daokan* (Citizen Journal), 2, 42–3.

'Feizhengfu zuzhi kanwu "Minjian" bei leling tingkan' (2007) ('Civilian' [a magazine reporting the news of NGOs] was ordered to close), *Da ji yuan* (The Epoch Times). Available online: www.epochtimes.com/gb/7/7/13/n1772281.htm (accessed 13 August 2007).

Feng, J. (2007) 'Rural re-education: The Chinese government is about to launch a civil servant training program on an unprecedented scale', *Beijing Review*, 29 March 2007, 20–1.

Fewsmith, J. (1996) 'Institutions, informal politics and political transition in China', *Asian Survey*, 36 (3), 230–45.

Frolic, B.M. (1997) 'State-led civil society', in T. Brook and B.M. Frolic (eds), *Civil Society in China*, Armonk, NY: M.E. Sharpe, pp. 46–67.

Fu, G. (2006) 'Lun shengzhiguanxian caizheng tizhi' (A discussion on managing county finance by provincial governments), *Caizheng Yanjiu* (Public Finance Research), 2, 22–3.

Fu, J. (2007) 'Wal-Mart tip of union iceberg', *China Daily*, 19 October.

'Fujian sheng gongbu 445 xiang xingzheng shenpi xiangmu' (2006) (Fujian province announced 445 administrative licensing items), *Fujian zhi chuang* (The Window of Fujian). Available online: www.66163.com/Fujian_w/bdxw/20060329/fj148889.html (accessed 4 April 2006).

Gao, J. (2007) 'Bu gongkai tingzheng daibiao xinxi zunzhong yinsi haishi qinfan ziyou?' (What does non-transparency of public hearing mean? Respect for privacy or infringement of freedom?), *Renmin wang* (PeopleNet). Available online: http://opinion.people.com.cn/GB/5834441.html (accessed 28 July 2007).

Gao, Y. (2006) 'Xingzheng xukefa shishi yinian, "min'gaoguan" anjian dafu shangsheng' (The cases of 'citizens suing officials' increase substantially after Administrative Licensing Law has been implemented for one year), *Sina xinwen zhongxin* (Sina News Centre). Available online: http://news.sina.com.cn/c/2005-07-04/11587125969.shtml (accessed 30 March 2006).

Garnaut, R. Song, L., Yang, Y. and X. Wang (2001) *Private Enterprise in China*, Canberra: Asia Pacific Press; Beijing: China Center for Economic Research.

Glaser, B.S. and Saunders, P.C. (2002) 'Chinese civilian foreign policy research institutes: Evolving roles and increasing influence', *China Quarterly*, 171, 597–616.

Goldman, M. and MacFarquhar, R. (1999) 'Dynamic economy, declining Party-state', in M. Goldman and R. MacFarquhar (eds), *The Paradox of China's Post-Mao Reforms*, Cambridge, MA: Harvard University Press, pp. 3–29.

'Gongkai shi yuanze, bugongkai shi liwai' (Open information is the principle. The Secrecy is the exception), *Liaowang dongfang zhoukan* (Oriental Outlook), 4, 2007, 1.

Grindle, M.S. (1980) 'Policy content and context in implementation', in M.S. Grindle (ed.), *Politics and Policy Implementation in the Third World*, Princeton, NJ: Princeton University Press.

Gu, X. (2001) 'Dismantling the Chinese mini-welfare state? Marketization and the politics of institutional transformation, 1979–1999', *Communist and Post-Communist Studies*, 34, 91–111.

'Guanche shishi xingzheng xukefa, Guangdong dafu xiaojian xingzheng shenpi shixiang' (Guangdong has substantially reduced licensing items to implement administrative licensing law) (2006), *Jinyangwang* (Golden Goat Net). Available online: www.ycwb. com/gb/content/2006-03/05/content_108015.htm (accessed 31 March 2006).

Guo, L. (2006a) 'How "Green GDP" becomes fashionable in China (I)', *EAI Background Brief No. 273*, Singapore: East Asian Institute, National University of Singapore.

—— (2006b) 'Politics of green GDP in China (II)', *EAI Background Brief No. 274*, Singapore: East Asian Institute, National University of Singapore.

'Guojia gongwuyuan gongzi gaige taobiao' (Civil service wage reform). Available online: www.trm.cn/view.asp?WZ=21030 (accessed 2 December 2007).

'Guowuyuan guanyu guli zhichi he yindao geti siying deng feigongyouzhi jingji fazhan de ruogan yijian' (2005) (Several opinions on supporting and directing the development of non-state sector such as private sector), *Zhonghua renmin gongheguo zhongyang renmin zhengfu* (The Central People's Government of the People's Republic of China). Available online: www.gov.cn/gongbao/content/2005/content_63162.htm (accessed 13 April 2006).

'Guowuyuan guanyu shenhua nongcun yiwu jiaoyu jingfei baozhang jizhi gaige de tongzhi' (2005) (A notice of State Council on deepening the reform on rural voluntary education funds), *Zhongguo fayuan wang* (China Court Web). Available online: www. chinacourt.org/flwk/show1.php?file_id=107416&str1=%B9%D8%D3%DA%C9%EE %BB%AF%C5%A9%B4%E5%D2%E5%CE%F1%BD%CC%D3%FD   (accessed   5 April 2007).

Haggard, S. (1995) *Developing Nations and the Politics of Global Integration*, Washington, DC: The Brookings Institution.

Hall, P.A. (1992) 'The movement from Keynesianism to monetarism: Institutional analysis and British economic policy in the 1970s', in S. Steinmo, K. Thelen and F. Longstreth (eds), *Structuring Politics: Historical Institutionalism in Comparative Analysis*, Cambridge: Cambridge University Press, pp. 90–113.

Hall, P.A. and Taylor, R.C.R. (1996) 'Political science and the three new institutionalisms', *Political Studies*, 44, 936–57.

Han, J. and Yang, J. (2006) 'Xingzheng xukefa zhixing zenmoyang?' (How is the implementation of Administrative Licensing Law going on?), *Sina Xinwen Zhongxin* (Sina News Centre). Available online: http://news.sina.com.cn/o/2005-07-29/02036555072s. html (accessed 30 March 2006).

Han, Z. and Zhao, C. (2002) 'Public hearing empowers citizens' (text), Beijing *Xinhua Domestic Service* (in Chinese) (12 January 2002), transl. Foreign Broadcast Information Service. FBIS Daily Report – China, 31 January 2002 (PrEx.7.10: FBIS-CHI-2002-0112).

Harding, H. (1981) *Organizing China: the Problem of Bureaucracy*, Stanford, CA: Stanford University Press.

Heady, C. (1997) 'The role of subnational governments: Theory and international practice', in Christine P.W. Wong (ed.), *Financing Local Government in the People's Republic of China*, New York: Oxford University Press, pp. 127–66.

Heilmann, S. (2005) 'Policy-making and political supervision in Shanghai's financial industry', *Journal of Contemporary China*, 14 (45), 643–68.

He, Y. (2006) 'Zhi jian bu zeng nan zai nali? You jian you zeng bian zi hechu?' (Why is it so difficult to prevent fee collection? How to deal with the problem of fee reduction but increase in the burden of work duties?), *People's Daily*, 19 September 2006.

Hilderbrand, M.E. and Grindle, M.S. (1997) 'Building sustainable capacity in the public sector: what can be done', in M.S. Grindle (ed.), *Getting Good Government: Capacity Building in the Public Sectors of Developing Countries*, Cambridge, MA: Harvard University Press, pp. 31–62.

Hira, A., Huxtable, D. and Leger, A. (2005) 'Deregulation and participation: an international survey of participation in electricity regulation', *Governance*, 18 (1), 53–88.

Holzer, M. and Zhang, M. (2004) 'China's fiscal reform: The issue of extra budgeting', *Journal of Public Budgeting, Accounting and Financial Management*, 16 (1), 19–39.

Ho, P. (2007) 'Embedded activism and political change in a semiauthoritarian context', *China Information*, 21 (2), 187–209.

Horsley, J.P. (2007) 'The rule of law in China: Incremental progress'. Available online: www.chinabalancesheet.org/Documents/05RuleofLaw.pdf (accessed 24 November 2007).

Howell, J. (2004) 'New directions in civil society: Organizing around marginalized interests', in J. Howell (ed.), *Governance in China*, New York; Oxford: Rowman & Littlefield Publishers, Inc, pp. 143–71.

Hu, A. and Guo, Y. (2002) 'Zhuanxingqi fangzhi fubai de zhonghe zhanlue yu zhidu sheji' (Corruption prevention strategies in transition period), in A. Hu (ed.), *Zhongguo zhanlue* (The Strategies of China), Hangzhou: Zhejiang People's Press.

Huang, D. and Wang, M. (eds) (1993) *Zhongguo xingzheng guanli dacidian* (Dictionary of Chinese Administration and Management), Beijing: Beijing Material Press.

Huang, H. (2004) 'Baokao gongwuyuan de re yu leng' (An analysis of applications for civil service positions), *Liaowang xinwen zhoukan* (Outlook Weekly), 47, 34–5.

Huang, P. and Di, P. (2003) *Zhongguo: guojia fazhan yu difang caizheng* (China: National Development and Sub-National Finance), Beijing: CITIC Publishing House.

Huang, X. (2007) 'Dangqian tudi wenti de shencengci yuanyin (The reasons for the problems of land management), *Zhongguo shuiwu* (China Tax), 2, 46–7.

Huang, Y. (2002) 'Managing Chinese bureaucrats: An institutional economics perspective', *Political Studies*, 50 (1), 61–79.

—— (2001) 'Political institutions and fiscal reforms in China', *Problems of Post-Communism*, 48 (1), 16–26.

—— (1995) 'Administrative monitoring in China', *The China Quarterly*, 143, 828–43.

Huang, Y. and Di, W. (2004) 'A tale of two provinces: The institutional environment and foreign ownership in China', MIT Sloan Working Paper No. 4482-04, William Davidson Institute Working Paper No. 667. Available online: http://ssrn.com/abstract=529142 (accessed 19 June 2006).

Hull, C.J. and Hjern, B. (1987) *Helping Small Firms Grow: An Implementation Approach*, London: Croom Helm.

Huntington, S.P. (1970) 'Social and institutional dynamics of one-Party system', in S.P. Huntington and C.H. Moore (eds), *Authoritarian Politics in Modern Society: The Dynamics of Established One-party Systems*, New York: Basic Books.

International Finance Corporation (2000) *Path out of Poverty: The Role of Private Enterprise in Development Countries*, Washington, DC: International Corporation Finance.

Janow, M.E. (1998) 'Policy approaches to economic deregulation and regulatory reform', in R.I. Wu and Y.P. Chu (eds), *Business, Markets and Government in the Asia Pacific*, London: Routledge.

Japan Bank for International Cooperation (2003) *Meta Analysis of Ex-Post Evaluation Reports by Country and Sector-Country Review Report: China*, Tokyo: JBIC.

Jia, X. and Pan, J. (2006) 'Shehui zhuanxingqi de zhili: zhongguo gongmin shehui zhishu' (Governance in transitional period: China civil society index), *Di er jie er shi yi shiji de gonggong guanli: jiyu yu tiaozhan guoji yantaohui* (The 2nd International Conference on Public Management in 21st Century: Opportunities and Challenges), 31 October–1 November 2006, University of Macau, Macao. Available online: www.umac.mo/fsh/pa/2nd_IntPAConference/JiaXijin&PanJianhui.doc (accessed 23 July 2007).

Jiao, X. (2005) 'Ease of incorporating open doors', *China Daily*, 2 March 2005. Available online: www.chinadaily.com.cn/english/doc/2005-03/02/content_420806.htm (accessed 1 January 2006).

—— (2004) 'Township structural reforms should not be compromised by the concern for job protection', *China Daily*, 17 November 2004. Available online: www.chinadaily.com.cn/english/doc/2004-11/17/content_392209.htm (accessed 14 May 2005).

Jin, L. (2006) 'Xingzheng xukefa shishi qingkuang qicheng beifangzhe buman' (70 per cent of the respondents are dissatisfied with the implementation of the Administrative Licensing Law), *Jinyangwang* (Golden Goat Net). Available online: www.ycwb.com/gb/content/2004-11/26/content_801758.htm (accessed 12 April 2006).

Jin, R. (2007) 'Yi kexue fazhanguan tongling caizheng gongzuo, dali cujin goujian shehui zhuyi hexie shehui' (Dealing with financial issues to construct a socialist harmonious society by using scientific view of development), *Zhongguo caizheng* (China State Finance), 1, 10–18.

—— (2006) 'Guanyu er ling ling wu nian zhongyang juesuan de baogao' (Concerning 2005 budget report of central government), *Zhongguo caizheng* (China Finance), 3, 8–11.

—— (2004) 'Guanyu er ling ling san nian zhongyang juesuan de baogao (jiesuan): Er ling ling si nian liu yue ershisan ri zai di shi jie quanguo renmin daibiao dahui changwu weiyuanhui dishici huiyi shang' (Concerning the approved central financial report in 2003 (abstract): In the tenth plenary meeting of the Tenth Standing Committee of National People's Congress convened on 23 June 2004), in Finance Yearbook of China Editorial Committee (ed.), *Zhongguo caizheng nianjian 2004* (Finance Yearbook of China 2004), Beijing: China Finance Journal Press, pp. 22–4.

Jin, Z. and Zhang, Y. (2006) 'Xianji caizheng kunnan de chengyin ji duice fenxi: yi Shandongsheng Yantaishi xianji caizheng zhuangkuang weili' (An analysis of the reasons and coping strategies of the fiscal problems at county level: A case study of the county finance at Yantai city of Shandong province), *Caizheng yanjiu* (Public Finance Research), 9, 61.

'Jingwu tousu shouli sanqianzhong, jucheng jin yi liu jiu qi shushi' (Only 169 out of 3,000 complaints about the police have grounds), *Nanfang dushibao* (Southern Municipal Post), 7 March 2002.

'Jintao zai zhongyang dangxiao fabiao zhongyao jianghua qiangdiao, jiandingbuyi zou zhongguo tese shehuizhuyi weida daolu, wei duoqu quanmian jianshe xiaokangshehui xinshengli er fendou: Wu Bangguo, Wen Jiabao, Jia Qinglin, Wu Guanzheng, Li Changchun, Luo Gan chuxi, Zeng Qinghong zhuchi' (In central Party school, Comrade Hu Jintao placed emphasis on steering along the road of socialism with Chinese characteristics with determination, as well as striving for reaching the horizon of better-off society. Attended by Wu Bangguo, Wen Jiabao, Jia Qinglin, Wu Guanzheng, Li Changchun, Luo Gan and chaired by Zheng Qinghong', *Renmin wang* (PeopleNet). Available online: http://cpc.people.com.cn/GB/64093/64094/5911131.html (accessed 23 August 2007).

Kahn, J. and Baroza, D. (2007) 'As unrest rises, China broadens workers' rights', *New York Times*, 30 June 2007. Available online: www.nytimes.com/2007/06/30/world/asia/30china.html?ex=1340856000&en=11e3c6f4c6445e93&ei=5088&partner=rssnyt&emc=rss (accessed 3 July 2007).

Kennedy, J.J. (2007) 'The implementation of village elections and tax-for-fee reform in rural Northwest China', in E. Perry and M. Goldman (eds), *Grassroots Political Reform in Contemporary China*, Cambridge, MA: Harvard University Press, pp. 48–74.

Keohane, R.O. and Nye, J.S., Jr. (2000) 'Introduction', in R.O. Keohane and J.S. Nye Jr. (eds), *Governance in a Globalizing World*, Washington, DC: Brookings Institution, pp. 1–44.

Klingner, D.E. and Nalbandian, J. (1998) *Public Personnel Management: Contexts and Strategies*, New Jersey: Prentice-Hall.

Lai, H.H. (2003) 'Local governments and China's WTO entry', *American Asian Review*, 21 (3), 153–86.

Lam, W.F. (2005) 'Coordinating the government bureaucracy in Hong Kong: An institutional analysis', *Governance*, 18 (4), 633–54.

Lan, X. (2006) 'Qiye banshi fudan jianqing yiban' (The burdens on enterprises were slashed by a half), *Zhongguo jingji shibao* (China Economics Times), 9 January 2006. Available online: www.cet.com.cn/20060109/GUONEI/200601096.htm (accessed 19 February 2006).

Langton, S. (1978) 'What is citizen participation?', in S. Langton (ed.), *Citizen Participation in America: Essays on the State of the Art*, Lexington, MA: Lexington Books, pp. 13–24.

Lardy, N. (2002) *Integrating China into the Global Economy*, Washington, DC: Brookings Institution Press.

Laurenceson, J. and Chai, J.C.H. (2003) *Financial Reform and Economic Development in China*, Cheltenham, UK; Northhampton, MA: Edward Elgar.

Law Committee, Standing Committee of NPC (1994) *Zhonghua renmin gongheguo falü fagui – xingzhengfa 1* (Laws and Regulations of the People's Republic of China: Administrative Law, Vol. 1), 3-4-1-IV.22.

Leach, W.D., Pelkey, N.W. and Sabatier, P.A. (2002) 'Stakeholder partnerships as collaborative policymaking: evaluation criteria applied to watershed management in California and Washington', *Journal of Policy Analysis and Management*, 21 (4), 645–70.

Leading Cadre's Office of Open Recruitment in Guangdong Province (2001) *Kuashiji gongxuan* (Open Recruitment at the Turn of the Century), Guangzhou: Guangdong People Press.

Lee, H.Y. (1991) *From Revolutionary Cadres to Party Technocrats in Socialist China*, Berkeley, CA: University of California Press.

Lei, X. (2008) 'Yi jijin zhen hou de erbai sishi xiaoshi' (One Foundation and 240 hours after the Earthquake), *Sina.Com.* Available online: http://finance.sina.com.cn/g/20080529/09484923805.shtml (accessed 23 July 2008).

Li, G. (2004) 'Lun cunmin weiyuanhui xuanju yu jumin weiyuanhui xuanju de qubie yu jingji chengyin' (The difference between the election in village committees and residents' committees and the economic factors underlying the difference), *Honghe xuebao baokan* (Journal of Honghe University), 3, 20–2.

—— (2000) 'Difang jigou gaige jinrui shishi jieduan' (Administrative reform in local governments is in implementation stage), *Zhongguo gongwuyuan* (Chinese Public Servants), 4, 15.

Li, J. (2006) 'Guanyu er ling ling wu nian zhongyang yusuan zhixing de shenji gongzuo baogao (jiexuan)- er ling ling liu nian liu yue ershiqi ri zai dishijie quanguo renmin daibiao dahui changwu lishihui di'ershierci huiyi shang' (An abstract of audit report of 2005 central budget execution presented to the twenty-second meeting of Standing Committee of the Tenth National People's Congress on 27 June 2006), in Finance Yearbook of China Editorial Committee (ed.), *Zhongguo caizheng nianjian 2006* (Finance Yearbook of China 2006), Beijing: China Finance Press, pp. 11–13.

Li, L.C. (2006) 'Embedded institutionalization: Sustaining rural tax reform in China', *The Pacific Review*, 19 (1), 63–84.

—— (2004) 'Political trust in rural China', *Modern China*, 30 (2), 228–58.

—— (2003) 'Towards a public and comprehensive budget: Public finance reforms in Guangdong', in J.Y.S. Cheng (ed.), *Guangdong: Preparing for the WTO Challenge*, Hong Kong: The Chinese University Press, pp. 51–80.

Li, P. and Xu, H. (2006) *Zhongguo zhengfu jian caizheng guanxi tujie* (A Graphic Explanation of Inter-governmental Fiscal Relationship in China), Beijing: China Finance Press.

Li, R. (2008) 'Schools don't get minimum legal funding, report says: education investment not keeping pace with economic boom', *South China Morning Post*, 1 January 2008.

Li, S. (2000) 'Competition in the sunlight – Party and government organs at all levels promote appointment to posts by competition' (text), Beijing *Xinhua Domestic Service* (in Chinese) (28 August, 2000), transl. the Foreign Broadcast Information Service. FBIS Daily Report – China (PrEx.7.10: FBIS-CHI-2000-0828).

Li, W., Qiang, C.Z. and Xu, L.C. (2005) 'Regulatory reforms in the telecommunications sector in developing countries: The role of democracy and private interests', *World Development*, 33 (8), 1307–24.

Li, X. (2007) 'Hubei shequ juweihui zhixuan jiang da wucheng' (Fifty per cent of the seats in Hubei's residents' committees will be returned through direct election), *Takungpao.com.* Available online: www.takungpao.com/news/07/07/19/ZM-767899.htm (accessed 19 July 2007).

Li, Z. (2004) 'Shenji zaixian fengbao zhenjing Zhongnanhai: youchachu weigui jin'e yu erwanyi' (Audit report shocked Zhongnanhai again. Abuse of public monies worth over 2 trillion yuan was uncovered), *Cheng Ming Yuekan* (Voice out Monthly), 9, 14–16.

Lieberthal, K.G. (1992) 'Introduction: The "fragmented authoritarianism" model and its limitations', in K.G. Lieberthal and D.M. Lampton (eds), *Bureaucracy, Politics and Decision Making in Post-Mao China*, Berkeley, CA: University of California Press, pp. 1–32.

Lin, S. (2003a) 'Shanghai moshi: jumin weiyuanhui yu shequ minzhu' (Shanghai model: Residents' committees and community democracy), in S. Lin (ed.), *Shequ minzhu yu zhili: anli yanjiu* (Research on Cases of Community Democratic Governance), Beijing: Social Sciences Documentation Press, 1–39.

—— (2003b) 'Shequ xuanju: xuanju dongyuan yu canyu jiegou' (Community democracy: electoral mobilization and the profile of voters), in S. Lin (ed.), *Shequ minzhu yu zhili*, (Research on Cases of Community Democratic Governance), Beijing: Social Sciences Documentation Press, 69–106.

Lin, Y. (2007) 'Nongcun zoujiao beihou' (Behind the part-time rural teachers), *Liaowang xinwen zhoukan* (Outlook weekly), 12 February, 7, 16–17.

Lin, Y. and Ren, L. (2007) 'Ganbu gongtuichaxuan zai kaocha' (A re-visit of mass nomination and election of cadres with candidates more than the number of seats contested), *Liaowang* (Outlook weekly), 5, 44–5.

Liou, Tom K.T. (1998) *Managing Economic Reforms in Post-Mao China*, Westport, CT: Praeger Publishers.

Liu, M. and Tao, R. (2007) 'Local governance, policy mandates and fiscal reform in China', in V. Shue and C. Wong (eds), *Paying for Progress in China: Public Finance, Human Welfare and Changing Patterns of Inequality*, New York: Routledge, pp. 166–89.

Liu, Q. (2006) 'Xian guan xiang yong huo le xiang cai' (Management of township-level treasury by county governments is conducive to the fiscal health of township-level governments), *Zhongguo caijing bao* (China Financial and Economic Times), 5 September 2006.

Liu, X. (2007) 'Tingzhenghui biancheng zhangjiahui. Gonggongchanpin weihe zhangbuxiu?' (Public hearing meetings have become price hike meetings. Why does the fee of public service keep rising?), *Renmin wang* (PeopleNet). Available online: http://finance.people.com.cn/GB/8215/80348/80771/5569541.html (accessed 15 September 2007).

—— (2006) 'Renli sanlunche paizhao shiyongquan ruci bi shouwei – dui yiqi xingzheng xuke anjian de falv fengshi' (A case study on a licensing issue over recalling business permits of man-powered tricycle), *Zhongguo wang* (ChinaNet). Available online: www.china.org.cn/chinese/law/603503.htm (accessed 20 January 2006).

Liu, Y. (2004) 'Zhangxin: gongwuyuan gai na duoshao qian' (Pay hike: How much salary should civil servants make?), *Zhongguo Xinwen zhoukan* (China News Weekly), 13 September, 26–7.

Liu, Y. and Pang, Z. (2003) 'Tingzheng zhidu: zhongguo gonggong juece minzhuhua de xinjizhi – yi tielu piaojia tingzheng hui wei li' (Public hearing: A new mechanism of democratic governance in China), in F. Li (ed.), *Zhongguo jiceng minzhu fazhan baogao* (A Report on the Development of China's Grassroots Democracy, 2002), Xian: Xibei University Press: 279–94.

Liu, Z. (2003) *Diqici geming: 1998 – 2003 Zhongguo zhengfu jigou gaige wenti baogao* (The Seventh Revolution: A Report on Structural Reform of Chinese Government 1998–2003), Beijing: China Social Sciences Press.

Lu, R. (1997) *Shenzhen ganbu zhidu gaigelun* (Discussions on the Reform of the Cadre System in Shenzhen), Guangzhou: Haitian Press.

Lü, X. (2000) *Cadres and Corruption: The Organizational Involution of the Chinese Communist Party*, Stanford, CA: Stanford University Press.

—— (1999) 'From rank-seeking to rent-seeking: Changing administrative ethos and corruption in reform China', *Crime, Law and Social Change*, 32 (4), 347–70.

Lü, X. and Perry, E. (eds) (1997) *Danwei: The Changing Chinese Workplace in Historical and Comparative Perspective*, Armonk, NY: Sharpe.

Lu, Y. (2007) 'The autonomy of Chinese NGOs: A new perspective', *China: An International Journal*, 5 (2), 173–203.

Lu, Z. (2006) 'Xingzheng weifa beihou de quli dongji' (A motive of profit seeking behind violating administrative laws), *Jinyangwang* (Golden Goat Net). Available online: www.ycwb.com/gb/content/2006-03/26/content_1093901.htm (accessed 31 March 2006).

Luo, B. (2005) 'Shenjizhang Li Jinhua yongzhan He Guoqiang (Auditor-General Li Jinhua confronted with He Guoqiang), *Cheng Ming Yuekan* (Voice out Monthly), 4, 10–11.

—— (2004) 'Gaoxinyanglian yansheng minfen' (Combating corruption by raising civil servants' salary lead to public outcry), *Cheng Ming Yuekan* (Voice out Monthly), 4, 11–12.

Luo, J. and Yu, G. (2005) 'Xingzheng xukefa dailai "guanli zhenkong"' (Has administrative licensing law result in 'management in vacuum'), *Zhejiang rendai* (Zhejiang People's Congress), 6, 21–3.

Luo, Y., Qiu, C. and Li, L. (2006) 'Guangzhou shishi xingzheng xukefa yi zhounian, suoyou tousu jiben dedao tuoshan chuli' (All complaints in Guangzhou city have been basically settled after Administrative Licensing Law was implemented for one year), *Jinyangwang* (Golden Goat Net). Available online: www.ycwb.com/gb/content/2005-07/06/content_935501.htm (accessed 31 March 2006).

Ma, H. (2006) 'Shuizai xuzhi xingzheng xukefa' (Who put aside Administrative Licensing Law?), in *Fashou* (Search of Law). Available online: www.fsou.com/html/text/art/3355744/335574481.html (accessed 20 January 2006).

Ma, J. (2006) 'Zero-based budgeting in China: Experiences of Hubei province', *Journal of Public Budgeting, Accounting and Financial Management*, 18 (4), 480–510.

Ma, Q. (2006) *Non-Governmental Organizations in Contemporary China: Paving the Way to Civil Society*, New York: Routledge.

Ma, Q. and Luo, X. (2005) 'Zuoda shouru dangao, tigao baozhang nengli' (Raising revenue and expanding welfare coverage), in Finance Yearbook of China Editorial Committee (ed.), *Zhongguo caizheng nianjian 2005* (2005 Finance Yearbook of China), Beijing: China Finance Press, pp. 54–7.

Ma, Y. (2004) 'Contract employees add new dimension to civil service', *China Daily*, 7 January. Available online: www.chinadaily.com.cn/en/doc/2004-01/07/content_296418.htm (accessed 14 May 2005).

Manion, M. (2000) 'Chinese democratization in perspective: electorates and selectorates at the township level', *China Quarterly*, 163, 764–83.

—— (1993) *Retirement of Revolutionaries in China*, Princeton, NJ: Princeton University Press.

Mao, H. and Yang, Y. (2007) 'Chengzhen yiliao baowang libucongxin' (The limitations of urban health care net), *Liaowang xinwen zhoukan* (Outlook Weekly), 12 February, 7, 62–3.

Mao, Q. and Ming, L. (2006) 'Xingzheng xukefa ke yianjiedu la' (Case studies of administrative licensing law are available), *Sina xinwen zhongxin* (Sina News Centre). Available online: http://news.sina.com.cn/o/2005-11-03/07047347027s.shtml (accessed 30 March 2006).

Matland, R.E. (1995) 'Synthesizing the implementation literature: The ambiguity-conflict model of policy implementation', *Journal of Public Administration Research and Theory*, 5 (2), 146–70.

Meng, Y. (2004) 'New licensing law streamlines bureaucracy', *China Daily*, 1 July. Available online: www.chinadaily.com.cn/english/doc/2004-07/01/content_344549.htm (accessed 24 February 2006).

Mertha, A.C. (2005) 'China's "soft" centralization: shifting *tiao/kuai* authority relations', *The China Quarterly*, 184, 791–810.

Ministry of Education (2005) *Zhongguo jiaoyu tongji nianjian 2005* (Statistics of Education in China 2005), Beijing: Beijing University of Technology.

Ministry of Finance (2005) 'Guanyu er ling ling si nian zhongyang he difang yusuan caoan de baogao' (A report on the execution of 2004 central and local budgets and 2005 central and local budget bill), *Zhongguo caizheng* (China State Finance), 4, 6–9.

Ministry of Health (2006) *Zhongguo weisheng tongji nianjian 2006* (Statistics of Health in China 2006), Beijing: Peking Union Medical College Press.

Ministry of Personnel, PRC (ed.) (1994) *Guojia gongwuyuan zhidu quanshu* (A Collection of Articles on State Civil Service System), Changchun: Jilin Literature and History Press.

Mueller, M. and Tan, Z. (1996) *China in the Information Age: Telecommunications and the Dilemmas of Reform*, Westport, CT: Praeger.

Murphy, R. (2007) 'Paying for education in rural China', in V. Shue and C. Wong (eds), *Paying for Progress in China: Public Finance, Human Welfare and Changing Patterns of Inequality*, New York: Routledge, pp. 65–95.

National Audit Office (2006) *Er ling ling liu nian di wu hao: Si shi er ge bumen 2005 niandu yusuan zhixing shenji jieguo gonggao (shang)* (2006 Directive No. 5 (The Audit Result on the Budget Execution of 42 Departments – First Volume)). Available online: www.audit.gov.cn/cysite/docpage/c516/200609/0911_516_17404.htm (accessed 20 November 2007).

National Bureau of Statistics (ed.) (2006) *Zhongguo tongji nianjian 2006* (China Statistical Yearbook 2006), Beijing: China Statistics Press.

National Bureau of Statistics (ed.) (1995) *Zhongguo tongji nianjian 1995* (China Statistical Yearbook 1995), Beijing: China Statistics Press.

'National People's Congress approves new Labour Contract Law', *China Labour Bulletin* (2007). Available online: http://iso.china-labour.org.hk/public/contents/news?revision%5fid=46521&item%5fid=46445 (accessed 28 July 2007).

Naughton, B.J. and Yang, D.L. (2004) 'Holding China together: Introduction', in B.J. Naughton and D.L. Yang (eds), *Holding China Together: Diversity and National Integration in the Post-Deng Era*, Cambridge: Cambridge University Press, pp. 1–28.

New China News Agency (ed.) (1996) *Zhongguo nianjian 1996* (Yearbook of China 1996), Beijing: Yearbook of China Press.

'New law to improve civil servant system', *China Daily*, 18 December 2004. Available online: www.chinadaily.com.cn/english/doc/2004-12/18/content_401238.htm (accessed 14 May 2005).

O'Brien, K.J. (2004) 'Villagers, elections, and citizenship in contemporary China', *Modern China*, 27 (4), 407–35.

—— (2002) 'Collective action in the Chinese countryside', *China Journal*, 48, 139–54.

OECD (2006) *Challenges for China's Public Spending: Toward Greater Effectiveness and Equity*, Paris: OECD.

—— (2002) *China in the World Economy: The Domestic Policy Challenges*, Paris: OECD.

—— (2001) *Citizens as Partners: Information, Consultation and Public Participation in Policy-Making*, Paris: OECD.

—— (1997) *Performance Pay Schemes for Public Sector Managers: An Evaluation of the Impacts*, Paris: OECD.

Ogden, S. (2002) *Inklings of Democracy in China*, Cambridge, MA; London: Harvard University Asia Center.

Oi, J.C. (1999) *Rural China Takes Off: Institutional Foundations of Economic Reform*, Berkeley, CA: University of California Press.

Ong, L. (2006) 'The political economy of township government debt, township enterprises and rural financial institutions in China', *China Quarterly*, 186, 377–400.

Organization Department of CCP Shanxi Provincial Committee (1999) 'Guanyu jinzhong diqu ganbu zhidu gaige de tiaocha' (A survey concerning cadre system reform in Jinzhong prefecture), in Research Office, Organization Department of CCP Central Committee (ed.), *Shisida yilai ganbuzhidu gaige jinyan xuanbian* (A Collection of Articles on Cadre System Reform since the 14th National Congress of the Communist Party of China), Beijing: Party Building Readings Press, pp. 41–8.

Ostrom, V. and Ostrom, E. (2000) 'Public choice: A different approach to the study of public administration', in M.D. McGinnis (ed.), *Polycentric Games and Institutions: Readings from the Workshop in Political Theory and Policy Analysis*, Ann Arbor, MI: The University of Michigan Press, pp. 34–55.

O'Toole, L.J., Jr. (1989) 'Alternative mechanisms for multiorganizational implementation: The case of wastewater management', *Administration and Society*, 21 (3), 312–39.

Painter, M. and Pierre, J. (2005) 'Unpacking policy capacity: Issues and themes', in M. Painter and J. Pierre (eds), *Challenges to State Policy Capacity: Global Trends and Comparative Perspectives*, Houndmills; New York: Palgrave Macmillan, pp. 1–18.

Paler, L. (2005) 'China's legislation law and the making of a more orderly and representative legislative system', *China Quarterly*, 182, 301–18.

Palumbo, D.J. and Nachmias, D. (1987) 'The preconditions for successful evaluation: Is there an ideal paradigm?', *Policy Studies Review*, 7 (1), 67–79.

Pan, P.P. (2004) 'China's orphans feel brunt of power: Party thwarts AIDS activist's unofficial school', *Washington Post*, 14 September, A01.

Pang, Z., Xue, L., Jin, O. and Shen, Y (2004) 'Zhongguo lifa tingzheng zhidu de shizhen fengshi' (A case study of public hearing over lawmaking in China), in Z. Pang, L. Xue and O. Jin (eds), *Tingzheng zhidu: touming xueche yu gonggong zhili* (Public Hearing Systems in China: Transparent Policy-Making and Public Governance), Beijing: Tsinghua University Press, pp. 99–157.

Pang, Z., Xue, L. and Shen, Y. (2004) 'Zhongguo tingzheng zhidu de diwei, gongneng yu chengxu' (The status, functions, and procedures of public hearing in China), in Z. Pang, L. Xue and O. Jin (eds), *Tingzheng zhidu: touming juece yu gonggong zhili* (Public Hearing Systems in China: Transparent Policy-Making and Public Governance), Beijing: Tsinghua University Press, pp. 26–40.

Peerenboom, R. (2001) 'Globalization, path dependency and the limits of law: Administrative law reform and rule of law in the People's Republic of China', *Berkeley Journal of International Law*, 19 (2), 161–264.

Pei, M. (2008) *China's Trapped Transition: The Limits of Developmental Autocracy*, Cambridge, MA: Harvard University Press.

Peng, Y. (1995) 'Yixie xiangzhen qiye renyuan suzhi piandi qianjing kanyou' (The low qualifications of employees in some township and village enterprises are worrisome), *Zhongguo renshi* (Chinese Personnel), 11, 48.

'Personnel reforms produce results', *China Daily*, 14 November 2001. Available online: www.chinadaily.com.cn/en/doc/2001-09/22/content_84847.htm (accessed 19 March 2005).

Pocha, J.S. (2007) 'The last "competitive advantage": Letter from China', *The Nation*. Available online: www.thenation.com/doc/20070604/pocha (accessed 28 July 2007).

'Public hearings system in China needs improvements: experts' (2004), *China Elections and Governance*. Available online: www.chinaelections.org/en/readnews.asp?newsid= {FDA1EC58–7565–45DE-AAD3–2165432CAD9B}&classid=16&classname=Govern ment (accessed 29 July 2007).

Pynes, J.E. (1997) *Human Resources Management for Public and Nonprofit Organizations*, San Francisco, CA: Jossey-Bass Publishers.

Qian, Y. and Weingast, B.R. (1995) *China's Transition to Markets: Market-Preserving Federalism, Chinese Style*, Stanford, CA: Hoover Institution on War, Revolution and Peace, Stanford University.

Qin, J. (1996) 'Guangxi, Henan officials disciplined for corruption' (text), Beijing *Xinhua* (in Chinese) (2 May), transl. Foreign Broadcast Information Service. FBIS Daily Report – China, 8 May 1996. (PrEx.7.10: FBIS-CHI-96-089).

'Quanfangwei kaizhan guojia gongwuyuan peixun gongzuo' (Civil Service Training in Full Swing), *Sichuan renshi* (Sichuan Personnel), 304, 2000, 12–13.

Read, B.L. (2003) '"Democratizing the neighbourhood?" New private housing and home-owner self-organization in urban China', *The China Journal*, 49, 31–59.

—— (2000) 'Revitalizing the state's urban "nerve tips"', *China Quarterly*, 163, 806–20.

'Reform civil servants' pay', *China Daily*, 10 November 2004. Available online: www. chinadaily.com.cn/english/doc/2004-11/10/content_390114.htm (accessed 14 May 2005).

Renmin ribao (People's Daily), 1 August 1988.

'Renshi gongzuo' (Personnel work) (2001), *People Daily*. Available online: www.peo-pledaily.com.cn/electric/hh50/1/1_3_1.html (29 December 2005).

Renshi zhengce fagui zhuankan (A Collection of Personnel Policies and Regulations), 1994, 68, 17–20.

Research Team on Improving the Mechanism of Financing Rural Voluntary Education (2005) 'Keguan pingjia nongcun yiwu jiaoyu caizheng baozhang jizhi fazhan de lishi guocheng' (An objective valuation of the historical development of rural voluntary education fund), *Caizheng yanjiu* (Public Finance Research), 7, 7.

Rojas, A. (2007) 'Unions in L.A., China team up', *Fresno Bee*. Available online: www. fresnobee.com/263/story/78728.html (accessed 9 July 2007).

Rothstein, B. (1996) 'Political institutions: An overview', in R.E. Goodin and H.D. Klin-gemann (eds), *A New Handbook of Political Science*, New York: Oxford University Press, pp. 133–66.

Ruttan, V.W. (1998) 'Designing institutions for sustainability', in E.T. Loehman and D.M. Kilgour (eds), *Designing Institutions for Environmental and Resource Management*, Cheltenham: Edward Elgar, pp. 142–64.

Sabatier, P.A. (1991) 'Towards better theories of the policy process', *PS: Political Science and Politics*, 24 (2), 147–56.

'Sanya paimai shijie changguan' (Sanya city auctioned the venue hosting Miss World Beauty Contest), *Mingpao Daily News*, 23 May 2007. Available online: http://hk.news. yahoo.com/070522/12/27yos.html (accessed 29 May 2007).

Sato, H. (2003) *The Growth of Market Relations in Post-Reform Rural China: A Micro-Analysis of Peasants, Migrants and Peasant Entrepreneurs*, New York: RoutledgeCur-zon.

Shang, X. (2007) 'Guojia zai shehui fuwu zhong de quewei: fuwuxing gongmin shehui zuzhi de ge an yanjiu' (The limitation of the state in social service provision), in X. Shang (ed.), *Chongji yu biange: duiwai kaifang zhong de zhongguogongmin shehui zuzhi* (Challenges and reforms: China's civil society in the reform era), Beijing: Chinese Social Sciences Press, pp. 298–309.

Shang, X., Wu, X. and Wu, Y. (2005) 'Welfare provision for vulnerable children: The missing role of the state', *China Quarterly*, 181, 122–36.

Shen, J. (2006) 'Shilun woguo lifa tingzheng chengxu de jiangou – cong geren suodeshui xiuding tingzhenghui shuoqi' (Institutionalization of legislation public hearing: Public hearing on revised Bill of Individual Income Tax), *Zhongguo baoan* (China Security Service), 160, 21–3.

Shen, Z. (2007) 'Shekeyuan baodao: Zhongguo shi rencai wailiu zui yanzhong guojia' (A report of Chinese Academy of Social Sciences: The brain drain problem of China is the most serious), *Lianhe zaobao* (United Daily), 7 April, 19.

Shi, T. (1997) *Political Participation in Beijing*, Cambridge, MA: Harvard University Press.

Shi, Z. (2006) 'Geren suodeshui fa tingzhenghui yu woguo shuishou lifa chengxu de wanshan' (Public hearing on Individual Income Tax Law and improvement of tax legislative procedures), *Shuiwu yanjiu* (Research of Taxation), 252, 53–6.

'Shizhengfu tisu xiaoguo xianzhu' (City government made progress in improving administrative efficiency), *Shenzhen tequ bao* (Shenzhen Special Zone Daily), 15 October 2001.

Shue, V. (1994) 'State power and social organization in China', in J.S. Migdal, A. Kohli and V. Shue (eds), *State Power and Social Forces: Domination and Transformation in the Third World*, Cambridge: Cambridge University Press, pp. 65–88.

Solinger, D.J. (2004) 'Policy consistency in the midst of the Asian crisis', in B.J. Naughton and D.L. Yang (eds), *Holding China Together: Diversity and National Integration in the Post-Deng Era*, Cambridge: Cambridge University Press, pp. 149–92.

Song, H., Jiang, Y., Liu, L., Yang, Y., Jia, Y., and Wang, T. (2004) *Zhongguo xiangcun cai zheng yu gonggong guanli yanjiu* (A Research of Finance and Public Management), Beijing: China Finance and Economics Press.

Speed, P.A. (2004) *Energy Policy and Regulation in the People's Republic of China*, The Hague: Kluwer Law International.

Stiglitz, J. (1999) 'Economics in government', a 1998 lecture, quoted from F. Forte, 'Government policies and the budget process', in S.S. Campo (ed.), *Governance, Corruption and Public Financial Management*, Manila: Asian Development Bank, pp. 21–46.

Study Group of Civil Service Examination and Appointment (1995) 'Gongwuyuan luyong: quanguo dazhuizong' (Civil service examination and appointment: A national overview), *Zhongguo rencai* (Chinese Talent), 11, 17–20.

Study Group of the Organisation Department of the CCP Guangxi Autonomous Region Committee (1999) 'Wending bianjiang he shaoshuminzu diqu ganbu duiwu duice yanjiu baogao' (A research report on stabilising the cadres in bordering regions and minority inhabited regions), in Research Office of the Organisation Department of the CCP Central Committee (ed.), *Zuzhi gongzuo yanjiu wenxuan (zhong)* (A Collection of Research Manuscripts of Organisation Work, Vol. 2), Beijing: Party Building Readings Press, pp. 335–49.

Study Group of the Organisation Department of the CCP Qinghai Provincial Committee (1999) 'Wending qingzhang gaoyuan ganbu duiwu duice yanjiu' (A research on stabilising the cadres in Qingzhang plateau), in Research Office of the Organisation Department of the CCP Central Committee (ed.), *Zuzhi gongzuo yanjiu wenxuan (zhong)* (A Collection of Research Manuscripts of Organisation Work, Vol. 2), Beijing: Party Building Readings Press, pp. 388–401.

Study Group of the Research Office of the Organisation Department of the CCP Central Committee (1999) 'Guanyu wending bianjiang he shaoshuminzu diqu ganbu duiwu duice yanjiu baogao' (A research report on stabilising the cadres in bordering regions and minority inhabited regions), in Research Office of the Organisation Department of the CCP Central Committee (ed.), *Zuzhi gongzuo yanjiu wenxuan (zhong)* (A Collection of Research Manuscripts of Organisation Work, Vol. 2), Beijing: Party Building Readings Press, pp. 293–302.

Study Group of Organisation Department, Liaoning Province Party Committee (1999) 'Guanyu wanshan xianshi dangzheng lingdao banzi gongzuo shizhi kaoke zibao tixi wenti de yanjiu baogao' (A research report concerning improving performance indicators for evaluating the leadership groups in county/ city governments), in Study Group of the Organisation Department of the CCP Central Committee (ed.), *Zuzhi gongzuo yanjiu wenxuan (shang)* (A Collection of Research Manuscripts of Organisation Work, Vol. 1), Beijing: Party Building Readings Press, p. 180.

Su, F. (2004) 'The political economy of industrial restructuring in China's coal industry, 1992–1999', in B.J. Naughton and D.L. Yang (eds), *Holding China Together: Diversity and National Integration in the Post-Deng Era*, Cambridge: Cambridge University Press, pp. 226–52.

Takahara, A. (1992) *The Politics of Wage Policy in Post-Revolutionary China*, London: Macmillan.

Tang, M. and Sun, S. (2004) 'Officials to be rated on pollution control', *China Daily*, 10 March. Available online: www.chinadaily.com.cn/english/doc/2004-03/10/content_313249.htm (accessed 25 April 2004).

'The greener the better', *China Daily*, 9 September 2006. Available online: www.chinadaily.com.cn/cndy/2006-09/09/content_684979.htm (accessed 12 October 2006).

Tian, S. (2007) 'Guan duo wei huan shuzi jingren: shengbu gaoguan yi wan san qian yu fanlan chengzai' (The bureaucracy size is astonishing: Officials at ministerial/provincial level number over 13,000), *Cheng Ming Yuekan* (Voice out Monthly), 4, 17–18.

'Tixian kexue fazhan yaoqiu de difang lingdao' (Local leadership groups living up to scientific outlook of development) (2007), *Nanyang Dangjian* (Nanyang Party Building). Available online: www.nydj.org.cn/Article/zcfg/200707/218.html (accessed 16 November 2007).

Townsend, J.R. (1969) *Political Participation in Communist China*, Berkeley and Los Angeles, CA: University of California Press.

Tran, E. (2003) 'From senior official to top civil servant: An enquiry into the Shanghai Party school', *China Perspectives*, 46, 32–47.

'Trial of Chinese "Green" activist postponed', the *Straits Times*, 9 June 2007.

Unger, J. and Chan, A. (1996) 'Corporatism in China: A developmental state in an East Asian Context', in B.L. McCormick and J. Unger (eds), *China after Socialism: In the Footsteps of Eastern Europe or East Asia*, Armonk, NY: M.E. Sharpe, 95–129.

—— (1995) 'China, corporatism, and the East Asian model', *The Australian Journal of Chinese Affairs*, 33, 29–53.

Walder, A. (1986) *Communist Neo-Traditionalism: Work and Authority in Chinese Industry*, Berkeley, CA: University of California Press.

Wang, D. (2005) 'Caizheng guoku guanli zhidu gaige' (Reform of public finance management), in Finance Yearbook of China Editorial Committee (ed.), *Zhongguo caizheng nianjian 2005* (2005 Finance Yearbook of China), Beijing: China Finance Press, pp. 34–6.

Wang, J. (2007) 'Xiamen mayor offers protesters some hope: Chemical plant might be axed after study', *South China Morning Post*, 7 June.

Wang, L. (1998) 'Reform of party and government organisations advances steadily' (text)

156   Bibliography

Beijing *Xinhua* (in Chinese) (7 May 1998), transl. by the Foreign Broadcast Information Service. FBIS Daily Report – China, 8 May 1998 (PrEx.7.10: FBIS-CHI-98-127).

Wang, M. (2002) *Fei yingli zuzhi guanli gailun* (An Introduction of NGO Management), Beijing: People's University of China Press.

Wang, S. (2008) 'Changing models of China's policy agenda setting', *Modern China*, 34 (1), 56–87.

—— (2006) 'Regulating death at coalmines: Changing mode of governance in China', *Journal of Contemporary China*, 46, 1–30.

Wang, S. and Hu, A. (1999) *The Chinese Economy in Crisis: State Capacity and Tax Reform*, Armonk, NY; London: M.E. Sharpe.

Wang, X. (2001) 'Assessing public participation in U.S. cities', *Public Performance and Management Review*, 24 (4), 322–36.

—— (2006) 'Zhongguo nongcun weisheng shiye fazhan de caizheng zhichi zhengce' (China's financial policy of towards rural health care), *Caizheng yanjiu*, (Public Finance Research), 3, 45–6.

Wang, X. and Wart, M.W. (2007) 'When public participation in administration leads to trust: an empirical assessment of managers' perceptions', *Public Administration Review*, 67 (2), 265–78.

Wang, Y. (2004) 'Xiangzhen jigou gaige de nandian ji duize' (Solutions to the problems of administrative reform in township-level governments), *Lilun guanche* (Theory Observe), 2, 25–7.

Wang, Z. (2007) 'Public support for democracy', *Journal of Contemporary China*, 53, 561–79.

Wang, Z. and Zhang, R. (2007) 'Gaoshoufei beihou' (The reasons for high fees), *Liaowang xinwen zhoukan* (Outlook Weekly), 8, 26–7.

'Wang Zhaoguo zai quanzong shisijie sici zhiweihuiyi shang de jianghua' (The speech of Wang Zhaoguo in the fourth executive committee of the Fourteenth National Congress of All-China Federation of Trade Unions), *Zhonghua quanguo zonggonghui* (All-China Federation of Trade Unions). Available online: www.acftu.org/template/10004/file. jsp?cid=318&aid=53833 (accessed 3 October 2007).

Wanna, J. (2003) 'Introduction: The changing role of central budget agencies', in J. Wanna, L. Jensen and J. de Vries, J. (eds), *Controlling Public Expenditure: The Changing Roles of Central Budget Agencies*, Cheltenham: Edward Elgar.

Weatherly, R. and Lipsky, M. (1977) 'Street-level bureaucrats and institutional innovation: Implementing special education reform', *Harvard Educational Review*, 47 (2), 171–91.

Wen, H. *et al.* (2001). *Zhongguo zhengfu rengong chengben* (Wage Cost of Chinese Government), Beijing: China Personnel Press.

Wen, H. and Chang, Y. (2004) 'Weixian shencha haizai yunchu' (Constitutional review is still looming), *Zhongguo xinwen zhoukan* (China News Weekly), 185, 31–3.

Western Development Office (2008) 'Bupingfan de wu nian: xibu dakaifa zhanlue shishi wunianlai jinzhan qingkuang' (The usual five years: The progress of western development in the past five years). Available online: www.chinawest.gov.cn/web/NewsInfo. asp?NewsId=28366 (accessed 13 February 2008).

White, G., Howell, J. and Shang, X. (1996) *In Search of Civil Society: Market Reform and Social Change in Contemporary China*, Oxford: Clarendon Press.

Wong, C.P.W. (2000) 'Central-local relations revisited: The 1994 tax-sharing reform and public expenditure management in China', *China Perspectives*, 31, 52–63.

—— (1997) 'Overview of issues in local public finance in the PRC', in C.P.W. Wong (ed.), *Financing Local Government in the People's Republic of China*, New York: Oxford University Press, pp. 1–26.

Wong, C.P.W., Heady, C. and Woo, W.T. (1995) *Fiscal Management and Economic Reform in the People's Republic of China*, Hong Kong: Oxford University Press.

World Bank (2006) *World Development Indicators 2006*, Washington, DC: World Bank.

—— (2005) *World Development Report 2005 – A Better Investment Climate for Everyone*, Washington, DC: The World Bank and Oxford University Press.

—— (2004) *Governance and Anti-Corruption 2004*. Available online: http://info.worldbank.org/governance/kkz2004/sc_chart.asp (accessed 18 April 2006).

—— (2004) *World Development Indicators 2004*, Washington, DC: World Bank.

—— (1994) *Rehabilitation Loan: Preidentified Import Component Distribution Monitoring Report*, Washington, DC: Russia Department, World Bank.

World Trade Organisation (2004) *Report of the Working Party on the Accession to China*. Available online: http://docsonline.wto.org/DDFDocuments/t/WT/min01/3.doc (accessed 17 February 2004).

Wu, J. (2007) 'Call for officials to be judged on housing efforts', *China Daily*, 19 September 2007.

Xi, L. (2002) *Zhongguo gongyuyuan zhidu* (Chinese Civil Service System), Beijing: Tsinghua University Press.

'Xiamen protesters demand scrapping of chemical plant', the *Straits Times*, 2 June 2007.

Xiao, H. (2006) 'Yanggang shi xingzheng xing shoufei xiangmu taiduo taigui yao zhengdun' (Yanggang city has to reduce the burdensome and expensive licensing items), *Jinyangwang* (Golden Goat Net). Available online: www.ycwb.com/gb/content/2004-11/05/content_789516.htm (accessed 31 March 2006).

'Xingzheng chufa fa' (Administrative Punishment Law), *China Court*. Available online: www.chinacourt.org/flwk/show1.php?file_id=24864&str1=%D0%D0%D5%FE%B4%A6%B7%A3%B7%A8 (accessed 12 April 2005).

'Xingzheng xukefa shishi, zhengfu zhi shou bude luanshen' (Government cannot arbitrarily intervene the daily lives of the citizens after Administration Licensing Law comes into effect), *Tom.Com*. Available online: http://news.tom.com/1002/20040630–1045934.htm (accessed 20 January 2006).

Xiong, L. (2007) 'NGOs finally accepted as valuable partners', *China Daily*, 13 April. Available online: www.mca.gov.cn/111/gongbao04.htm (accessed 28 July 2007).

Xu, B. (1999) 'Jumin weiyuanhui: zai guojia yu shehui zhi jian – Shanghai shi changheyuan xiaoqu gean yanjiu' (Residents' committees: Between the state and society – A case study of Changhe small community in Shanghai), *Huadong ligong daxue xuebao – sheke ban* (Journal of East China Polytechnic University – Social Sciences), 3, 87–8.

Xu, S. (1994) 'Zhongguo gongwuyuan zhidu de jianli yu tuixing' (Establishment and implementation of Chinese civil service system), in Ministry of Personnel, PRC (ed.), *Guojia gongwuyuan zhidu quanshu* (A Collection of Articles on State Civil Service System), Changchun: Jilin Literature and History Press, pp. 216–23.

Xue, X., Feng, J. and Wei, J. (2005) 'Dui Wanrong xiangzhen caizheng de diaocha' (A Survey of the financial status of the township-level governments under Wanrong county), *Shanxi Caizheng* (Shanxi Finance), 8, 41–2.

Yan, B. (2005) 'Shixian cong guanzhi dao fuwu de zhuanbian: xingzheng xuke fa shishi hou de daolu yunshu xingzheng shenpi gaige linian' (Transformation from regulation to service delivery: Reform of licensing in road transportation after Administrative Licensing Law comes into effect), *Tongling xueyuan xuebao* (Journal of Tongling College), 1, 43–5.

Yang, D.L. (2004) 'Economic transformation and state rebuilding in China', in B. Naughton and D.L. Yang (ed.), *Holding China Together: Diversity and National Integration in the Post-Deng Era*, West Nyack, NY: Cambridge University Press.

—— (2004) *Remaking the Chinese Leviathan: Market Transition and the Politics of Governance in China*, Stanford, CA: Stanford University Press, pp. 120–48.

Yang, G. (2005) 'Environmental NGOs and institutional dynamics in China', *China Quarterly*, 181, 46–66.

Yang, K. (2003) 'Assessing China's public price hearings: Symbolic aspects', *International Journal of Public Administration*, 26 (5), 497–534.

Yang, K. and Callahan, K. (2007) 'Citizen involvement efforts and bureaucratic responsiveness: participatory values, stakeholder pressures, and administrative practicality', *Public Administration Review*, 67 (2), 249–64.

Yang, S. (2006) 'Putong nongmin shangshu quanguo rendai, difang tudi fagui huode xiuzheng' (Local regulations have been amended because of a peasant's appeal to National People's Congress), *Jinyangwang* (Golden Goat Net). Available online: www.ycwb.com/gb/content/2005-06/07/content_916874.htm (accessed 31 March 2006).

Yang, X. and Gao, C. (2005) 'Mei bianzhi biexiang chihuangliang' (The payroll of officials who are not hired according to establishments plan cannot be covered by budgetary fund), *Zhongguo caijingbao* (China Finance and Economics Post), 13 September.

Yang, Y. and Zhang, B. (2001) 'Zhongguo chengzhen jumin xintai de diaocha yanjiu' (Social attitudes of urban residents), in X. Yu *et al.* (eds), *Zhongguo shehui xinxi fenxi yu yuce* (An analysis and forecast of Chinese society), Beijing: Social Sciences Documentation Press, pp. 27–43.

Yan, Z. (2005) 'Chengshi jumin shequ canyu zhi tezheng tanxi – yi Wuhan shi Yangyuan jiedao de shidi diaocha weili' (Analysis on characteristics of community participation of urban residents), *Huazhong keji daxue xue bao – shehui kexue ban* (Journal of Huazhong University of Science and Technology – Social Sciences Edition), 4, 61–5.

Yao, Z. and Hao, C. (2007) 'Xiao caizheng, da touru: Hainansheng shixian xinnonghe zhidu quansheng fugai' (Small budget but high government expenditure: The new rural cooperative system has been covered the whole Hainan province), *Zhongguo caizheng* (China State Finance), 2, 27–8.

Yearbook of China Audit Editorial Committee (2005) *Zhongguo shenji nianjian 2005* (Yearbook of China Audit 2005), Beijing: China Audit Press.

Yep, R. (2008) 'Enhancing the redistributive capacity of the Chinese state? Impact of fiscal reforms on county finance', *The Pacific Review*, 21 (2), 231–55.

—— (2004) 'Can "tax-for-fee" reform reduce rural tension in China? The process, progress and limitations', *China Quarterly*, 177, 42–70.

Yin, J. (2007) 'Yusuan shencha jiangcheng renda xinjiaodian' (Budget examination has become the focus in people's congress meetings), *Liaowang dongfang zhoukan* (Oriental Outlook), 12, 26–7.

Young, N. (2007) 'Move to prevent green protest shows uneven distribution of free speech', *China Development Brief*. Available online: www.chinadevelopmentbrief.com/node/1157 (accessed 18 July 2007).

'You yang chi gongkuan shuo kai qu' (A story about goats eating public funds), *Zhongguo caijing bao* (China Financial and Economic Times), 1 September 2006.

Yu, K. and Li, L. (2006) 'Shui zai canyu shequ gonggong shiwu – dui Wuhan shi 750 ming shequ jumin de diaocha yu fenxi' (Who participates in community affairs? An analysis of a survey of 750 residents in Wuhan), *Shequ* (Community), 4, 14–16.

Yu, X. (2006) 'Wo sheng nongzi zhuanying zhi sida guaizhuang' (Four strange issues in the monopoly of agricultural input), *Nanfang wang* (NanfangNet). Available online: www.southcn.com/nflr/nydkt/kandian/200512280247.htm (accessed 23 January 2006).

Yu, X. and Tan, Y. (2006) 'Huizhen nongzi zhuanying zhi liubi' (Collectively finding out the roots of monopoly of agricultural inputs), *Nanfang wang* (NanfangNet). Available online: www.southcn.com/nflr/nydkt/kandian/200512280248.htm (accessed 25 January 2006).

Yu, Y. (2007) 'Quanzong yu woerma juxing gaoceng huitan' (All-China Federation of Trade Unions held talks with Wal Mart), *Zhonghua quanguo zonggonghui* (All-China Federation of Trade Unions). Available online: www.acftu.org/template/10004/file. jsp?cid=222&aid=63830 (accessed 3 October 2007).

Yuan, Y. (2006) 'Caogen "NGO" yu gangguo "GONGO"' (Grassroots NGOs and government-organised NGOs), *Zhongguo xinwen zhoukan* (China Newsweek), 23 October, 44–5.

Yue, S. (2006) 'Jing, Hu, Yue, E zhengji zaojia' (Beijing, Shanghai, Guangdong and Hubei governments falsified working reports), *Cheng Ming Yuekan* (Voice out Monthly), 7, 16.

—— (2005) 'Li Jinhua yu jinrong jutou de yingzhang' (Li Jinhua in conflict with big shots in financial sector', *Cheng Ming Yuekan* (Voice out Monthly), 9, 16–18.

Zhang, B. (2007) 'Zhongguo caizheng zhengce fenxi' (An analysis of China's fiscal policy), in G. Bai and W. Shi (eds), *Zhongguo gonggong zhengce fenxi 2007* (Analysis of Public Policies of China 2007), Beijing: Chinese Social Sciences Press.

Zhang, M. (2007) 'Nongcun jiaoshi de linglei shengcun' (The alternate income of rural teachers), *Liaowang xinwen zhoukan* (Outlook Weekly), 7, 12 February, 17–18.

—— (2006) 'Assessing China's 1994 fiscal reforms: An intermediate report', *Journal of Public Budgeting, Accounting and Financial Management*, 18 (4), 453–77.

Zhang, S. (2006) 'Fahui caizheng zhineng zuoyong, cujin keji chuangxin nengli de tigao' (Fully utilising fiscal strength to promote innovation), *Zhongguo caizheng* (China State Finance), 9, 20–1.

Zhang, Z. (2005) 'Jiage tingzheng kunjing de jiejue zhi dao' (Solutions to the problems of implementing price hearing), *Fashang yanjiu* (Research of Law and Business), 2, 32–3.

Zhao, H. (2007) 'Juweihui zuzhifa' (Urban Residents' Committees Law), *Neimengu xinwen wang* (Inner Mongolia News Web). Available online: http://js116114.cn/ information/article/20051104/24604_2.html (accessed 15 September 2007).

—— (1997) 'Ruci "jiangli" jixu zhizhi' (This kind of 'reward' should be ruled out), *Renshi* (Personnel), 136, 34–6.

Zhao, J. and Yang, M. (2006) '"Sanbao" bao Jiangxi nongcun yiwu jiaoyu jingfei' (Three measures to guarantee Jiangxi province's rural education fund), *Zhongguo caizheng* (China State Finance), 3, 14–15.

Zhao, Y. (2006) 'Rang xingzheng xukefa yingqilai' (Enforcing administrative licensing law with vigor), *Zhongguo wang* (ChinaNet). Available online: www.china.org.cn/ chinese/law/650395.htm (accessed 19 January 2006).

Zheng, C. (2004) 'Civil servants' study allowance sparks', *China Daily*, 7 September. Available online: www.chinadaily.com.cn/english/doc/2004-09/07/content_372260.htm (accessed 15 December 2004).

Zheng, J. and Su, X. (2007) 'Weirao tigao "liangge nengli" jiji tuijin hezuo yiliao jiankang fazhan' (Proactively promoting the development of health cooperative system through strengthening 'two capabilities'), *Zhongguo caizheng* (China Finance), 2, 29–31.

'Zhengfu shouzhi fenlei gaige fangan: Caizhengbu yusuan [2006] shisan hao' (A blueprint of reforming the classification of government expenditure: Ministry of Finance Budget No. 13' (2006), *Caizheng jiandu* (Financial Scrutiny), 5.

Zhong, Y. (2003), *Local Government and Politics in China: Challenges from Below*, New York: M.E. Sharpe.

'Zhonggong zhongyang guanyu yinfa "dangzheng lingdao ganbu xuanba renyong gongzuo tiaoli" de tongzhi' (Notice from Party centre about the promulgation of 'Regulations on the Appointment of Leading Cadres'), *China Court*. Available online: www. chinacourt.org/flwk/sho1.php?file_id=76185&str1=%B8%C9%B2%BF   (accessed   6 May 2005).

'Zhongguo chengli jieneng jianpai lingdao xiaozu' (China established a leading group on energy saving and emission reduction), *Lianhe zaobao* (United Press), 28 April 2007.

'Zhongguo juweihui shixing 'yixingfenli' (China's residents' committees separated the mechanisms of implementation from decision-making bodies), *Takungpao.com*. Available online: www.takungpao.com/news/07/07/17/ZM-766728.htm (accessed 23 September 2007).

'Zhongguo shenji baogao: 2006 niandu zhongyang yusuan zhixing he qita caizheng shouzhi de shenji gongzuo baogao zongshu' (Audit report of China: A working report of execution of central budget and other budgetary revenue and expenditure), *Zhongguo shenji* (China Audit), 332, 2007, 16.

'Zhonghua renmin gongheguo gongwuyuan fa' (The Law of Civil Servants, the People's Republic of China), *Zhonghua renmin gongheguo renshibu wangzhan* (Ministry of Personnel Website). Available online: www.mop.gov.cn/gjgwy/content.asp?id=48 (accessed 14 May 2005).

Zhonghua renmin gongheguo guowuyuan ling di siyier hao (Directive No. 412 of The State Council of the People's Republic of China). Available online: www.gov.cn/ zwgk/2005-06/20/content_7908.htm (accessed 8 February 2006).

'Zhonghua renmin gongheguo huanjing yingxiang pingjia fa' (PRC Environmental Impact Assessment Law), *China Court*. Available online: www.chinacourt.org/flwk/show1. php?file_id=77627&str1=%BB%B7%BE%B3%D3%B0%CF%EC%C6%C0%BC%D B%B7%A8 (accessed 12 April 2005).

'Zhonghua renmin gongheguo jiagefa' (PRC Price Law), *China Court*. Available online: www.chinacourt.org/flwk/show1.php?file_id=29493&str1=%BC%DB%B8%F1%B7% A8 (accessed 15 February 2005).

'Zhonghua renmin gongheguo lifa fa' (PRC Legislation Law), *China Court*. Available online: www.chinacourt.org/flwk/show1.php?file_id=34719&str1=%C1%A2%B7%A8 %B7%A8 (accessed 12 April 2005).

'Zhongzubu renshibu yaoqiu jinzhi bu jianmian kaoshi zuowei xiyin gongwuyuan rencai de youhui zhengce' (Organisation Department of CCP Central Committee and Ministry of Personnel Prohibited Exemption of Civil Service Examination), *People Daily*. Available online: www.people.com.cn/GB/jiaoyu/1053/1973867.html (accessed 18 July 2004).

'Zhongzubu yinfa shishi difang lingdao banzi he ganbu kaohe shixing banfa' (Organisation Department of CCP Central Committee issued a decree on implementing the performance evaluation of local leaders and cadres), *Renmin ribao* (People's Daily), 7 July 2007.

Zhou, C. (2005) 'Tuijin caizheng tizhi gaige, huanjie xianxiang caizheng kunnan' (Alleviating the fiscal problems and reforming the fiscal systems at county and township levels), *Zhongguo caizheng* (China State Finance), 12, 17–18.

Zhu, C. (2004) 'Gongwuyuan zhaokao chaore chudong' (A craze in civil servant recruitment), *Zhongguo rencai* (China Talent), 12, 12–14.

Zhu, Q., Li, R. and E, G. (1996) *Guojia gongwuyuan guanli* (Management of state civil servant), Beijing: China Personnel Press.

Zou, K. (2004) 'Harmonising local laws with the central legislation: One critical step in China's long-march towards rule of law', *China Perspectives*, 53, 44–55.

Index

Routledge
Taylor & Francis Group

Governance for Harmony in Asia and Beyond

Edited by **Julia Tao**, City University Hong Kong, **Anthony B. L. Cheung**, **Martin Painter** and **Chenyang Li**

Part of the Comparative Development and Policy in Asia Series

In the context of increasingly multi-religious, multi-racial and multi-ethnic modern societies, the achievement of harmony is emerging as a major challenge. This book examines the idea of harmony, and its place in politics and governance, both in theory and practice, in Asia, the West and elsewhere.

Selected Contents:

December 2009: 234x156: 288pp
Hb: 978-0-415-47004-9: £80.00

To order this title visit:
www.routledge.com/asianstudies

Routledge
Taylor & Francis Group

Challenges for the Regulatory State in Asia
Governance Change in Telecommunications, Higher Education and Health Management

Edited by **Martin Painter**, City University of Hong Kong, **Ka Ho Mok,** University of Hong Kong and **M. Ramesh**, National University of Singapore

Part of the Comparative Development and Policy in Asia Series

Exploring the rise of the regulatory state in Asia, especially on governance and state capacity, this volume examines the challenges when policy areas become more market-oriented, comparing different policy instruments, adopted for example in telecommunications, education and health. It argues that the Asian regulatory state is always shaped by local circumstances.

Selected Contents: 1. Introduction: An Outline of Major Aims and Objectives, Research Questions, Research Methodology, and Brief Background for the Book 2. Theoretical Framework: Neo-Liberalism, Pro-Competition Policy Tools and Changing Regulatory Regime 3. Policy Backgrounds: Privatization, Deregulation and Re-Regulation in Telecommunications, Higher Education and Health Management in Asia 4. Telecoms Liberalization and Regulatory Reform 5. Corporatizing and Privatizing Higher Education and Regulatory Reform 6. Marketizing Health Management and Regulatory Reform 7. Challenges for Regulatory State: A Comparative Analysis 8. Conclusion: Varieties of Regulatory State: An Asian Perspective

February 2010: 234x156: 240pp
Hb: 978-0-415-44757-7: £85.00

To order this title visit:
www.routledge.com/asianstudies